Walk with Us and Listen

Walk with Us and Listen

POLITICAL RECONCILIATION IN AFRICA

CHARLES VILLA-VICENCIO

FOREWORD BY DESMOND TUTU

Georgetown University Press
Washington, D.C.

Georgetown University Press, Washington, D.C. www.press.georgetown.edu
© 2009 by Georgetown University Press. All rights reserved. No part of this book
may be reproduced or utilized in any form or by any means, electronic or mechanical,
including photocopying and recording, or by any information storage and retrieval
system, without permission in writing from the publisher.

Library of Congress Cataloging-in-Publication Data

Villa-Vicencio, Charles.
    Walk with us and listen : political reconciliation in Africa / Charles Villa-
Vicencio.
        p. cm.
    Includes bibliographical references and index.
    ISBN 978-1-58901-572-2 (pbk.: : alk. paper)
    1. Reconciliation—Political aspects—Africa.   2. Peace-building—Africa.
3. Conflict management—Africa.   4. Africa—Politics and government—1960–
I. Title.
    JZ5584.A35V55 2009
    303.6'9096—dc22   2009008225

15 14 13 12 11 10 09   9 8 7 6 5 4 3 2
First printing

Printed in the United States of America

For Lwazi and Oliver

—Two young boys living at different ends of the Earth.

CONTENTS

FOREWORD

This book provides an important corrective to the tendency among some participants in the transitional justice debate to relegate reconciliation to the status of a poor cousin of punitive justice. Reconciliation, in the cautious sense discussed in this book, is essential for a successful political transition in the aftermath of violent conflict and authoritarian rule. To reach out to your former enemies is not merely altruistic. It is central to self-interest and sustainable peace building. What dehumanizes you dehumanizes me. And the outcomes of this dehumanization are anger, resentment, greed, and revenge, which constitute a sure and certain recipe for ongoing conflict.

If a political transitional does not result in the creation of a society within which former enemies are willing and able to work together to overcome a nation's woes, it is likely to do little more than fuel the fires of the very conflict it seeks to overcome. In this sense reconciliation is the summum bonum, the most likely notion of the common good that nations are likely to experience this side of the grave.

Charles Villa-Vicencio builds his argument around "political reconciliation," providing social substance for a category that critics often dismiss as religious nonsense and political obscurantism. He suggests that reconciliation does not necessarily involve forgiveness and that former enemies and adversaries need not forgive one another in order to live together in an acceptable manner. This level of political reconciliation is, of course, an essential start to any peace process. I continue, however, to believe that we need to strive for more. This is why I chose to title my book on the South African Truth and Reconciliation Commission process *No Future without Forgiveness*. Forgiveness in the fullest sense involves a change of heart and mind, which takes a special effort from all concerned and much mutual understanding. So traumatic is the hurt suffered that some are indeed never quite able to forgive. Understandable as this is, the option for forgiveness is an ideal that the world cannot afford to give up on. It is a lure that draws us increasingly forward to deeper levels of integration and healing.

For former enemies to work together in the healing of nations, there can be no justice without the level of political reconciliation described in this book. For justice to prevail, it can be neither your justice nor mine. It needs to be a form of justice that unites us. It must be "our" justice—a form of justice that reconciles our different perspectives and interests. This takes time, hard work, and the transformation of both us and our enemies. This is what reconciliation is all about. It unites "us" and "them" into "our." To get to this point and to agree on a common understanding of justice to which we are all prepared to submit ourselves, we must engage in serious political, moral, and intellectual work. We are required to think through and understand the contours that have shaped our different views, driven us into conflict, and caused us to exploit one another. Reconciliation is a process or gradual growing into a common space that allows us to trust one another enough to work together, eventually to be friends and neighbors, and, yes, even to forgive and love one another. This is what makes this book so important. It points the way to the beginning of a process that by God's grace can reach beyond its goal, which is "political reconciliation," to a deeper level of forgiveness, harmony, and love. But I am now into theology, which is where this book chooses not to go!

In South Africa we opted for amnesty as a way of drawing perpetrators into the new society. We did not fully succeed in this regard. It is, at the same time, clear that we would not have succeeded in persuading the country's former political leaders and generals in the security forces to sit down at the negotiation table if they knew they would have their day in court and be required to spend time in prison. So, on balance, I think we did the right thing. We said peace is more important that fulfilling the niceties of punitive justice. In so doing we required those who applied for amnesty to acknowledge their crimes. We traded truth for justice. The South African Truth and Reconciliation Commission did not offer blanket amnesty or crass impunity, and I continue to believe that there is a place for the prosecution of those who refuse to acknowledge their complicity in evil. Sometimes it takes the imposition of punishment to bring criminals to their senses. If those guilty of gross violations of human rights do, however, seek to live a new life and contribute to transforming the country, then we need to talk with them and where necessary strike a deal. This is sometimes the only way of putting a stop to the brutality of the past, as a basis for initiating the kind of society within which hatred and revenge are replaced by respect for one another. This, in principle, was what we tried to do in South Africa. We still have a long way to go, but we have made a start.

Drawing together the insights of scholars and practitioners of political negotiations, conflict resolution, and peace building, this book reflects the importance of engaging one's adversaries in dialogue and participatory decision making. It provides insights into the views of Western seers and scholars on the possibilities of human encounter, and, of particular importance, it integrates the wisdom of African traditions and grassroots people into Western thought patterns. In so doing it provides practical guidelines for people who have lived in conflict over many years to assist them in learning to listen to one another and speak honestly as a basis for building both trust and lasting peace. The chapter on the national conversation in South Africa provides an insightful account of the successes and failures of the dialogue leading to the establishment of the Truth and Reconciliation Commission as well as the debate during the commission's process, which was at times as acrimonious as it was healing. The chapter on *ubuntu* reaches beyond the simplistic and romantic understandings of a vital African contribution to conflict transformation. The discussion on traditional African forms of justice provides important perspectives on how people in different parts of the continent have resolved conflicts over the years. These practices are discussed in a thoughtful and critical manner, probing ways in which international norms of justice and traditional African practices can enrich and complement one another in the quest to bring lasting peace to a continent torn apart by decades of colonial rule and postcolonial dictatorships.

Peace building is not an easy process. No single intervention by the United Nations, the International Criminal Court, or the African Union is enough to give Africans the cherished prize of peace and relative prosperity. The book fits into the philosophy that underlies the international Council of Elders that it is my privilege to chair. It poses vital questions concerning the need for the Court and local initiatives for justice and peace to find common ground. The international community can help bring peace to situations such as those in the Democratic Republic of the Congo, Sudan, and Zimbabwe. Indeed, the United Nations, the African Union, and neighboring countries have often been far too reluctant to confront tyrants, dictators, and warmongers in such countries. Where dictators, criminals, and perpetrators fail to respond to reason, the international community needs to pressure them to do so, and where necessary they need to face the International Criminal Court's full wrath. If, conversely, political leaders are ready to comply with international human rights standards, as was the case in South Africa in the early 1990s, we need to seek a way of settling the conflict in a manner that is as mutually beneficial as possible for all concerned. This is the most likely way of making and sustaining peace between former enemies. Where offenders are not prepared to acknowledge past wrongs, as is the case with President Robert Mugabe, they need to be removed from office. They cannot have it both ways.

This does not, however, mean that the international community should be allowed to dictate the terms for local and regional peace settlements. There can be no lasting peace if local populations and their leaders feel that a peace settlement fails to take their moral and cultural values into account, or if it fails to address their priorities. International agencies and the legitimate leaders in situations of violent conflict *both* have a role to play in peace building. This is clearly emphasized in this book.

Reconciliation is an inherent part of a holistic understanding of justice and sustainable peace. It is an essential ingredient for forging meaningful, respectful, and participatory democracy between former enemies. My prayer is that this level of peace may descend on Africa in the manner that its people so richly deserve.

Desmond Mpilo Tutu
Archbishop Emeritus of Cape Town

ACKNOWLEDGMENTS

It is never possible to acknowledge all those who contribute to a process that results in a publication. The participants in many struggles on the African continent, most of whom remain unnamed, are a constant inspiration to my work. I shall forever carry the memory of many of those whom I have been privileged to meet.

This book was conceived within the context of the work of the Institute for Justice and Reconciliation in South Africa and in other African countries. I spent eight challenging and productive years as executive director of the institute and am extremely grateful to my colleagues there. The institute, however, grew out of the work of the South African Truth and Reconciliation Commission, and I readily acknowledge with deep gratitude the impact of my colleagues there. These include Desmond Tutu, without whose leadership the commission could have shipwrecked; Alex Boraine, deputy chair of the commission and a long-standing friend; Mary Burton; Dumisa Ntsebeza; Yasmin Sooka; and other colleagues who assisted me in my attempts to hone a viable balance between justice and reconciliation. My conversations with Johan van der Vyver, professor of international law and human rights at Emory University, have been invaluable in reflecting on the Rome Statute and related matters in transitional justice.

Some of this book was written during my time as Claude Aké Visiting Professor, located jointly in the Department for Peace and Conflict Research of Uppsala University and in the Nordic Africa Institute. The book was completed during the 2008 Northern Hemisphere fall semester, when I was a research fellow at the Berkeley Center for Religion, Peace, and World Affairs at Georgetown University. The support of Thomas Ohlson, professor of peace and conflict research at Uppsala University, and Carin Norberg, the director of the Nordic Africa Institute, is acknowledged with gratitude, as is that of John DeGioia, president of Georgetown University, and Thomas Banchoff, head of the Berkeley Center. I am also grateful to Fathali Moghaddam and colleagues in the Conflict Resolution Program at Georgetown University.

Fanie du Toit, the present executive director of the Institute for Justice and Reconciliation, has worked with me since the institute's fragile inception and has become a close friend. My colleagues over the years in the institute's Transitional Justice in Africa Programme—especially Marian Matshikiza, Tyrone Savage, and Zola Sonkosi—have contributed to my thinking on what it takes to make peace in Africa. Erik Doxtader, a senior research fellow at the institute who migrates between teaching in the United States and doing research work in South Africa, has been a wonderful colleague in dialogue during several research projects over the years. He read the book and offered his usual profound insights before it went to press. Arlene Stephenson assisted with the early editorial process. Julie Bleeker, a research assistant, helped in tracking down very stubborn references and in finalizing the manuscript. Richard Brown and the staff of Georgetown University Press undertook the final editing and production of the book with sensitivity and professional care. Archbishop Tutu has written a generous and thoughtful foreword. My sincere appreciation to them all.

The writing of this book has also been enriched by my family—and has made its inevitable inroad into family time. The support and long suffering of my wife, Eileen, is acknowledged with deep gratitude.

Walk with Us and Listen

INTRODUCTION: WHERE PAST AND PRESENT MEET

Don't tell us what to do. Walk with us and listen. . . . You will never fully understand the journey of our suffering. We suffer alone and we must heal our own wounds. But we need your presence, so stay with us.

—Tendai Nkomo, a survivor of the Matabeleland massacre
in Zimbabwe, Bulawayo, September 2003

I wonder how both sides can reconcile if one side is the victim and the other the perpetrator. . . . If they admit their actions, it would be up to me to forgive them or not. It also depends on how they confess. I almost died. They have merely said "sorry." . . . The fact that I haven't killed them means perhaps I have already forgiven them.

—Tang Kim, in the DVD by Rachana Phat, *The Khmer Rouge Rice
Fields: The Story of Rape Survivor Tang Kim*

Political reconciliation is the litmus test of a successful political transition and peace endeavor. If all the niceties of procedural and punitive justice as demanded in international human rights law are implemented without contributing to meaningful cooperation between former enemies living in the same national or geographic area, there is little chance that the victims of past atrocities will be able to attain a measure of human and social dignity.

Moral sensitivities aside, this is a process that requires perpetrators, victims, and bystanders to be drawn into a society committed to the rule of law, political participation, social stability, and economic development. Sustainable human rights require political stability and institutional accountability. My concern is that this can be undermined by those who draw on the tenets of the

International Criminal Court to insist that perpetrators who bear the greatest responsibility for international crimes must, *of necessity in all cases*, be prosecuted. The burning question is how to achieve a balance between justice and reconciliation. This is a balance that does not simply involve a trade-off between peace and justice. The trade-off is rather between different forms of justice within the context of circumstances inherited from the past.

Reconciliation, as addressed in the pages that follow, does not necessarily involve forgiveness. Forgiveness implies the healing of the psychological and spiritual scars of past suffering. In the words of Pope John Paul II, forgiveness involves "the purification of memory"—a situation within which the past no longer has a negative impact on the present.[1] Most nations never attain this deeper level of inner peace—and perhaps they should not.

Political reconciliation constitutes a more modest endeavor, involving a minimum level of political harmony and cooperation between former enemies as a basis for pursuing holistic justice, which includes accountability, human rights, economic development, and the rule of law. This was the goal of the South African negotiated settlement leading to the nation's first democratic elections in 1994. Nelson Mandela, released from prison after twenty-seven years, was elected president in the country's first democratic election. The former apartheid political leaders and generals, in turn, committed themselves to support and uphold the new Constitution. In brief, the South African settlement favored political justice over criminal justice.[2] The agreement offered amnesty to perpetrators for truth, which resulted in the transfer of political power from the apartheid regime to a democratically elected government. This government created a democratic space within which the equal treatment of all South Africans could be pursued on the basis of constitutional government, the rule of law, and the affirmation of broad, inclusive human rights. Despite the long and bitter struggle that brought about the South African settlement, Desmond Tutu described the outcome as a "miracle."

South Africans clearly have a lot more to do to promote participatory democracy, to fight crime and corruption, to enhance economic equality, and to deliver on the ideals of the Constitution. The decision not to prosecute perpetrators who formally acknowledged their crimes through the Truth and Reconciliation Commission (TRC) was, however, a turning point in bringing the apartheid conflict to an end. Without qualified amnesty, the advances in political change and structural transformation would not have been possible.[3]

The attainment of change of this kind is invariably a morally and politically messy affair, leaving some ethnically minded citizens asking whether the price paid for peace was too high. The rejoinder is to ask whether a peace that holds the potential to entrench sustainable reconciliation between those who have been killing one another can ever be held ransom to moral or legal forms of idealism. The answer may well be related to one's station and geographical location in life. The words of Tendai Nkomo quoted in the prologue weigh the dialectic between justice and peace. The reflection of Tang Kim quoted above captures the ambivalence of postconflict peace building and reconciliation.

Johan Galtung's reflection on the parallel between peace and health is a useful one. He argues that "health can be seen as the absence of disease," but also as something more positive: as the "building of a healthy body capable of resisting diseases, relying on its own health forces or health sources." Peace is not only the absence of violence, nor is it realized merely by removing those responsible for past atrocities from society. It includes the capacity of societies to deal with conflict nonviolently and to be willing to build healthy structures and institutions to deal with the underlying causes of conflict.

Activists often speak of *negative* and *positive* peace to distinguish between the two concepts of peace. Distinctions are also made among peacekeeping, peacemaking, and peace building. Peacekeeping refers to military interventions aimed at bringing an end to hostilities. Peacemaking involves efforts, usually at a diplomatic level, to help opponents arrive at a peace agreement. Peace building has as its goal the creation of a sustainable positive peace. It has a long time line, involving the demobilization and reintegration of soldiers; the rebuilding of functioning political, economic, and educational systems; and the restoration of relationships. It involves multiple actors from every sector of society, working for material and institutional changes as well as subjective or attitudinal changes among individuals and communities.

In what follows, I argue that transitional justice is a process that needs to be holistically understood, offering an integrated program that addresses the past, present, and future challenges that face nations undergoing transition. This inevitably raises concerns by those who regard transitional justice as an imperative to intervene at the first opportunity to prosecute those seen to be primarily responsible for past atrocities. My unease is that the International Criminal Court has to date concentrated its attention on the atrocities of certain African countries to the neglect of the world's major powers and their allies, whose track record on human rights abuses is decidedly not beyond question. Interventions by the Court in Africa and elsewhere are important in terms of international jurisprudence, but they frequently fail to give sufficient attention to building relations between the communities involved in conflict, which is a prerequisite for sustainable peace. My intent is not to exonerate perpetrators or to encourage a culture of impunity; it is to explore alternative and additional options for holding perpetrators accountable and to promote peace building in societies facing deep conflict.

The centrality of truth telling in such a process is vividly seen in a High Court indictment preventing the South African president from granting pardons for crimes committed during the apartheid era, before giving victims an opportunity to respond. The Court ruled that the inquiry into the granting of pardons ought to be undertaken in "an open and transparent way" and "in the spirit of the TRC" as undertaken by President Thabo Mbeki in 2008.[5] This resulted from an application to the court by a coalition of organizations of civil society acting on behalf of the victims of gross violations of human rights, after it became clear that victims would not be consulted. Their concern is not necessarily to prevent all pardons for apartheid-era crimes, but that there is full public disclosure of details concerning the deeds of the perpetrators, that the reasons for granting these pardons are made public and that victims are given an opportunity to respond to the process before any decision concerning pardons is made—as was the case in amnesty applications to the TRC.

This book, which was written at the interface between transitional justice and peace building, seeks to correct the emerging tendency to prioritize prosecutions at the cost of reconciliation by some exponents of transitional justice. I do so by emphasizing the need for former enemies, adversaries, and strangers to engage one another in rigorous political conversation and decision making as a basis for exploring solutions to the underlying causes of the conflict they face. In brief, prosecutions need to be balanced against the need for political stability. Justice and reconciliation need to be inherently linked to ensure sustainable peace.

This is particularly true in situations of intrastate violence where issues of ethnicity, historical memory, and inherited material inequality are major contributing factors to the conflict. For peace to emerge in a positive and enduring sense, it needs to be negotiated and agreed to by those who are required to live with its consequences—whatever the intentions or judgment of the international community. Kofi Annan, the former UN secretary-general, makes this point in observing that "[peace] programmes that emerge from national consultations are . . . more likely than those imposed from outside to secure sustainable justice for the future in accordance with international standards, domestic legal traditions and national aspirations."[6]

Communities that have killed one another in wars that have sometimes lasted for generations are, however, often neither ready nor able to make peace without international interventions. It is this that makes political reconciliation such an arduous and difficult process. Political reconciliation is never an easy option. Neither is it a mysterious or ineffable process. It is grounded in hard negotiations, tough policymaking, accountability, and invariably moral compromises.

Interpersonal reconciliation often results in antagonists needing to dwell on the healing of psychological wounds of a deep and personal kind. In the wake of prolonged political violence and war, political reconciliation requires people to focus less on the past. Despite the persistence of emotionally charged memories that cannot be ignored or brushed aside, the focus needs to be on the creation of a new and different kind of future. The immediate goal for societies

[handwritten marginal note: How to do so]

seeking to recover from a terrible past is what Rajeev Bhargava so aptly describes as a "minimally decent society."[7]

Political reconciliation does not provide an immediate or quick solution to the social, economic, political, and other causes of conflict. It involves a commitment to the long haul of building political confidence as a basis for social cohesion. For this process to be sustained, adequate progress needs to be made at the level of social transformation and reconstruction—failing which, any attempt to cooperate across old divisions is likely to give way to an escalation of social discontent, if not political collapse.

Reconciliation is a process that ebbs and flows. It often begins with little more than a cautious openness toward others. As trust and confidence grow, the possibility of a deeper and more honest relationship may develop. This enables participants in a reconciliation process to manage and deal with conflict in a manner that ensures relationships remain intact. Reconciliation is often the only realistic alternative to escalating social conflict and political violence.

Affirming the importance of a realistic kind of reconciliation, this book is rooted largely, although not exclusively, in the continental African experience—where, it is argued, individual healing traditionally involves the entire community. The members of the local community are required to consider together their complicity in the crimes of individuals, to each personally take responsibility for his or her restoration, and to ensure that victims receive reparations. I do not focus on a specific African case study, although the contemporary South African nation-building endeavor figures prominently.

A Personal Reflection

It has been suggested that a story is a letter an author writes to himself or herself. Here, I endeavor to turn into language my transient thoughts, experiences, hunches, unarticulated ideas, and restless pursuits in seeking to understand the meaning of reconciliation. This I do in order to be confronted by them again and in the hope that others involved in peace building will correct, fine-tune, and add to what is offered.

My role in the South African struggle has been a varied one. Having been born several years before the white-supremacist National Party came to power in South Africa in 1948, I was raised to believe in the inherent superiority of whites. In time, a diversity of experiences and encounters imprinted on me a deep sense of the unjust, racist, and oppressive nature of the socioeconomic privilege I enjoyed. I became aware that white fears were driven essentially by racist propaganda. I also discovered how difficult it is for people to surrender the social status and privilege that have been entrenched by centuries of colonialism and decades of apartheid rule.

My early academic training was in theology. Increased involvement in the political struggle against apartheid, and the opportunity to minister in poor and alienated communities that suffered the direct effects of an unjust system, drove my quest for tools with which to effect change in South Africa. I later taught social ethics for several years at the University of South Africa, and in time I became a professor of religion and society at the University of Cape Town.

Beyond my engagement in liberation theology and other forms of theology, I read history, sociology, politics, conflict resolution, and negotiation theory, seeking to link theory and practice as I was drawn deeper into the struggle for a just South Africa. More of an activist than a scholar, I nevertheless continued to search for the perfect fit between theory and practice—that never quite came. I was later appointed national research director of the South African TRC. Thinking back on that experience, I realize to what extent the TRC, despite its limitations, offered a rare opportunity to link theory and practice. Its mandate was to ground practice in the moral and legal principles enshrined in the new South African Constitution. As the work of the TRC unfolded, the complexities of making concrete and viable decisions that linked ethical goals to working practices constituted what Reinhold Niebuhr (on whom I wrote my PhD thesis) in the early 1970s called a "possible impossibility."

Reflecting on the journey I have traveled, a thread of continuity can sometimes be discerned amid the gains and losses of struggle. The thread is difficult to name. I write around it and do not always fully grasp it, hoping to create a level of sensitivity in myself and in those who read these pages to see and nurture the capacity of people who, for a variety of reasons, are driven by the forces of history to learn to live together in a relatively peaceful way.

Political reconciliation has not received the kind of methodological attention that its professional cousins—conflict transformation, restorative justice, and mediation—have received. This book is partly an attempt to address this neglect, and yet it is not primarily about method or theory. Nor is it a scholarly book, although the narrative draws on the insights of many perceptive scholars and wise activists. It is primarily about context and story. It is about finding words to describe processes unfolding in particular conflicts, and distilling the essence of particular political processes that have enabled people to overcome a hostile past and work toward a solution that may not yet be at hand.

Privileged to have participated in peace initiatives in several African countries, I have in some situations worked directly with community-based activists. In others my engagement has been with political leaders. Elsewhere I have observed political settlements from the outside. I have come away from these different experiences realizing that despite the animosity and violence that is part of the African political scene, there are profound ethical insights and resources for peace building embedded in African memory and tradition.

Irae Baptista Lundin, a human rights activist in Mozambique, spoke about the kind of reconciliation that led to a political settlement in her country in 1992:

> Some level of reconciliation is the only viable basis for lasting reconstruction and development. This has to do both with remembering past opportunities to make peace that we failed to grasp, as well as the anticipation of a new future. It involves engaging both our ancestors and grandchildren yet to be born. It is a celebration of the human spirit that has the capacity to rise above the past, in making possible what seems impossible. It is about people demanding life in the midst of death. It is about not giving up. It is about refusing to die. It involves truth-telling, justice and a shared future.[8]

Ancestors, future generations, rituals, talks, negotiations, settlements, accords, justice, reconciliation, and transitional mechanisms are ultimately metaphors and endeavors that involve a process that is as much about building relationships with others as it is about finding ways to deal justly with past atrocities.

Some of the wisest peace builders and negotiators I have had the privilege of meeting in Africa and elsewhere have little or no formal training in negotiations or peace-building skills. What they do have is a deep and vested commitment to resolve what often appears at the time to be an irresolvable problem. Coupled with a serious measure of common sense, they intuitively draw on different experiences, moral and political commitments, and personal and communal insights into what lies behind the conflict.

In reflecting on initiatives in a number of countries across the African continent, I am mindful that some of these initiatives appear less than adequate from the perspective of established principles of conflict resolution theory or Western notions of justice. The latter, conversely, sometimes not only fails to make a positive impact on African conflicts but also are counterproductive to sustainable peace building on the continent. Western-oriented lawyers, activists, and advocates of peace would do well to seek a more empathetic understanding of the traditional African worldview, which promotes political inclusivity and legal compromise. They would also do well to inquire to what extent African moral values and practices could contribute to making peace in some of the most intractable conflicts in the Middle East, Iraq, Afghanistan, and other theaters of Western engagement.

The distinguishing, if not defining, characteristic of peacemaking and nation building in Africa involves the function and importance of words. Words are a formative and energizing part of African rituals and celebrations. They are also the defining characteristic of focused discussion—what in South Africa is called an *indaba* (Zulu), *imbizo* (Xhosa), or *bosberaad* (Afrikaans).

Although the South African settlement obviously has had an impact on my thinking, this model is decidedly not seen as a panacea for all situations. There was a joke going the rounds in South Africa at the height of the conflict in the middle to late 1980s. It suggested that South Africans faced two options: a realistic one and a miraculous one. The realistic option was for us to fall on our knees invoking God to send a band of angels to sort out the conflict. The miraculous option was for enemies to talk. We chose the latter.

The Book in Outline

This introduction is followed by a theoretical prologue. It is effectively an extended note on the affinities and tensions that tend to emerge between lawyers and peace-building proponents regarding international crimes. The three chapters that follow address peace-building and negotiation practices within an African context. The final five chapters address issues of transitional justice and political reconciliation in a more specific way. I argue that the reluctance of proponents of transitional justice to address substantial concerns relating to economic development need to be redressed by giving more attention to the concerns of peace builders. It is not enough for the advocates of transitional justice to say that postconflict development is not central to *their* mission, any more than peace builders can afford to show indifference to impunity. The challenge is to ensure that what is done or left undone in the name of transitional justice does not jeopardize the development work and other nation-building initiatives in societies that are endeavoring to take the first steps toward participatory democracy. Peace builders need, in turn, to accept that impunity is the enemy of sustainable peace. The question is whether and to what extent it is necessary to live with one's enemies in both the literal and figurative sense.

Chapter 1 provides a brief overview of the context within which African nations seek self-realization and political fulfillment. Without allowing for the African encounter with colonialism and its aftermath, it is difficult to understand the current attitudes of many African people toward Western interventions on the continent. The memory of colonialism in the latter part of the nineteenth and first half of the twentieth centuries is for Africans what the memory of the Holocaust is for Jews, the Battle of Kosovo in 1389 is for Serbs, and the 1690 Battle of the Boyne is for Irish Protestants. Chapter 2 considers the complexities of peace building in Africa. It draws on the literature of conflict mediation, suggesting a level of affinity between some insights in this literature and African peace endeavors, which is often overlooked. Chapter 3 offers a more systematic consideration of active talking and listening as part of peace-making and nation-building processes. Again the link between Western and African endeavors in peace building is considered. Chapter 4 considers the journey toward political reconciliation traveled by South Africans through the TRC and beyond. Here the discussion moves beyond the language of conflict mediation and transformation to the concerns of transitional justice. Chapter 5 explores *ubuntu* as an underlying ethos for the South African transition and its relevance for nation-building initiatives elsewhere. Chapter 6 addresses traditional African justice and reconciliation initiatives, inquiring as to what extent they can be adapted to meet the challenges and demands of established forms of international justice. On the basis of these chapters, chapter 7 reflects again on the nature of political reconciliation. Chapter 8 provides several suggestions as a possible consensus between international law and traditional African structures for justice and reconciliation.

Sensitivities are inevitably involved in a project of this kind. In some instances my recollection of discussions and insights may not be precise at the level of verbal accuracy. In these situations, I have avoided direct quotations and attributions. I have also curtailed the use of notes in an attempt to limit technical and scholarly debate. The acknowledgment of the debate and insights that I have gained from others has at the same time necessitated the more extensive notes at some points.

Most of the activists and practitioners of peace building whom I have encountered in the cut and thrust of the politics of transition are not "scholars" in the conventional sense of the word. My conversation is primarily with them, recognizing the need to remember words spoken and events that often pass by without time for adequate reflection. In this regard the words of William Stafford deserve pondering:

> So, the world happens twice—
> Once we see it as is;
> Second, it legends itself deep,
> The way it is.[9]

The essential word here is "legends." It suggests storytelling, reflection, thoughtfulness, meditation, and empathy as well as critique and revision, which individually and collectively provide a second chance to understand and to discover a basis for developing peace-building endeavors. The problem is that legends often include myth and political spin—which need to be discerned and identified as such.

PROLOGUE: AFFINITIES AND TENSIONS IN DEBATE

Several years back the standard prescription for overcoming armed conflict, war, and mass atrocities was to offer blanket amnesty to all perpetrators on all sides of a dispute. Today the dominant theory, promoted through the International Criminal Court (ICC), is that those bearing major responsibility for genocide, crimes against humanity, and war crimes should be prosecuted.

The shift in the international law debate toward the obligation to prosecute was already gaining ground at the time of the South African Truth and Reconciliation Commission (TRC), which sought to forge a middle path between prosecution and blanket amnesty. The intent of the ICC, which did not come into force until April 2002 with the necessary sixty ratifications of the Rome Statute, was to close down impunity and to strengthen the hand of new democracies in countering the indomitable influence of perpetrators of human rights violations.[1] It was not to promote prosecutions to the point of the potential collapse of newly emerging democracies. In this respect the ICC constitutes a major step forward in the international struggle for human rights.

The holding of perpetrators responsible for massive human rights violations assists many victims and survivors to "move on"—perhaps even open themselves to the possibility of reconciliation with those responsible for their suffering. The fact that Charles Taylor is facing trial in The Hague for his role in the Mano River subregion affirms the dignity and rights of those who suffered his brutality. The refusal to prosecute perpetrators in Chile until recently has clearly undermined the reconciliation process in that country, and in South Africa the government's general reluctance to hold accountable or prosecute those who were refused amnesty by the TRC has left many victims angry and perplexed.

At the same time, there is growing concern among peace builders that some in international human rights circles are seeking to shift the ICC's attention away from prosecutorial discretion and increasingly toward an obligation to prosecute, without adequate consideration being given to the political consequences that prosecutions may have in a particular context. This raises a host of contextual questions.

These questions include: Would there have been a peace settlement in South Africa had the architects and implementers of apartheid—politicians and generals—faced extended jail sentences? Probably not. Does the arrest of Jean-Pierre Bemba, leader of the Congolese Liberation Movement and runner-up to Joseph Kabila in the presidential elections, undermine the democratization process and further polarize the country, as is suggested by his supporters?[2] The trial of the rebel leader of the Union of Congolese Patriots, Thomas Lubanga, in The Hague for war crimes related to the forced recruitment of child soldiers sends a strong message that warlords in the Democratic Republic of the Congo (DRC) are not beyond the law. His trial could at the same time inflame the already fragile ethnic relations in Ituri, where he is seen as a protector of Hema rights in the rivalry for control of the region's vast mineral resources. The arrests of Mathieu Ngudjolo Chui, the former senior commander of the National Integrationist Front, and of Germain Katanga, a senior commander of the Patriotic Resistance Forces in Ituri, have in turn raised the ire of the Lendu/Ngiti ethnic groups to which they belong. Will the possible trial of Laurent Nkunda, head of the National Congress for the Defence of the Congolese People, following his arrest in Rwanda, whether in The Hague or Kinshasa, contribute to peace building or further alienate his ethnic Tutsi followers?[3] Recognizing the deep Tutsi/non-Tutsi social divisions in the DRC, the latter may well be the case if the atrocities committed by the Congolese government forces, the Hutu-based Democratic Forces for the Liberation of Rwanda, and other rebel groups in the area go unpunished. The fact that longtime enemies Rwanda and the DRC were able to change tactics and thus cooperate in an effort to disarm the rival militias each nation has backed as proxies is at the same time a victory for local and regional solutions to vexing problems involving war crimes and related atrocities.

Shifting the focus to Uganda, it is improbable that Joseph Kony and other leaders of the Lord's Resistance Army will agree to any cease-fire agreement with the Ugandan People's Defence Forces while facing ICC warrants for their arrest. The extension of violence, including the abduction of children in neighboring countries, at the same time demonstrates a continuing blatant disdain for human rights by the Lord's Resistance Army leaders. In Sudan the proposed ICC warrant for the arrest of President Omar al-Bashir signals the world's outrage at his behavior in Darfur and elsewhere. The question is to what extent an ICC warrant would undermine peace efforts in that country. Would the indictment of President Robert Mugabe, in turn, scuttle the fragile peace settlement between the Zimbabwean African National Union and the leaders of Movement for Democratic Change, Morgan Tsvangirai and Arthur Mutambira?[4]

There are no easy answers to these and similar questions. Reflecting on the transitional justice debate from a perspective of political science, James McAdams comes to an "uncomfortable realization [that] for every argument that can be summoned in favour of doing more to address a past wrong, we can find an equally compelling argument to do less."[5] He argues that the ability of democratic leaders to control the future political agenda of any country is always less than is either hoped for or assumed. History, in turn, suggests that the outcome of interventions by the international community in conflict situations is equally open to question. This is what makes the continuing debate on issues of justice, truth telling, and reconciliation so important. Options for peaceful transition can never be taken off the table. Trial and error, adjustment and rethinking, debate and negotiation—all are part of the dogged process required in the pursuit of sustainable peace. There will always be differing views on what is required to build a nation in the wake of dictatorial rule. Atrocities need to be acknowledged and victims' rights affirmed. The politically aggrieved, including those perpetrators who endeavor to contribute to rebuilding the society they helped destroy, also need to feel that their views are being addressed in order to be persuaded that politics has more to offer than war.

There are invariably different interpretations of the past. Even where the goals and objectives of a struggle are morally beyond question, people pursuing the noblest of goals often resort to desperate means to attain them. The South African TRC declared that the armed struggle against apartheid was morally just and that the defense of apartheid constituted an unjust war. In so doing, however, it declared that unjust means were at times employed by both sides in pursuing their goals. It argued that there are different levels of culpability in any struggle, acknowledging that victims often become perpetrators. In these situations, the boundaries between good and evil begin to blur and there are opposing views of what constitutes moral responsibility under dictatorial rule. Combatants and others separated by ideology, custom, legal restraints, and war invariably need time to get to the point where they can recognize and accept the moral ambiguity of the tactics they used in times of war. They need to be drawn into a national conversation, without which social cohesion is made that much more difficult in most postconflict situations.

The leaders of democratic states, not least emerging democracies, invariably have less capacity to control the political agenda than is so often ascribed to them. To use Bernard Williams's phrase, a successful transition involves a significant amount of "moral luck" and political flexibility.[6] Success in such situations is, however, inevitably accompanied by inclusive, transparent, and open-ended debate—a process that needs to include everyone who has an interest in the nature of the emerging state and is prepared to participate constructively in its realization: victims and survivors of past abuse, perpetrators, enemies, adversaries and political opponents, as well as human rights activists. The involvement of international experts and organizations in a transitional process is often helpful in promoting the rule of law and a culture of human rights. In a given situation, however, international agents are often unable to fully understand the level of trauma and the cost of civil war—so it is crucial to ensure that transitional justice programs are owned and executed by local participants.

An important factor in dealing with a transition is clearly whether the perpetrators are ready to contribute to the peace process in a serious manner by turning away from violence and by responding in a positive manner to the needs of victims and survivors of past practices and abuse. Despite the limitations of the South African negotiated settlement, the political and military leaders of the apartheid regime were ready to end the war, end apartheid rule, honor the outcome of democratic elections, and protect the Constitution.

Where dictators, rebel leaders, and other perpetrators are, however, not prepared to make peace, persisting in the execution of violence and/or oppression, it is inconceivable that they should be allowed to perpetuate their behavior with impunity. In such situations the international community may well need to intervene with prosecutions. Yet it continues to be clear that more is required than prosecutions to ensure appropriate forms of institutional transformation to promote both justice and sustainable peace. The challenge facing the international community in dealing with recalcitrant individuals, groups, and nations is not necessarily to refrain from all prosecutions but to become more involved in postconflict reconstruction as a basis for countering future gross violations of human rights. Prosecutions are not enough.

Recognizing the importance of prosecution for crimes as stipulated by the ICC, Diane Orentlicher moderates the position taken in her earlier formative essay, "Settling Accounts: The Duty to Prosecute Human Rights Violations of a Prior Regime," in arguing that there is no one-size-fits-all approach to transitional justice.[7] She stresses the need to recognize "the unique historical experience of each society that has endured serious violations of human rights [that] will inevitably shape its citizens' understanding of justice."[8]

The balance required for a successful transitional justice program cannot be a tame compromise between a preoccupation with past injustices and fears about the future. It can decidedly not be a balance between good and evil. It needs to be a bold and creative exercise in addressing the demands for both justice and peace. José Zalaquett captures the essence of traditional justice by suggesting that it has two overall objectives: to prevent the recurrence of abuses and—to the extent possible—to repair the damage they caused.[9] Alex Boraine favors a five-component holistic approach to transitional justice: accountability of the perpetrators, truth recovery, reconciliation, institutional reform, and reparations.[10] Yasmin Sooka provides her own five benchmarks: the depolarization of society, institution building, economic stability, civic trust, and the rule of law.[11] Nuances aside, few working in the broad area of peace building will disagree with these emphases. The United Nations *Agenda for Peace* identifies the many meeting points of engagement among the different levels of conflict management, peace building, postconflict reconstruction, and, by implication, transitional justice.[12]

Reflecting the complexity of most peace processes, the 2004 UN report to the secretary-general, *The Rule of Law and Transitional Justice in Conflict and Post-Conflict Societies*, defines transitional justice as "processes and mechanisms associated with a society's attempts to come to terms with a legacy of large-scale past abuses, in order to ensure accountability, serve justice and achieve reconciliation."[13] A 2006 document from the Office of the United Nations High Commissioner for Human Rights, *Rule of Law for Post-Conflict States: Truth Commissions*, conversely provides a much narrower focus for transitional justice and truth commissions that fails to adequately affirm the necessary link between justice and reconciliation.[14] In brief, the implication of the *Truth Commissions* document is that justice is more important than reconciliation, accountability is more important than truth, and reparation is more important than reconstruction.

If this understanding of truth commissions is an adequate reflection of the dominant trends in the transitional justice debate, a report by Karen Brounéus on reconciliation and development cooperation, commissioned by the Swedish International Development Cooperation Agency, provides a necessary corrective to the neglect of reconciliation. This report provides a sober reminder that a holistic understanding of justice in a postconflict situation demands a long and often tiresome program involving institutional reconstruction, human development, and political reconciliation. "Planning support for reconciliation," writes Brounéus, "should begin with analysis including: the context of the conflict, root causes, consequences (including psychological trauma), and the existence of initiatives for reconciliation at different levels in society (top-level, middle range and grassroots)."[15] This echoes the recommendations of the *Report of the Dag Hammarskjöld Symposium on Respecting International Law and International Institutions*, which advocates that "more support needs to be given to the rule of law budgets in Africa for building institutions and practices of good governance, and less on showy projects of interest to the international community." The report argues for "a balance [to] be struck between the universal norms associated with the rule of law and respect for local, national and regional values, and that greater reliance be placed on local and regional associations of lawyers and judges."[16]

Peace initiatives around the world suggest, however, that the balance being sought needs to extend beyond the legal profession.[17] The recently established Council of Elders under the leadership of Desmond Tutu, for example, draws on the expertise of a wide range of peace builders, including Graça Machel, Mary Robinson, Jimmy Carter, Nelson Mandela, Li Zhaoxing, Kofi Annan, and Muhammad Yunus. The essence of the Dag Hammarskjöld report, nevertheless, stands. It calls for overcoming "detrimental and myopic competition among donors that promotes their own view of the rule of law without deference to local attitudes and conditions."[18]

An imposed form of justice that fails to enjoy local ownership and that fails to build positive and constructive relationships between former enemies as a basis for redressing past wrongs is unlikely to stand the test of time. By the same token, reconciliation is not possible where the rights of individuals are not protected and those responsible for their suffering are able to prosper in their impunity. Though this interdependence may seem like common sense, the on-the-ground reality often belies these fundamental truths. Indeed, in societies emerging from extended periods of human rights abuses, advocates for reconciliation and human rights are sometimes fundamentally divided in their approach to nation building. The recognition of the need for complementarily between the ICC's demands and broader peace-building endeavors is at the heart of the pages that follow.

This in essence is captured in the debate surrounding the response of the African Union (AU) Heads of States summit, held in Libya in July 2009, to the indictment of President Omar al-Bashir by the Pre-Trial Chamber of the ICC for atrocities committed in Darfur. Despite heated and sometimes bitter exchanges between the most ardent supporters of the ICC prosecutions and their critics, both have cause to take the draft statement of the summit seriously. It reiterates the commitment of AU Member States "to combating impunity and promoting democracy" while expressing "grave concern" about the impact of the al-Bashir indictment on the "delicate peace processes underway in Sudan".[19] Politicking aside, the statement captures a concern that is central to the pages of this book. African nations need to be held accountable to the commitment they have made to redress impunity. The complexities of peace building need at the same time to be kept central to the transitional justice debate.

1

AN AFRICAN JOURNEY

The effect of the policy of the colonial powers has been the economic isolation of peoples who live side by side, in some instances within a few miles of each other, while directing the flow of resources to the metropolitan countries. For example, although I can call Paris from my office telephone here in Lomé, I cannot place a call to Lagos in Nigeria only 250 miles away. Again, while it takes a short time to send an airmail letter to Paris, it takes several days for the same letter to reach Accra, a mere 132 miles away. Railways rarely connect at international boundaries. Roads have been constructed from the coast inland but very few join economic centres of trade. The productive central regions of Togo, Dahomey (Benin) and Ghana are as remote from each other as if they were on separate continents.

> —Sylvanus Olympio, first president of Togo,
> quoted by Martin Meredith, *The State of Africa:*
> *A History of Fifty Years of Independence*, shortly
> after the nation's independence from France

We must face the matter squarely that where there is something wrong in how we govern ourselves, it must be said that the fault is not in our stars but in ourselves. . . . We know that we have it in ourselves, as Africans, to change all this. We must assert our will to do so, we must say that there is no obstacle big enough to stop us from bringing about an African renaissance.

> —Nelson Mandela, *Long Walk to Freedom*

Africa stands arguably at the cutting edge of the international debate on transitional justice. This is exemplified nowhere more clearly than in three current attempts on the continent to move beyond war to the beginning of peace: The first is the now-aborted Juba talks between the Government of Uganda and the

Lord's Resistance Army (LRA) that juxtapose local initiatives for justice and reconciliation with international demands for prosecutorial justice.[1] (This will be discussed further in chapters 6 and 8.) The second is the indictment of Sudanese president Omar al-Bashir by the International Criminal Court (ICC), which raises questions concerning the appropriateness of the ICC's intervention into peace initiatives in Sudan. The third is the fragile peace initiative between Robert Mugabe's Zimbabwean African National Union and the Movement for Democratic Change in Zimbabwe, which may yet raise its own set of questions concerning the prerogatives of the ICC. Because Zimbabwe, like Sudan, is not party to the ICC, the involvement of the ICC would involve the recommendation of the Security Council of the ICC, which is subject to the veto power of its permanent members.

As other African states move toward political transition, attempts to impose the ICC's demands for the prosecution of those alleged to be most responsible for acts of genocide, crimes against humanity, and war crimes are likely to provoke increasing concern among some peace builders on the continent. Confronted by decades of impunity that have spiraled into civil wars, regional conflict, genocide, and oppressive rule, the international community insists that perpetrators of such deeds have their day in court. The fact that thirty African states (out of fifty-three sovereign states) have ratified the Rome Statute indicates a general acceptance of the statute by most African countries.

The level of political instability that characterizes many African peace initiatives is, however, such that even the most fervent proponents of prosecutions recognize the need to ensure that legal action against perpetrators does not throw the country back into war. Article 16 of the Rome Statute allows the Security Council of the United Nations to suspend ICC investigations for renewable one-year increments if those investigations relate to situations with which the Security Council is engaged under its Chapter VII powers relating to matters of peace and stability.[2] Article 53, in turn, allows for a stay of prosecutions triggered by a state party or Security Council referrals if, taking into account the seriousness of the crime and the interests of victims, this is judged to be "in the interest of justice" which presumably includes situations where prosecutions might impede peace initiatives.[3]

Luc Huyse and Mark Salter warn that the notion of the "interests of justice" is an "extremely technical and diffuse concept."[4] If this means that the criteria by which these technicalities are to be unraveled are solely those of international law, to the exclusion of the judgment of governments and others directly involved in peace building, then effectively the ICC has the final word—reducing local and regional African peace initiatives, at best, to poor cousins in the peace process.

It is argued in the chapters that follow that the choice is not, however, primarily between international and African options for peace building; it is rather to find ways in which local and international communities can cooperate in ensuring that perpetrators of gross violations of human rights are held accountable for their deeds and where necessary brought to trial, while ensuring that local and other peace-building initiatives do not slide back into conflict. For this to happen and for the West to understand suspicions concerning international interventions on the continent, it is necessary to locate current African conflicts within the history of colonialism—which constitutes a dominant memory within African politics. "The memory of colonialism continues to impose itself on the African continent like a body of death. Too many Western scholars and leaders fail to take this into account in offering their solutions to our problems," suggests Dani Nabudere, a veteran Ugandan scholar. "Africa needs to rise above its past, ensuring that corrupt rulers and dictators can no longer hide in the shadow of its impact. The reality of colonialism and its aftermath needs, however, to be remembered to ensure that dominance of its kind never happens again."[5]

It is, for example, impossible to understand the Zimbabwean crisis without taking the continuing aftermath of colonialism into account, along with the exploitation of colonial memory by Mugabe and his cronies, to justify the odious rule that characterizes Zimbabwe today.[6] It is similarly not possible to understand the suspicion of many in other parts of Africa regarding the involvement of the West, and what are seen as "Western legal presuppositions" expressed through the ICC, without taking into account the long shadow of colonialism.

The Scramble for Africa

The effects of the scramble for Africa at the end of the nineteenth century constitute a crucial part of this historical context.[7] When the would-be colonial masters at the Berlin Conference in 1885 parceled out land among themselves, they did so without regard to kith, kin, tribe, ethnicity, monarchies, chiefdoms, language, culture, or religion. The map on the conference table included large sections of territory simply designated terra incognita, with boundaries between colonies being decreed by the drawing of geometric lines and the tracing of rivers—tearing clans, communities, and nations asunder. The Bakongo were divided between the French Congo, Belgian Congo, and Portuguese Angola. Somaliland was carved up between Britain, Italy, and France. In many instances, diverse and separate groups—each with its own hierarchy of rulers, and devoid of a common history, culture, language, or religion—were compelled to live within common colonial borders. Nigeria contained 250 ethnolinguistic groups. The Belgian Congo consisted of six thousand chiefdoms. Antagonistic kingdoms such as the Buganda and Bunyoro in Uganda became part of the same British colony. In Sudan, Chad, and Nigeria, Muslims, Christians, and traditional religionists were expected to find a common destiny. In Rwanda and Burundi, myths of origin and legends of identity were used to promote division between Hutus, Tutsis, and Twa.

The British colonized what would become Northern and Southern Rhodesia, Nyasaland, Ghana, Uganda, and more. There were German South West Africa, Portuguese Zambesia, French Equatorial Africa, the Spanish Sahara, and the Belgian Congo. Italy colonized Abyssinia; the Germans and later the French occupied Cameroon; and the British defeated the Dutch, African chiefdoms, and later the Boer republics to make what is today South Africa a part of the British Empire.

This colonial division of Africa began to change in the wake of World War II. Independence came first to Ghana in 1957 and then to other African colonies, and, eventually in 1994, democracy came to South Africa, the last bastion of white domination on the continent. An expectation in each of these situations was that human rights and prosperity would follow. These hopes in many situations soon gave way to disillusionment, with neocolonial and authoritarian rule resulting in levels of exclusion not vastly different from what prevailed in colonial times.

There are also African success stories in the face of extremely difficult circumstances. However, it is excesses of independent African states fueled by neocolonialism and global economic imbalance—along with postindependence greed, corruption, political cronyism, and military exploitation—that continue to characterize many African countries. An Oxfam Report shows that since the end of the Cold War, for example, conflicts in Africa have cost the continent $306 billion, the equivalent to all the foreign aid it has received over the same period.[8]

The African experience needs to be assessed in all its brutality, extremes, degradation, squalor, and special pleading, as well as beauty, creativity, perseverance, and determination, in much greater detail than can possibly be undertaken here. It is wrong to romanticize precolonial Africa or for Africans to portray themselves as helpless victims of history. It is equally wrong to ignore or play down the impact of colonialism.

Speaking at a Gorée Island conference on vitalizing African cultural assets, Breyten Breytenbach focused on the need to discern and understand the values that independence and liberation brought to the continent.[9] He asked to whom present African reality belongs. Are Africans living in borrowed clothes? Is there a particularly African way of understanding and administering power? Is this essentially a negative or potentially a positive thing? How do colonialism, global realities, contemporary African politics, and talk of an African renaissance affect each other? Is there an African notion of peace and coexistence? To what extent do contemporary responses to conflict, including contemporary manifestations of the African renaissance, carry the marks of traditional African mechanisms for justice and reconciliation (as will be discussed in chapter 6)? Do African notions of peace offer positive incentives to the global quest for peace? These are questions that underlie the narrative of the chapters that make up this book.

The Challenge of Independence

Newly independent African states had little experience in modern forms of representative democracy. Nations needed to be welded together from an array of tribes and clans whose members spoke different languages and were at different stages of political and social development. Colonialism had fueled and exploited these divisions. Urbanization was exploding. Economies were owned largely by foreign companies and developed in accordance with the needs of the former colonial powers and their allies. The transportation infrastructure was designed to facilitate the exporting of raw materials and the importing of manufactured goods. There was an acute shortage of skilled workers, and little attempt was made to remedy the situation.

Kwame Nkrumah, the first president of Ghana, addressing the inaugural meeting of the Organization for African Unity (OAU) in 1963, spoke of the challenge facing Africa:

> African unity is, above all, a political kingdom that can only be gained by political means. The social and economic development of Africa will come only within the political kingdom, not the other way around. . . . In independent Africa we are, however, already reexperiencing the instability and frustration which existed under colonial rule. We are fast learning that political independence is not enough to rid us of the consequences of colonial rule. The movement of the masses of the people of Africa for freedom from that kind of rule was not only a revolt against the conditions it imposed. Our people supported us in the fight for independence because they believed that African governments could *cure the ills of the past* in a way that could never be accomplished under colonial rule.[10] (emphasis in original)

"Without freedom there can be no development. Without development there can be no freedom," was Nkrumah's persistent message. He spoke within a context in which African leaders frequently disregarded the most fundamental ingredients of good governance, thereby throttling development, stifling democracy, and undermining peace. Coups, attempted coups, and human rights abuses were slowly squeezing the democratic life out of African nations while Nkrumah himself was increasingly involved in apparently corrupt business deals and surrounded by enemies. Having survived an assassination attempt, he was overthrown in a military coup in February 1966. This was not only because of government corruption or his own grandiose lifestyle amid the desperate economic plight of his people, but also primarily because of his attempt to subordinate the army to serve his own ends. Most counterrevolutionary moves to correct political ineptitude elsewhere on the continent ended in dictatorships or failed states, whereas subsequent attempts at democratization and reconstruction were slow and contested.

The pursuit of the political kingdom more often than not degenerated into chauvinistic forms of nationalism and dictatorial rule, wrapped in the familiar cry of "noninterference in the affairs of a sovereign state." It was a cry heard across Africa from Idi Amin's Uganda and General Sani Abacha's Nigeria to apartheid South Africa, with an inevitable disregard for civil liberties, the promotion of autocratic rule, the violation of basic human rights, and economic collapse. Frantz Fanon, writing during the first wave of African independence, observed that such petty nationalistic agendas and corruption by the political elite were "quickly copied by street vendors and cobblers"—all in contradistinction to the expectations that prevailed on the eve of independence, as well as the essential principles that formed the basis of the Pan-Africanist agenda.[11] It was a culture soon entrenched in postindependence Africa, within which African prophets and critics reminded their leaders that democracy is about more than holding elections. It is about the right of citizens to participate in the shaping of the way in which they are governed and the obligation of a ruling party that loses an election to surrender power and sit in the opposition benches of parliament.

The ultimate failure of visionary African leaders who brought hope as well as achievement to their nations and the continent as a whole—ranging in different ways and at different levels of intensity from Nkrumah to Thabo Mbeki—has resulted in a sense of African pessimism. It has also generated a determination among a generation of Africans to see their nations rise above the burden of the past as well as the divisiveness of the present. This has resulted in an African milieu that makes the continent both a fertile environment for international interventions and an African endeavor to find African solutions to African problems of conflict, war, genocide, and crimes against humanity. The Zimbabwean crisis illustrates both challenges. With African leaders having failed to arrest the steady slide of that country into crisis, "international diplomatic and economic interventions were initiated precisely because African leaders failed to deal with the situation," argued Tendai Biti in Cape Town, shortly before his arrest on returning to Zimbabwe in June 2008. "The surest way to keep what some call 'interference by the international community' in the affairs of Africa is for Africa to take responsibility for dictators like Mugabe."[12] Against the background of international sanctions as well as a groundswell of protests in Zimbabwe, South Africa, and elsewhere, a fragile peace settlement was subsequently, however, negotiated by President Mbeki on behalf of the African Union (AU), providing some evidence of Africa beginning to pick up on its responsibility to its own that has long been neglected.

In brief, African peace requires a level of intrastate cooperation and interstate interdependence, and an affirmation of international human rights' standards, that many African states have failed to realize. For this to happen, suggests Adele Jinadu, Africa is required to find ways of "containing and defusing the destabilizing political and social tendencies" of ethnically split societies, imposed by the Berlin conference, that were used by colonial powers and exploited by African leaders through ethnic, tribal, and economic systems of stratification.[13] Quoting Amilcar Cabral, he argues that Africa is "to return to the source," in the sense of the preindependence struggle by Africans who transcended ethnic and class divisions in protest against economic exclusion and political oppression by their colonial masters.[14]

For this to happen African politics needs to be rerooted in a commitment to change that allows and encourages grassroots engagement in the challenges of the day. Above all, it requires strong and patient leaders who are ready to deal with the corruption and political abuse that make their countries unattractive investment places for former colonial masters and industrial countries. It further requires a global economic system that allows vulnerable countries to participate in global trade as equal partners.

The call for renewal is today more urgent and widespread among those excluded from the political and economic benefits enjoyed by the political elite in Africa than at any time since the beginning of the independence movement at the end of the 1960s. It is this that has resulted in the affirmation of an African renaissance that has reproduced for some both the hope and expectation that greeted African independence, as well as a sense of political skepticism by those who have observed the African journey from both within and outside the continent.

An African Renaissance

The dawn of an African renaissance was articulated by Thabo Mbeki, quoting the first-century Roman philosopher Pliny the Elder, in an important speech in 1998: "*Ex Africa semper aliquid novi!*" (Something new always comes out of Africa). Mbeki challenged Africans to rise to the political, economic, and developmental challenges they face, with subsequent events seeing the transformation of the OAU into the AU. The decision to make this change was agreed to at the OAU's Lusaka summit in July 2001, and the AU was formally launched in Durban in 2002.

The projection of a renaissance and the birth of the AU are dismissed by critics in Africa and elsewhere as insufficiently robust to deal with the crisis of African politics. In essence the AU provides a structural manifestation for a restorative approach to justice that favors inclusivity and reform rather than radical change. While allowing for direct involvement in the affairs of delinquent member states, the AU's early conduct reflects the approach of communal, participatory traditional African mechanisms for justice and reconciliation. This gradualist approach to reform has laid the foundation for the conflict with the ICC in which many African leaders are engaged in Uganda, Sudan, and elsewhere.

The AU does, however, provide guidelines for promoting collective security in conflict and postconflict situations and a new commitment to democratic reform and social development. The shift in focus is away from the independence that was needed in the immediate postcolonial period and toward a sense of interdependence between African states. Simply put, the OAU addressed challenges related to political liberation, whereas the stated intent of the AU is development, democracy, and peace through the New Partnership for Africa's Development (NEPAD) and the African Peer Review Mechanism. No transition is easy, few transitions are uncontested, and implementation is the proof of the pudding. The AU and NEPAD face all these challenges. Nelson Mandela had earlier insisted that "Africa has a right and a duty to intervene to root out tyranny." At the time of the AU's' launch, Thabo Mbeki and Olusegun Obesanjo promoted an interventionist policy that gave the AU "legislative powers to act against member states acting against the ethos of good governance and the rule of law."[15] The situations in Sudan and Zimbabwe, conversely, suggest a reluctance by African leaders to implement this policy, favoring a traditional approach to conflict via mediation.

In an attempt to create a new relationship between Africa and the developed world, the promotion of NEPAD was central to the making of the AU. Chris Landsberg sees it as both a "marketing tool" to turn around Africa's global image and an attempt to correct the "power imbalances" between Africa and the industrial global North.[16] Although the verdict is still out on the success or otherwise of NEPAD, it is dismissed by many as a neoliberal ploy that fails to give adequate attention to the continent's developmental issues. NEPAD does not enjoy continental support, and it has not delivered on the demands being made by Africa's poorest countries.

More than half the fifty-three African states have signed the memorandum of understanding on the African Peer Review Mechanism. Reviews have been undertaken in Ghana, Kenya, Tanzania, and Rwanda. In South Africa, the presidency has been criticized by civil society and other organizations both within the country and abroad for its perceived control of the review process in an attempt to limit political damage, and also for its failure to address a number of pertinent issues such as unemployment, poverty, HIV/AIDS, land reform, and violence against women.

Central to the mission of the AU are good governance, conflict resolution, and peacekeeping through the establishment of the AU Peace and Security Council. The Pan-African Parliament's president, Gertrude Mongella, suggested at the close of the Parliament's second session in September 2004 that the objectives and values of the AU could only be successfully instituted at a continental level to the extent that they "enjoyed the credibility that can only come from being effectively implemented within member states." Pointedly, she stated that the objectives and values of the AU were the "only viable antidote to intrastate conflict that plagued many African countries." She noted further that "without political stability, there will be no development or economic growth on the continent."

The inevitable challenge facing Africans is how to ensure that policy and good intent are translated into practice and resolve, in order for what Cyril Obi describes as a "third independence for African people" to become reality.[17] The tasks for the first postcolonial generation of African leaders were to transform liberation movements into political organizations, to establish political stability, and to promote the rule of law. The formative African leaders of this generation included Kwame Nkrumah (Ghana), Jomo Kenyatta (Kenya), Julius Nyerere (Tanzania), Leopold Senghor (Senegal), António Agostinho Neto (Angola), Seretse Khama (Botswana), Samora Machel (Mozambique), Kenneth Kaunda (Zambia), Robert Mugabe (Zimbabwe), and Sam Nujoma (Namibia). Later came Nelson Mandela as South Africa established democratic rule in 1994. This generation of leaders, in many instances, offered charisma and inspiration to expectant nations, while in others they manipulated ethnic concerns and, in some instances, in the words of the Dani Nabudere, they "put the rules for corruption in place for the next generation of leaders to perfect."[18] Like many leaders in world politics, this generation's legacies have been both positive and negative. Some succeeded in laying the foundations for democratic rule. Some failed. Others deliberately undermined democracy.

Many in the next generation of leaders were different. In some instances their commitment was to arrest internal dictatorships. In others it was to perpetuate the entrenchment of executive power. This generation included Joaquim Chissano (Mozambique), José Eduardo dos Santos (Angola), Mobutu Sese Seko (Zaire), Yoweri Museveni (Uganda), Jerry Rawlings (Ghana), Meles Zenawi (Ethiopia), Isaias Afeweiki (Eritrea), Paul Kagame (Rwanda), John Garang (Sudan), Laurent Kabila (Democratic Republic of the Congo), and others. Some came to power in military takeovers. Some were elected to leadership. Some committed themselves to correcting the excesses and failures of their predecessors. Others fell into deeper levels of corruption. Again, some succeeded and some failed.

Now a third generation of leadership shows signs of emerging in Africa. Coming forth from resurging civil societies in different situations of conflict, this generation of Africans rejects the conflation of party and state promoted by many earlier leaders. Seeking to transform democracy from a top-down approach to a movement from below, this third generation refuses to reduce the state to the government of the day, let alone to the executive branch of that government. Drawing on international human rights principles, the support of international nongovernmental organizations, and long-suppressed political dissidence at home, it enjoys growing support among citizens. In many African countries, heads of state and governments that continue to suppress criticism from dissident voices are obliged to do so with an increasingly heavy hand. In other situations, leaders are being compelled to respond positively, although hesitantly, to the demands coming from their critics.

What is significant is that individuals and groups *outside* government—in civil society, trade unions, the media, and academia—are claiming a space in which to influence political developments for the better. This suggests a shift away from the "African strongman syndrome" to the possibility of democratic inclusivity. Driven by a similar vision to that which drove the most dynamic of the first-generation liberation leaders, they demand a change in political culture. Some have broken away from the political movements that gave them birth. Others are pushed to the margins of these organizations. Their role is crucial to the birth of a brand of African politics that refuses to leave politics to the politicians.

This process is seen in the rejection of the disputed results of the December 2007 elections in Kenya that resulted in a coalition government between President Mwai Kibaki's Party of National Unity and Rail Odinga's Orange Democratic Party, negotiated by a team of African leaders under the former UN secretary-general, Kofi Annan. "The settlement may not be perfect, but it shows a willingness to move beyond the government through the barrel of a gun," the *East African Standard* reported when the agreement was reached in February 2008. The negotiated settlement in Zimbabwe provides further indications of an African state endeavoring to move beyond confrontation. And the political developments in South Africa, in turn, suggest that the exclusion of large sections of the population from the benefits of the 1994 political settlement is being publicly resisted.

Despite the limitations of the Kenyan and Zimbabwean developments and recent setbacks in South African politics, the suggestion is that the voice of civil society, invariably at huge human cost, is being heeded in a way that has not been seen in these countries since the time they first won their independence. In brief, there are indications that participatory democracy is reemerging as a means of redressing the conflicts that constitute contemporary African politics. The annual publication of the Nigeria-based African Centre for Development and Strategic Studies (ACDESS) is helpful in mapping the extent and nature of intrastate conflict and postconflict reconstruction on the continent. It identifies four essential areas that need to be addressed as the basis for overcoming the different levels of conflict: a culture of democracy and peace; good political, economic, and social governance; democratic elections; and the prevention of unconstitutional changes of government.

The ACDESS report indicates that African politics has moved forward since its early heady days of independence to the recognition by an increasing number of states that political stability, good governance, economic development, human rights, and political reconciliation are inherently and inextricably linked. The UN secretary-general's report of March 21, 2005, *In Larger Freedom: Towards Development, Security and Human Rights for All*, stresses the need for an integrated approach to implementing a number of "actions that are both *vital* and *achievable*." It is important in that it extends the secretary-general's 1998 report, *Causes of Conflict and Promotion of Durable Peace and Sustainable Development in Africa*, which similarly emphasized the need to address conflict transformation and human development in a coordinated and complementary manner.

Conflict prevention and postconflict reconstruction involve *justice* in dealing with gross violation of human rights, *reconciliation* in the sense of enabling former enemies to coexist peacefully, *human security* as a way of ensuring sustainability, and *economic development* as a basis for correcting past inequalities. They involve balancing political sensitivities, deliberate compromises, and considered pragmatism. At the same time, they involve calls for moral integrity and the pursuit of possibilities that militate against the prevailing political climate. They involve a level of "realistic idealism" that pursues solutions that are possible in the immediate to short-term period as a basis for reaching toward ideals that are not immediately possible. All these, as suggested above, place the African renaissance and the AU's contemporary approaches to conflict mediation in continuity with traditional African restorative mechanisms.

Limitations aside, there are signs of things beginning to go right in the designs of several African states that are seeking to mend their former ways. We see this commitment in the Dar es Salaam Declaration on Peace, Security, Democracy, and Development in the Great Lakes of November 2004 and in the draft Policy Framework for Post-Conflict Reconstruction and Development of the African Union of 2005. A concern is that human rights purists, strident in their critique of the limitations of countries in transition, often undercut the progress that is being made in countries struggling to deal with a terrible past. Critiques and the exposure of failure are vitally important. But the cliché is also true: In striving for the best, we sometimes undermine the good by failing to realize the limits of what is possible at the time. We need to push the limits of the possible while ensuring that we both grasp and build on the small victories that are there for the taking.

Popular political change is necessarily driven by a sense of impatience, as seen in Kenya, Zimbabwe, South Africa, and elsewhere. Time and patience are, at the same time, important dimensions of political reconstruction. It would have been obscene to suggest that Jews be reconciled with Germans in 1945— even in the modest political sense suggested in the introductory pages to this book. The miraculous thing is that there were some Jews who, in the wake of the Holocaust, were able to explore the meaning of reconciliation at a deeper level than this political one.

Reconciliation was reasonably the furthest thing from the minds of Rwandans in the wake of the 1994 genocide, and yet there were Rwandans that sought to put an end to what Michael Ignatieff calls the "zero-sum game of ethnic competition" for social, political, and economic privilege that thrust Hutu and Tutsi into internecine slaughter.[19]

In South Africa, Nelson Mandela came out of jail after twenty-seven years offering to negotiate with a regime that he had dedicated his life to overthrowing. The long-awaited revolution became a negotiated revolution, and political power shifted decisively. Although economic change has been slow and criticism of the South Africa macroeconomy is both strident and unrelenting, Saki Macozoma, a leading black business entrepreneur, defends government economic policy: "I shudder to think where any of us, the poor included, would have been had we torn down the last remnants of the badly faltering economy at the time of the democratic transition, as some suggested we should. Instead we built on what we had, turning a moribund economy into the most vibrant economy in Africa."[20] Conceding that the majority of South Africans do not yet benefit from this growth, Macozoma suggests that "at least we had an economy to broaden. This is more than can be said about some developing economies."

The burning question is how to ensure political stability and the need to redress past injustices in societies seeking to move away from an autocratic and violent past to the beginning of democratic rule. "When we talk about political transition, two things are necessary," argues Macozoma. "These are democratic elections and political stability. Get these right and you are in a position to address economic and other inequalities. Fail to do so and all else will fail."

Justice and Reconciliation

Democracy and access to basic material resources go hand in hand. These are essential ingredients of social injustice and political polarization in countries struggling to transcend long periods of conflict and autocratic rule. Countries such as South Africa have attained an important level of political democracy by conducting free and fair elections. The struggle for economic justice is more elusive.

Perhaps in the crudest form, those arguing for neoliberalism naively assume a perfect market, while the proponents of the developmental state naively assume a perfect state. Neoliberals assume that everybody has the same access and the same information about what is being traded, whereas developmentalists believe that state interventions are always in the common interest, shrewdly informed, well implemented, and free of unintended consequences. It is at the interface of the two that the South African and perhaps the African economic debate is happening.

Within the context of this book, it is important to ask to what extent political programs built around the African renaissance and transitional justice initiatives can facilitate the kind of stability needed for some form of economic justice to emerge. The Truth and Reconciliation Commission (TRC) in South Africa and similar initiatives in Ghana, Sierra Leone, Morocco, and elsewhere—as well as related but more traditionally African approaches to justice and reconciliation in the Rwandan *gacaca* courts—all aim at the need for democracy and stability as a basis for social and economic development. Similarly, indigenous cleansing ceremonies also exist, both adjacent to formal truth-seeking structures and as standalone initiatives sponsored by local communities and traditional leaders. These are discussed further in chapter 6. The aim of these initiatives is to integrate justice and reconciliation through communal restorative procedures. Questions abound concerning the effectiveness of these initiatives in contemporary political situations. Chief among these is whether grassroots communities, which have often been locked in violent conflict for decades, are being drawn into the nation-building and reconciliation processes.

Inherent to the vision that underlies African political renewal in renaissance thinking and through structures of the AU is the realization that the rule of law, nation building, social cohesion, and reconciliation go hand in hand. The need for this holistic approach to nation building is, of course, not limited to the African context. Xanana Gusmão, a former resistance leader and the first president of Timor-Leste (East Timor), argues that reconciliation is the essence of an inclusive sense of justice. His response to the recommendation (which was ultimately not implemented) by a UN Commission of Experts at the Stockholm International Forum in 2004 that there be an International Criminal Court for Timor-Leste was that reconciliation is the basis of justice: "The report by judges [the UN Commission of Experts] I greatly respect, but it also impressed me because it considers nothing other than trying and punishing people. For those experts, life operates according to the scales of justice—as though there is justice in the world, with universal principles regulating all countries on an equal footing, as though under-developed, developing or smaller countries do not feel the law of the strong hanging over their heads."

Speaking further on the relationship between justice and reconciliation, he continued:

Many believe that justice is a necessary condition for reconciliation—that without justice there can be no reconciliation. In my view, it is precisely the opposite—without reconciliation there is no real justice. We cannot pursue justice merely based on revenge and hatred. Japanese generals were executed after the Second World War, but today there is still no real reconciliation between China and Japan. In the context of Timor-Leste, the great justice achieved was the international community's acknowledgement of our right to self-determination and independence, and consequently the right of our people to live in peace and harmony. We need to create the conditions for peace and harmony, and reconciliation is the proper way to achieve these goals.[21]

A few years after Gusmão's optimistic words, it is difficult to assess the extent to which sustainable peace is a possibility in Timor-Leste, recognizing that a range of judicial and social reforms still wait to be implemented.

When Some Refuse to Make Peace

Gusmão's concern raises the pertinent question of what to do with individuals and groups that refuse to explore any form of conciliation or to participate in a search for political accommodation, or who seek to use negotiations as a ruse behind which to pursue violent or oppressive goals. Are there occasions when there is no alternative but to impose retribution or to allow a conflict or war to continue to unfold until a mutually painful stalemate occurs that makes some form of accommodation and the beginning of a reconciliation process possible?

In a provocative article titled "Give War a Chance," Edward Luttwak suggests that "although war is a great evil, it does have a virtue: it can resolve political conflicts and lead to peace." Though NATO or regional peacekeeping initiatives are able to protect civilians to a limited extent, in many instances they have the destructive consequence of prolonging the state of war. Luttwak's argument is that peace invariably comes only when all the belligerents become exhausted or when one wins decisively. "Either way the key is that the fighting must continue until a resolution is reached."[22] His reminder that many endemic conflicts linger because the transformative effects of decisive victory and/or exhaustion are blocked by outside intervention is sobering. More frightening are the human cost and the sense of a return to the survival of the fittest in a bully-takes-all context. Given the realities of the global milieu, it is also unrealistic to think that any local war can be fought in a hands-off environment with the hope of a victory for those who have a just cause on their side.

From a transitional justice perspective, the question is whether the AU has the will to act decisively against rogue states that refuse to abide by the principles of good governance and human rights required of AU member states. To date the AU has been reluctant to take the kind of stand against such states for which the broader international community is asking. "The involvement of the international community in African affairs continues to be regarded by leaders who are driven by Africanist ideals as a form of colonialism," observes Fantu Chenu, the research director of the Nordic Africa Institute. "Add this to what has emerged over the years as a culture of impunity and you begin to understand the suspicion that prevails in Africa concerning the ICC. African opposition to international engagement in African conflicts is sometimes not because of neocolonialist perceptions but because it is a way of perpetuating a form of impunity from which they benefit."[23]

Reflecting on the "seductiveness of moral disgust" that tempts peacemakers to simply walk away from a fray, Michael Ignatieff offers a more nuanced assessment of outside peace initiatives. He writes of the visit in 1995 of Boutros Boutros-Ghali, then secretary-general of the UN, to several troubled African states—Rwanda, Angola, Zaire, and Burundi. In a frank discussion, Boutros-Ghali told Burundian Hutu and Tutsi leaders: "You seem to assume that the international community will save you. You are deceived by the assumption. The international community is quite content to let you massacre each other to the last man. . . . You are mature adults—*majeurs et vaccinés.* God helps those who help themselves." Relaxing later in the Hôtel Source du Nil in Bujumbura, he told Ignatieff: "We are only the doctors. If the patient won't take the medicine, what can we do?" The metaphor is inaccurate, suggests Ignatieff. These patients were not refusing to take the medicine; they were setting fire to the clinic.[24] Is there a point where moral disgust requires that we simply allow the conflict to continue?

Two slightly different questions arise: Ought one ever to negotiate with those responsible for the slaughter of innocents? Is military intervention—and the subsequent consequences in certain situations—perhaps the only viable option that can be ethically justified? There are no easy answers. The Lancaster House negotiations on Zimbabwean independence in 1980 led to the end of minority rule and a brutal bush war that lasted for more than fifteen years. Twenty-seven years later, questions of land claims continue to fester. In 1993 nineteen American troops were killed in Mogadishu in a firefight with Somalian warlords. A year later, this had a direct bearing on the U.S. decision to block a UN resolution to intervene in the Rwandan genocide. In South Africa negotiations with the apartheid regime led to an end of legalized racial discrimination and armed conflict in 1994. At the height of the Kosovo War in 1999, the United States argued that to end the conflict it was necessary to deal with

Slobodan Milošević. "If this is what peace takes," a diplomat noted, "then pragmatism needs no defending, even if it violates our sense of justice." Things went horribly wrong, and the UN's ICC for the former Yugoslavia later indicted Milošević for crimes against humanity in Kosovo, for violations of the laws of war in Croatia and Bosnia, and for genocide in Bosnia. A year later Milošević was extradited to stand trial in The Hague, where he died before a verdict could be reached. In 2003 under an international deal to end Liberia's fourteen-year civil war, Charles Taylor was granted asylum in Nigeria, from where he was later extradited to stand trial in The Hague for war crimes in Sierra Leone. The U.S.-led invasion of Iraq led to the collapse of Saddam Hussein's regime, but peace has decidedly not been brought to that country in the process. It is difficult to know when external interventions are appropriate and what form they should take.

Were these failed interventions perhaps too restrained—in Ignatieff's words, "not imperial enough?" Alternatively, should peace initiatives be led by local leaders and communities that have the option of looking for regional or international support without surrendering ownership of the peace process? Suffice it to say that war and outside intervention are insufficient to solve entrenched political conflicts. It takes words of one kind or another to end a dispute. For peace to prevail, the war ultimately needs to be fought in words across a table. Violence, killing, guns, ambushes, rape, assault, and pitched battles need to be confronted in open and frank talks. They need to be addressed and resolved in nouns and verbs.

Pauline Baker's reflection on the tension between "conflict managers" and "democratizers" is pertinent to contemporary African peace endeavors.[25] The former tend to favor interventions, ranging from preventive diplomacy to various types of mediation and dispute resolution. They argue that war needs to be brought to an end before justice can be attained. The latter favor the principled prosecution of human rights offenders, the rule of law, and the imposition of democracy as the end against which to measure the termination of hostilities. For them, Baker suggests, peace is no longer acceptable on any terms. It needs to result in justice.

Peace and Justice

There must be peace for justice to prevail and there must be justice for peace to endure—requiring a form of justice that addresses the demands of transition and restoration along with accountability, which may include prosecutions. For this to occur, three salient principles need to be followed. First is the need to find an appropriate balance between accountability and human rights on the one hand and peace and reconciliation on the other. This invariably involves a compromise with which those directly involved in the conflict are prepared to live. Recognizing that external interventions in pursuit of human rights can rarely, if ever, be ruthlessly interventionist, the second principle reiterates the caveat that transformation can only achieve what is acceptable to those involved and what is possible at a given time and in a given place. Third, to ensure that neither justice nor reconciliation is sacrificed under the guise of good intentions by all who are party to the negotiations, peace pacts need to be subjected to relentless scrutiny—with special attention being given to the needs and demands of the oppressed who are struggling to overcome past abuses. For justice to endure and become part of the national fabric, it needs to be embodied and executed in functioning institutions.

These principles require a balance between demands for trials as a basis for establishing the rule of law and a level of political reconciliation that is likely to entail legal compromises. Kofi Annan, speaking on the relationship between the ICC and the South African TRC shortly after the TRC's closure, stressed that the ICC's purpose is to intervene only where the state is unwilling or unable to exercise jurisdiction over perpetrators:

> It is to ensure that mass murderers and other archcriminals cannot shelter behind a state run by themselves or their cronies, or take advantage of a general breakdown of law and order. No one should imagine that it would apply to a case like South Africa's, where the regime and the conflict which caused the crimes have come to an end, and the victims have inherited power. It is inconceivable that in such a case the Court would seek to substitute its judgment for that of a whole nation which is seeking the best way to put a traumatic past behind it and build a better future.[26]

Moreno Ocampo, the ICC's chief prosecutor, speaking in Cape Town more recently, stated that his aim is a "zero-sum case goal" or the absence of trials by the ICC as a consequence of the effective functioning of national judicial systems and political reconciliation. As suggested above, however, there is an ingredient to African peace building that simply does not prioritize retribution in the way it is prioritized in Europe, the United States, and elsewhere. This means that Ocampo's zero-sum case goal, at least in the sense of Western forms of justice, will probably always be difficult to attain in Africa. There is a need to find a point at which justice and reconciliation sustain one another. The late South African chief justice Ismael Mohammed spoke of this as an "agonizing balance," designed to address the demands of everyone involved in the conflict, drawing former enemies into a nation-building process. He stated that victims and perpetrators need to cross the "historic bridge" from the past to the future. This, he suggests, should *not* be "with heavy dragged steps delaying and impeding a rapid and enthusiastic transition to the new society."

Probably few Liberians who suffered under Charles Taylor's rule, or Sierra Leoneans who had their country torn apart through his involvement in their civil war, are not grateful that he is now appearing before an international tribunal in The Hague. Before Taylor's arrest, he was given asylum in Nigeria. "Asylum in Nigeria ended the Liberian civil war and we had to live with the classic tension that exists between the desire for justice and the desperate need for some form of peace," observed Joe Rahal, a Sierra Leonean human rights campaigner and activist. "The fact that he now has his day in court is important. I wonder, however, whether the Taylor case will not be used elsewhere to dissuade dictators to surrender power."

In seeking to describe ways in which peace and political reconciliation are sometimes forged, my aim is to explore African contributions to the international debate, recognizing that in many African and other developing-world conflicts the immediate adoption of human rights ideals and international law imperatives is simply not possible. And yet human rights are universal and in urgent need of implementation to ensure sustainable peace. This requires peacemakers to focus on the practical realization of these ideals, to the extent that that is possible, rather than on keeping a checklist of violations that sometimes does little more than result in a public scolding by human rights purists of those who deviate from their norms. It is, in fact, becoming increasingly clear that imposing established Western transitional justice measures, to the exclusion of indigenous initiatives and more pragmatic African solutions, renders transitional justice processes that much less effective. The need facing all developing-world countries in transition is sustainable peace and reconciliation as a basis for addressing economic and other needs. The concern of peace builders in Africa is that international funding is simply not forthcoming in the way in which it is for Western driven prosecutorial messages. "We are often told that international interventions should not prevent us from doing our own thing. The reality is that financial resources are simply not available in the same way that it is for Western initiatives," a senior Rwandan justice official notes. He continues:

> Compare the budget for the International Criminal Tribunal for Rwanda in Arusha with that of the *gacaca* courts and the National Unity and Reconciliation Commission inside the country. Alternatively, consider the budget of the Sierra Leone Special Court in relation to the budget of the Sierra Leonean TRC. I become increasingly frustrated with international nongovernmental organizations and UN officials jetting in to tell us what to do. The world needs to give us a chance to solve problems in our own way. The West has much to offer but needs to understand there are useful resources outside of its domain that can be nurtured and promoted as part of the African reconciliation process. Our peace-building initiatives are too often undermined by interna-

tional interventions that are backed by Western financial resources. This borders on yet another brand of neocolonialism.[27]

Justice and national reconciliation are deeply interdependent. In the aftermath of violent conflict, it is not possible to sustain the rule of law and a culture of human rights without the active and ongoing work of reconciliation. By the same token, reconciliation—even in a modest sense of beginning a political process that can only be completed in the indefinite future—is not possible among those who disregard one another's humanity and continue to abuse human rights. The link between building and reconciliation, on the one hand, and human rights, the rule of law, good governance, and morality, on the other, needs to be seen as an inherent part of peace building.

Peacemaking no less than peace building is primarily about what is realistically possible. To succeed, it must at the same time recognize the need to stretch the boundaries of what is possible—a process that comes about through both understanding and tolerance, as well as by demands that sometimes come in the form of ultimatums or through legal interventions by international, regional, and/or national courts. Ultimately, however, the participation of the people who are living the reality of a local conflict is needed to bring about peace and to explore reconciliation.

The Ethnic Challenge

Reflecting on these and related challenges in South Africa and elsewhere on the continent, the South African novelist and academic Njabulo Ndebele powerfully and yet simply suggests that reconciliation and inclusion have not so much to do with present realities as with "who we can become." He reminds us that for reconciliation to survive and for cultural tolerance to prosper, there needs to be material and economic development. At the same time, he stresses that this cannot be achieved if former enemies fail to commit themselves to working together toward national reconciliation. The subjective and the material must be promoted as two sides of the same coin. The former includes issues of identity and culture as well as human coexistence. The latter involves socioeconomic change. Important in this regard is timing. The sequencing of these developments within the context of fragile and slow transitional processes is often not addressed with sufficient sensitivity by the "evangelists for prosecution," who often give the impression that prosecutions alone will solve the problems of the world.

Prosecutions are appropriate and probably necessary in most transitions from dictatorial rule to democracy and the establishment of the rule of law. However, it is equally important to strengthen an inclusive national identity and to establish the kind of economic transformation that draws yesterday's victims and survivors into the new society. Also, social and ethnic groups that historically have been isolated from one another need to learn to live together in a cooperative and peaceful manner.

W. E. B. du Bois was correct in defining the problem of the twentieth century as the problem of the color line. The problem of the twenty-first century may well be ethnic separation—a social dynamic that necessarily involves more than observable characteristics such as color and appearances. It includes memory and history, language and culture, worldviews, ideologies, religions, and related self-images. An analysis of African political conflict shows that these differences also invariably include strong dimensions of intrusive economic privilege. Class and identity are intertwined.

A common enemy often generates a measure of unity in a splintered opposition. In at least some African states, this has been evident, where a semblance of preindependence unity gave way to latent ethnic, class, and ideological divisions after independence. Félix Houphouët-Boigny observed: "We have inherited from our former masters not nations but states, states that have within them extremely fragile links between ethnic groups."[28] Social cement was required to unite these states, with ethnic consciousness often becoming more dominant than it had been before independence. This continues to be a factor in contemporary African politics. There is a growing realization of an urgent need to deal with ethnicity in a politically realistic manner in states ranging from Rwanda, Burundi, and the Democratic Republic of the Congo in the African Great Lakes region, to the countries of the Greater Horn, West Africa, and the southern African region. For peace and development to coexist, not least on the African continent, there is a need for a form of national unity within which differences are both recognized and celebrated.

Perhaps more so than in the West, the African sense of belonging is more organic, more culturally driven, more clan oriented, and more family centered. This is not obvious to many well-intentioned would-be peacemakers from the developed world. This makes understanding the dynamics of patriarchal or matrilineal family hierarchies, extended family, ancestral loyalty, and ethnic allegiance an important ingredient in an African nation-building process. Put differently, given the memories of colonialism and the experience of ethnically based economic privilege that prevail in many postcolonial situations, in Africa it is no easy task to establish liberal democratic structures that cut across race and class. For example, it is more difficult than in the United States and some European countries where, despite their deficiencies, democracies have been built over many generations based on ideologies and ideas that may not obviously have been rooted in traditional entities of belonging. (Note that many European nations were assembled out of differing ethnic, linguistic, and religious entities, which were held together by a combination of nationalism and a centralized state with a monopoly on military power.) And yet the United States and most European countries are today again experiencing difficulties in ensuring that their centers hold as excluded groups, immigrants, and new nationals challenge dominant political ideologies and the economic privileges associated with them.

The overwhelming majority of notable conflicts beyond the African continent, not least in Eastern Europe and the former Yugoslavia, are also between communities within failed or failing national states rather than between national states. This makes African experiences in nation building significant to nation building elsewhere in the world where conflicts are also often rooted in the failure of ethnic, cultural, and religious communities to coexist peacefully. It is at the same time important to recognize that such conflicts are almost invariably intertwined with some form of material deprivation and/or political exclusion. It is essentially when individuals and groups experience a sense of marginalization from the body politic and its material benefits that they draw on identity concerns to drive and legitimate their political and material agendas.

The intriguing question is that if alienation is at least partially, if not significantly, grounded in economic imbalances, why do dissident groups resort to using cultural and religious language, rituals, and practices to give expression to their alienation? It has, perhaps, something to do with the depth of marginalization and alienation they experience, which leads to a need for both subjective needs and material restitution to be a national priority. This alienation is often so deep that it takes on a sense of spiritual or metaphysical exclusion that resonates with questions of identity. Historic and enduring, it has an impact on both body and soul, with implications for social identity, individual purpose, and hope itself. It is a cry from and to the very ground of being itself. It is an appeal to the most essential sources of life—ancestors, spirits, the soil, tradition, and the gods. A more political observation is that for the purposes of mobilization, emphasis on a separate identity as grounds for grievances and a basis for organization often has grassroots appeal. This is especially the case where other forms of social cohesion in a central state are crumbling.

The briefest survey of African conflicts echoes this organic, metaphysical, or spiritual cry. It is present in the Hutu/Tutsi conflict in Rwanda and Burundi. The source of Mai-Mai deprivation and exclusion in the Kivu provinces in the eastern part of the Congo is largely socioeconomic, and yet the Mai-Mai draw on cultural and traditional religious forces, magic, ancestor veneration, and traditional forms of spirituality to give expression to their exclusion. The Casamance people, alienated by the dominant Senegalese culture and social economy, draw on Diola culture to justify their struggle for political and economic independence. Material essentials such as land, rice, and rain are spoken of almost in the same breath as ancestors, spirits, and a supreme being. The Lord's Resistance Army in Northern Uganda emerged out of the ethnically based

Holy Spirit Movement under Alice Lakwena, while being grounded in political and economic exclusion. These realities are discussed further in chapter 6.

Twelve years after Nelson Mandela delivered his inaugural presidential address, titled "Many Cultures One Nation," there is an indication that this oneness is being challenged in South Africa by a growing sense of particularism. The Khoi-San celebrate their origins, there is a growing pride among those who trace their identity to the arrival of sixteenth-century slaves, Afrikaners claim their place as a tribe of Africa, South African Indians affirm their cultural origins, and Muslim women are increasingly seen in public in traditional black veils. Where a state is strong and seen to serve all, this could embody dynamic diversity; when central state weakness or discrimination drives group grievances and divisions, it can become destabilizing.

International instruments on group and minority rights, seen as early as in the 1954 recommendations of the UN Subcommittee on the Prevention of Discrimination and the Protection of Minority Rights, signaled an increasing awareness by the international community of the place of ethnicity, religion, and culture in national and regional peace efforts. This underlines the need to include in the nation-building process all those who have the capacity to undermine peacemaking and democracy, without allowing them to jeopardize the emergence of an equitable and just new order.

The challenge of identity, despite its manifestation at times as tribal or ethnic chauvinism, provides a serious challenge to "difference-blind" liberal inclusivity. African nation-building initiatives, despite limited successes and some disastrous failures, identify the difficulty and importance of political, cultural, and social inclusion. Martin Luther King's famous dictum that we need either to learn to live together or die together is a reality that Africa and the world would do well to consider. This calls for peace builders, proponents of transitional justice, African politicians, and international human rights communities to give special attention to how people with differences can peacefully coexist. To embrace these differences while serving all alike is perhaps the only viable option for nation building in a modern context.

African Peace

Ultimately, the African continent is not more given to war or to peace than any other part of the globe. It has been subjected to centuries of colonial and structural violence, and in more recent years it has known a level of violence, abuse, and exploitation by its leaders that must not be ignored or glossed over.

The underlying question is how best to attain sustainable peace on a continent burdened with the memory of colonialism and internationally imposed "solutions" to domestic problems that have resulted in the endless suffering of

African people. Can an appropriate level of complementarity be developed between international demands for prosecutorial justice and an African level of tolerance and negotiation? To what extent do international and African notions of justice differ? What impact does this have on peace-building initiatives in Africa? Is there is a peculiarly African set of values embedded in African culture that underlies African peace-building initiatives? To what extent have colonialism and globalization affected these values, negatively or positively? To what extent can African values enrich the transitional justice debate and Western models of peace building? Perhaps most important, how can the deep suspicion toward the ICC in many African circles be overcome? These and similar questions are addressed in the chapters that follow.

2

SHARED PEACE

We cannot confront de Klerk's people with terms so severe that they
will continue the war in their hearts. We want them to be good citizens
in a new South Africa. We have to learn to live together, otherwise we all
lose. The challenge is to create a shared peace within which to pursue
our goals, knowing it is inevitable that we will influence one another
and in so doing reshape our goals.

—Govan Mbeki, Cape Town, April 1995

It is hard to conceive of a situation in Western society where someone who has
played the role of Ian Smith in the former Rhodesia or P. W. Botha in South
Africa is able to coexist with past enemies who are the victors in a new order.
Smith was able to walk the streets of Harare with impunity; and when Botha
died, the African National Congress (ANC) government offered to give him a
state funeral. The focus of this chapter is not, however, on such events that
characterize some African political transitions—on what some regard as a sense
of "African exceptionalism." It is on the broader discussion among scholars and
practitioners of peace building, on what is seen to be universally required for
sustainable peace to be achieved in postconflict societies. The particular African contribution to this process is returned to in later chapters.

The mix of justice and reconciliation required in societies seeking to overcome deep conflict often sits uncomfortably with the principles of legal and
moral purists. In the words of Ramesh Thakur, "the fate of defeated leaders is
primarily a political question, not a judicial one."[1] Henry Kissinger expresses a
similar sentiment: "It is the temptation of war to punish; it is the task of policy
to construct. Power can sit in judgment, but the statesmen must look to the
future."[2] In Juba a Dinka elder told me, "Young men make war. It is the elders of the tribe that make peace. We look for a way in which anger and suffering can be calmed so that the cycle of revenge can be ended. . . . What we
say is not always popular among our people but because it is sometimes the
only alternative to terrible suffering our people accept it."[3] South Africa's

apartheid conflict drew to a climax in a historic settlement, forged essentially between black Africans and white Boers. The settlement was designed to stop an escalating war that threatened to destroy the very identity, infrastructure, and promise of a nation yet to be born. In the words of Shakespeare's Macbeth: "As two spent swimmers that do cling together," South Africans came to see political reconciliation as the only viable alternative to an escalation of war.

As suggested in chapter 1, transitional justice decisions in Africa on how to balance justice and peace invariably need to be made in situations where opposing forces have the capacity to harm the other but not to win the war and institute sustainable peace—situations characterized by what Thomas Ohlson calls "mutually hurting stalemates."[4]

A pragmatic approach to peace building within this kind of context invariably leaves some protagonists less than satisfied with the terms of a settlement. Peace agreements and political settlements also frequently evoke a measure of tension between leaders and grassroots communities. For a peace agreement to get off the ground, it needs the formal consent of the leaders of the major groups involved in the settlement. Those opposed to it tend to question the extent and depth of support for the agreement, arguing that the political and economic leaders stood to gain the most from the process and thus dismiss the agreement as a self-seeking "settlement of the elite." Indeed, women frequently remain marginalized, the poor alienated, and young people excluded from such benefits that might flow from the settlement, with the dominant or privileged classes of the past carrying that privilege with them into the future. Community or second-tier leaders who question the agreement often feel obliged to support it out of loyalty to first-tier leaders or as a result of political pressure, hoping (sometimes against their own better judgment) that the settlement will ultimately benefit their communities. In turn, alienated grassroots members either get caught up in the euphoria generated by those leaders who support the settlement or accept it with a sense of resignation, albeit questioning to what extent the quality of their lives will change for the better.

Where Top and Bottom Meet

John Paul Lederach, emphasizing the importance of holistic or multilevel peacemaking, tells the story of a member of a nongovernmental organization (NGO) in Somalia cajoling his cousin who was chairperson of a key political party in Mogadishu. "How is it that you warlords think that one of you can be president?" asked the NGO leader. Stressing the need to build peace from below, he reminded his cousin that "without a solid frame, the roof of the house will collapse." Shifting the metaphor, his cousin replied that "the key to a healthy body is a good head," arguing that he had never seen "legs walk or arms move without a head."[5] Peace building calls for cooperation and collaboration between enemies and opponents at both the top and bottom ends of society. A settlement at top-level leadership is not enough, but leadership is important. Put differently, for peace to succeed, a multitrack strategy is required that integrates interventions from track one (top leaders), track two (middle-level leaders), and track three (grassroots community leaders). This integrated approach needs dispassionate political analysis that includes political trade-offs and hard-nosed cost-benefit assessments at the level of international, regional, national, and communal leadership. To address the social and economic needs of those who feel excluded from the political settlement, constituency building is necessary, which needs to involve leaders in civil society, faith communities, business, and academia. For negotiations at the top and middle levels to succeed, grassroots communities must be drawn into the process. The burning question is how to synthesize these different levels and still keep up the complex momentum needed for further transformation.

The needs, local cultures, and interests of grassroots people, not least the poor and socially alienated sections of society, must be kept firmly on the political agenda. Structures need to be rebuilt and an economy developed for job creation to take place, the poor to be fed, and alienated members of society to be drawn into the emerging state. The problem is that all this takes time. It can inevitably only happen in stages that both overlap and follow on one from the other. At best, political reconciliation begins with a commitment to coexistence that recognizes the need for educational reform, skills development, and the beginning of institutional change aimed at drawing as many individuals and groups into the settlement as possible. This requires a specific commitment to sensitize and mobilize people, with a view to ensuring their vigilance in the monitoring and promotion of their needs and concerns. The complexities and dangers inherent to this process are huge. On the one hand, this could result in a clash of interests that, if left unmanaged, might undermine the political climate needed to build a new political dispensation. On the other hand, the essence of the demands made by different sectors of society could be so restrained and diluted that the political process would be undermined to the point that in the interests of compromise and consensus critique would be closed down. The outcome would be a society built on soft mediocrity and compliance that would fail to provide the space and social structures through which people could give expression to their needs and promote their interests. The challenge is to build a national consensus while encouraging a level of debate that ensures that progress can be made toward political and other ideals that either are not immediately attainable or are desirable.

In an attempt to minimize the conflict related to the forming of governments, an increasing number of African and other new democracies are building participatory governments both by design and as a necessary transition mechanism. The perceived need is for government to include as many political, racial, ethnic, and cultural groups as possible—especially such militants who have the capacity to prevent a political settlement. Burundi has opted for a quota-based system of representation. South Africa (discussed below) has its own way of including minority groups in the parliamentary and nation-building process. Rwanda has chosen to bar any racially exclusive political parties, insisting that the Hutu/Tutsi divide make way for Rwandan inclusivity. These different models of peace building await the judgment of history. What is clear is that political exclusivity in Africa and elsewhere, whether explicitly imposed or disguised by ideologies of deception, is a source of intensifying anger, brooding rebellion, and open violence.

Suffice it to say that where ethnic, racial, economic, religious, and cultural exclusion are accentuated by economic exclusion, the recipe is in place for violence to intensify. It is this that makes socioeconomic reconstruction, designed to open economic opportunities to all groups that constitute the nation, so vitally important. Remedial efforts, which may demand some form of affirmative and corrective action, are needed to convince those who have been historically excluded from the material benefits of society that their material needs will be met. Clearly the impatience and grievances of the poor can only escalate where new rulers are seen to be flaunting new levels of personal and class prosperity. Political reconciliation and economic reform are the flip sides of the same national currency, and they need to extend from the highest to the lowest echelons of society. It takes strong and inclusive leadership for this to happen.

Leadership

The nineteenth-century philosopher G. W. F. Hegel once argued that a successful leader needs to be one step ahead of his or her people, but never more than one step—ahead in order to lead, but not too far ahead in order to understand and give expression to the needs of the community. The South African breakthrough in negotiations came as a result of the leadership of Nelson Mandela. After he emerged from twenty-seven years in prison, his example and attitude enabled many who were victims of apartheid to rise above bitterness in building an inclusive democracy, while simultaneously enabling the perpetrators and benefactors of apartheid to be drawn into the settlement. The pragmatic leadership of President F. W. de Klerk provided a different kind of guidance in the white community. He initiated an important departure from the rule of his predecessors Hans Strijdom, Hendrik Verwoerd, B. J. Vorster, and P. W. Botha, all of whom had either rejected or ignored Mandela's calls from prison for negotiations. In the wake of severe opposition in his party concerning the release of Mandela and other political prisoners, de Klerk presented whites with a choice in the form of a referendum that would be the last "whites-only" poll in the country. He won the referendum and provided an opening for peace.

De Klerk's popularity among his Afrikaner followers soon waned, while his initial support among black South Africans showed a temporary escalation. Some waved placards in support of "Comrade de Klerk." However, this soon disappeared as a result of the Boipatong and Bisho massacres, which his critics saw him as having allowed if not provoked.[6]

Mandela was able to provide the leadership he did because he enjoyed the support of grassroots communities. This was consolidated by strong civil society leaders who were capable of persuading the majority of people to endorse the negotiated settlement, declaring their support for him. The politicized nature of South African society—together with the structures that mobilized people through trade unions, religious organizations, cultural initiatives, sports clubs, and other organizations of civil society—drew people into the political process. The result was that they felt it was *their* settlement, at least to the extent of having shared in the buildup to it and in the celebration of its implementation.

Mandela provided the kind of leadership that made popular inclusion across the political spectrum possible. He lay the foundation for the kind of economic reconstruction that was not fully addressed during his presidency but that his successor, Thabo Mbeki, was able to take up in a more direct manner. Yet this, too, necessitated compromises and trade-offs among different interest groups, both to avoid unnecessary conflict and to promote economic transformation. As Mbeki noted early in his presidency, "It's a very delicate thing to handle the relationship between these two elements [transformation and reconciliation]. It's not a mathematical thing; it's an art. . . . If you handle the transformation in a way that doesn't change a good part of the status quo, those who are disadvantaged will rebel, and then goodbye reconciliation."

It is also important for ordinary people to see their leaders relating in a cordial manner to their political opponents. The Convention for a Democratic South Africa (Codesa) talks that led to the interim Constitution and democratic elections received massive media coverage. Proposals on sunset clauses were debated in the media. Pictures of political leaders from opposite sides of the political divide embracing one another were part of daily television coverage. This assisted those removed from the actual negotiation process in accepting the settlement that followed. A hardened and zealous young opponent of apartheid who was skeptical of the negotiation process commented of the time: "When I was in prison, I vowed never to trust a white person again. When I saw Madiba [Mandela] shaking hands with de Klerk on television, I realized that I too needed to make peace with those whom I regarded as my political opponents."[7]

Rapprochement of this kind is but a first step. In 1980, when Robert Mugabe was elected president of Zimbabwe in the wake of a vicious bush war, he too showed magnanimity: "If yesterday you hated me," he observed, "today you cannot avoid the love that binds you to me and me to you. . . . The wrongs of the past must now stand forgiven and forgotten. Our majority rule would easily turn into inhuman rule if we oppressed, persecuted, or harassed those who do not look or think like the majority of us."[8] But gracious words are not enough. Cheap reconciliation solves nothing, and a failure to deal creatively with the causes of past conflict ultimately results in further conflict. Reconciliation can never be an excuse to live with past injustices or to gloss them over. It offers an opportunity to transform past wrongs in a reasoned and purposeful manner. In Zimbabwe the issues of land, governance, and democratic participation still wait to be resolved. It will take hard, enduring, and creative political work and leadership for this to happen. Reconciliation can never be accomplished, and certainly cannot endure, where the causes of conflict and alienation are not addressed.

It is this reality that South Africans face as a fourth term of democratic government begins to unfold. The majority of black South Africans continue to feel alienated from the economic gains that came in the wake of apartheid. The level of political transparency and the overt gestures of political reconciliation that characterized the Mandela years have, with the ousting of Thabo Mbeki as president, given way to confrontation and deep-seated tensions in the ANC. Capitalizing on global economic growth, Mbeki's biggest policy success had been the nation's rapid economic growth since the end of apartheid and the rise of a black middle class. Yet, to the anger of the lower classes, wealth is more unevenly distributed than ever before. Mbeki failed to convince the trade unions and the poorest South Africans that government has acted in their interest, which enabled his opponents to mobilize against him and see him driven out of office in September 2008.

Structures and Participation

Multilevel participation in peace building necessitates both the machinery of democratic politics and the engagement of citizens as political actors. The former demands structures that allow for maximum communication and participation in the decision-making process. In functioning democracies, this includes universal franchise, free and fair elections, a free press, the protection of human rights, and an independent judiciary. Political engagement, in turn, calls for citizens not only to exercise their right to vote but also, at best, to be actively engaged in the political process through, for example, voluntary organizations, community activity, and other forms of political engagement. It further needs consultative encounters between grassroots people and political leaders.

Inclusive democracy and political reconciliation are inherently linked—there cannot be one without the other. Both seek to promote multileveled, open-ended processes of continuous interaction that engage clusters of citizens both in and out of government in resolving public problems.

The difficulty is that despite the breadth of political inclusivity, only rarely is everyone drawn into this process. Some choose not to be drawn into it, and this poses the question as to how those who are part of the process ought to relate to those who are not. This is vividly illustrated in the tension that prevailed between Joshua Nkomo's Zimbabwean African People's Union (ZAPU) and Robert Mugabe's Zimbabwe African National Union (ZANU-PF). This tension came to a head in 1983, when Mugabe unleashed the notorious fifth brigade to brutally crush an alleged Matabeleland rebellion in Operation Gukurahundi. Nkomo, a weakened and ailing man, eventually consented to the absorption of ZAPU into ZANU-PF and was appointed by Mugabe as vice president of Zimbabwe. Accused by some of his followers of selling out, he explained shortly before his death that he had submitted to Mugabe's demands to stop the murder of the Ndebele (his political support base) and of the ZAPU politicians and organizers who had been targeted by Zimbabwe's security forces. In Burundi the Forces Nationales de Libération (FNL) resorted to armed attacks on the new government. For peace to prevail, the FNL still needs to be drawn into government. The Democratic Republic of the Congo continues to be threatened by divisions. In Uganda the armed response of the Lord's Resistance Army to the government since 1989 has entrenched the country in ongoing war.

In South Africa the response to the country's settlement by the white Afrikaner right wing and the largely ethnically based Inkatha Freedom Party in KwaZulu-Natal threatened to undermine a peaceful transition to the beginning of democracy in 1994. These threats vividly illustrated the need for diversity and inclusivity to be promoted both constitutionally and politically—through, for example, the official recognition of eleven languages and the representation of minority parties in the national assembly via a process of proportional representation. This resulted in some parties gaining representation in parliament on the basis of receiving less than 1 percent of the national vote. In addition, the government promoted discussions on language and cultural concerns with white Afrikaner nationalists. It also granted a measure of self-determination to those Afrikaners favoring an independent Afrikaner Volkstaat by allowing the emergence of what is effectively a "privatized" Afrikaner cultural community called Oranje in the Northern Cape Province. Furthermore, the Inkatha Freedom Party was persuaded to participate in government. And last, the Commission for the Promotion and Protection of the Rights of Cultural Religious and Linguistic Communities was established to address the concerns of those who feel their interests and concerns are not adequately addressed.

Feelings of exclusion and alienation are often deep-seated and necessitate a level of inclusivity that constitutes the burden of this book. Above all, political participation demands grassroots as well as minority communities to be involved in the process. The words of Mongesi Guma, the chairperson of the Commission for the Promotion and Protection of the Rights of Cultural Religious and Linguistic Communities, are important is this regard:

> Political leaders are engaging one another, business leaders meet on a daily basis and students from different racial groups are encountering one another in urban schools and universities. The problem is that rural communities are simply not being exposed to people from different groups. It is very difficult to make a subsistence farmer in the agrarian parts of KwaZulu-Natal or the deep rural Eastern Cape, let alone small Venda tribe in the Limpopo Province, feel part of a state that does not give sufficient expression to Zulu, Xhosa or Venda values. These include issues ranging from language usage and national symbols to same-sex marriages, polygamy and the role of traditional leaders in the democratic process. It is equally difficult to persuade an Afrikaner Volkstater that there is room in a multicultural South Africa for Afrikaners to feel at home. These are simply realities that we need to keep working at. The challenge is to create an inclusive state that maintains space for traditional communities to do their own thing.[9]

Divisionism, as suggested in the previous chapter, haunts many African states. Unlike many established democracies, the social and economic survival in Africa continues in several instances to be dependent on leaders and local chiefs facilitating the granting of land, services, and social welfare. Traditionally grounded in a familial relationship between the chief and his or her subjects, the familial factor continues to influence perceptions and expectations of leaders in some African situations today. It is this that makes the new level of commitment to political democracy that addresses issues of national inclusivity in a number of Africa countries so difficult and so vital. The Ugandan scholar Dani Nabudere explains the importance of this:

> Politics in Africa is about relationships. Africans expect their leaders to protect them—and at the time of independence, democracy was seen as a secular form of tribal politics. There was a somewhat romantic hope and expectation that political leaders would function in a protective, albeit paternalistic, way as tribal chiefs. They saw the president as a paramount chief—not least within a traditional community or tribe that he or she represents. Kinship lies at the heart of traditional African politics and a leader is expected to deliver more than knowledge, man-

agement capacity and leadership skills. The African leader needs, in addition to all else, to be a paterfamilias. That's what made Julius Nyerere, Jomo Kenyatta and Nelson Mandela different from those who may well be more skilled in other aspects of state craft. Women leaders need to be matriarchs. There is a longing for kinship.

Voters look for a sense of trust and many are happy to live with dependency and paternalism if trust is there. This is grounded in the assumption that one's own [kin] is more able than someone else—however gifted the outsider may be. Contemporary politics in Africa still carries this bias. Presidents and leaders who ignore and fail to draw leaders from different tribes and communities into government are often required to pay a high price. Grassroots Africans are prepared to overlook a lot of leadership indiscretion if they feel a political leader understands their ways and identifies with their customs. They want to see their leaders in traditional dress, participating in their rituals and singing their songs. This sometimes enables corrupt leaders who exploit this expectation to survive. It also places obligations on leaders to show familial care and protection; when they do not, they are resented. A father is expected to care for his family. A mother must nourish her own. Those who do not do so are resented in a harsher manner than what any stranger or non-familial leader will experience—and when that point is reached, the community will again instinctively look for one of their own to replace the rejected leader. The elephant matriarch is replaced from within the herd. The lion king is replaced by his own.[10]

Questioned on the impact of modernity, the weakening of traditional African structures, and the demand for human rights and good governance, Nabudere spoke of the "partial transcending of ethnic loyalties" while insisting that "tribal, ethnic, cultural, and religious" factors are realities that African leaders, however progressive they might be in seeking to transcend these divisions, still need to take into account when directing the affairs of state. "The successful leader has got to address these concerns. It takes a special kind of person, especially in emerging and fragile democracies, to be seen as leader of all the people." Such a leader needs to recognize and embrace the aspirations of all ethnic and other groups with a view to minimizing the kind of conflict that has torn so many African (and other) societies asunder.

Mutual Understanding

This willingness to understand and respond to the aspiration of others is essential in deeply divided societies. It is also a difficult and often time-consuming process that often collapses into an illusion of peace that prevails where the defeat or weakening of one side is interpreted by the victors as the solution to the conflict. Anatol Rapoport suggests that in reality this often becomes the basis for prolonging the conflict, with the win-lose game giving rise to a lose-lose situation.[11] In what have been called "deadly quarrels" involving complex underlying causes—tribal, economic, and cultural—the only alternative is a mutually acceptable, what is sometimes optimistically called a win-win situation. Realistically, this means that the parties to the conflict must accommodate one another on the basis of a cost-benefit analysis, allowing everyone to feel that there is something in a peace settlement for them—a concern discussed in the next chapter.

Change in a political context is rarely without conflict, and that conflict is often of a deadly or radical kind capable of destroying an emerging opportunity for peaceful transition. This begs the question as to whether and how disputants can engage one another in a manner that minimizes hostilities. The numerous important conflict resolution theories available in print and in practice are not addressed in depth here. To provide theoretical context to what follows, two observations must suffice.

The first concerns the place and importance of culture and local practice in the pursuit of sustainable peace, which is described in various ways. Johan Galtung speaks of "positive peace," in the sense of a social context within which the structures of domination and exploitation that give rise to a conflict are replaced by participatory democracy and the rule of law.[12] John Burton invented the word "provention" to describe this level of resolution.[13] John Paul Lederach, wanting to move the debate beyond the semantics of management, technique, and settlement, speaks of "conflict transformation."[14] The range of theorists and practitioners of conflict resolution in pursuit of such high goals is wide, with Burton and Lederach effectively located at the two ends of the debate.[15]

Burton roots his approach in a social scientific understanding of human behavior that identifies a number of unalterable and nonnegotiable universal human needs necessary for any successful conflict resolution exercise. Without suggesting that culture should be ignored or that the facilitator has nothing to learn from culture-rich participants, Burton states that the role of the third-party facilitator is to assist participants to "excavate through" their culture, religion, and related organic practices in order to identify and make explicit (for themselves as much as for others) their essential needs—which include material concerns as well as identity and security needs. For this to happen and for a conflict to be resolved, he argues that relationship building between disputants is unnecessary—simply focus on need and the rest will follow.

Lederach, conversely, argues that the very culture that Burton seeks to excavate through needs to be examined and tested as a way of releasing insights, resources, and a will to address and settle a conflict. This "thicker" approach to conflict transformation, which draws on indigenous poetry, storytelling, proverbs, and other forms of the arts, locates the facilitator of a resolution or transformation process next to the disputants as they plumb the depths of their cultures and memories. For Lederach, an empathetic engagement with and understanding of the culture of disputants is "an additional level of sophistication and expertise," which the "already trained" facilitator would do well to add to his or her resources. To understand another's culture is to enter into his or her world. To enable disputants to do so can be the beginning of mutual understanding and relationship building. A wise person once observed that if you do not wish to reconcile too much, it is better not to understand too much! Crossing the barrier of otherness and, by implication, the building of relationships is an important ingredient of Lederach's model of conflict transformation.

In their book on negotiation theory, *Getting to Yes*, Roger Fisher, William Ury, and Bruce Patton define this difficult process as the "jungle of people problems," within which they separate relationships from substance as a basis for dealing with substantive needs. Their counsel is to deal with the people problem. Negotiators and disputants are not abstract representatives of opposite sides. They are human beings: "They have emotions, deeply held values and different backgrounds and viewpoints; and they are unpredictable."[16] Emotions (both positive and negative) are inherent to a decision-making process. Few if any of us have the capacity to negotiate purely at a rational level. Integrity and relationship building between disputants enables both sides to handle and temper their emotions.

Typologically, if Burton's approach is *prescriptive* in its affirmation of the universality of analytical human reasoning, Lederach's approach is *elicitive*. It reaches into the depths of ethnoconflict theory and practice. Culture is seen as the carrier of important ethical values and local ways of dealing with conflict. For Lederach, cultural analysis is an irreducible part of those problem-solving processes that give expression to the concerns, priorities, constraints, hopes, fears, and possibilities for conflict transformation among disputants. In a memorable comment on the intertwining of human reason and culture, F. G. Bailey notes: "In the end the best conflict managers will not be cultural outsiders. They will be those for whom the culture is second nature. The enlightened outsider, laboriously searching for the relevant cultural constructs, has too much to learn. The willful outsider, who disdains the search and thinks he has a formula good for all occasions and all cultures, has everything to learn from them."[17]

The second observation builds on the first. It is seen through the lens of Gharajedaghi's four classical ways in which conflicts can be addressed: (1) A course of action that yields the best possible result for the winning party at the expense of the other. This *win-lose situation* invariably fails to transform or address the cause of the conflict. (2) A process that produces minimum satisfaction for everyone involved. A *grim compromise* ultimately satisfies no one. At best, it postpones or curtails hostilities. (3) Ignoring or neglecting a conflict in the hope that it will disappear. *A situation of lingering* invariably escalates a conflict rather than addresses it. (4) Removing or transforming a conflict and solving problems by introducing a redesigned or new way of engaging one another. A *win-win situation* of this kind addresses the cause of the conflict.[18] The rules of engagement encapsulated in Gharajedaghi's fourth way of dealing with conflict are explored in chapter 5, where the African notion of *ubuntu* is considered. In brief, shared peace is ultimately the only lasting option for sustainable peace.

For this level of peace building to be realized in complex political conflicts, opposing groups need to feel that their convictions and values are considered, that their cultural identity is respected, and that their essential needs are met. It demands a holistic approach to peace building that recognizes the insights of Burton while appropriating the context sensitivities of Lederach. This requires that participants move beyond a particular problem or *episode* to the *epicenter* of conflict, which Lederach defines as "the web of relational patterns, often providing a history of lived episodes, from which new episodes and issues can emerge."[19] He argues that while particular episodes release conflict energy, the epicenter is where the energy is produced. It is this "energy" that needs to be transformed in order to address the substantive issues involved. As this begins to happen, new options for living together are envisaged and shared. In a word, a transformational approach to conflict is grounded in the dynamic generated through positive human relations. It is here, in relation to others, that what Lederach calls a "moral imagination" is born.[20]

This involves engagement, trust building, and mutual respect, which can only be realized though dialogue, action, and response—a process addressed more systematically in chapter 3. Cyril Ramaphosa, the ANC's chief negotiator in the South African transition, spoke of relations between the ANC and the South African government at the time and the ANC having reached a point of social trust and cooperation that prompted them to endeavor to accommodate one another's needs in order to take the process forward. This came slowly and necessitated hard work by people on all sides of the conflict. There were generations of mistrust to overcome. A staff member of the ANC's negotiating team who was privy to the negotiations reports that the two sides challenged one another's presuppositions and arguments until they realized they were unable to "outspin" one another. She tells of a late-night session after negotiations had concluded for the day when this was acknowledged: "Time was running out, and neither side could afford to return to the past hostilities. It became clear that both sides began to look for options of settlement that neither side would earlier have accepted. The atmosphere changed, and a new level of talking began. I suppose we needed confrontations in order to be accommodating. In retrospect, there were several cycles of standoff and adaptation. That's at least how I saw it." Ramaphosa endorsed this: "Once both parties came to the conclusion that they could not vanquish each other, accommodation started. Each problem was seen to have a solution."[21] Such accommodation needs necessarily to be inclusive. It involves a continuum of different needs, interests, and concerns, ranging from the material and economic to issues of identity, language, culture, spirituality, and aesthetics. It can probably also only emerge, suggests Theuns Eloff, who headed the Process and Secretarial Services in the South African negotiations (formerly known as Codesa), when both sides have their backs to the wall or are in trouble deeply enough to know there is no alternative but to find a compromise solution.[22] Somewhat controversially, Eloff has suggested that the Northern Ireland dispute lasted as long as it did because neither side wanted a solution badly enough!

In different situations, different needs and interests take priority. Sustainable peace needs to address prioritized as well as lesser concerns. It is, of course, essential to ensure that a starving person has food to eat. And yet with that need met, the person or community concerned will demand housing and education for children and, in time, cultural and language rights. "Take the hierarchy of needs seriously, but not too seriously," a wise woman argued at a seminar on development in Kigali. "People need to eat. But once they have food, they demand more. They cannot be paid off with a slice of bread, not even an occasional fillet mignon!"[23]

In peace settlements, there are invariably multiple groups with multiple needs, with different groups prioritizing different rights. Dealt with sensitively, the affirmation of these rights can provide space within which to address or even transcend the exclusivity that comes from focusing only on issues of, say, identity or material deprivation to the exclusion of other interests that one may share with members of a different group. To explore the possibility of creating space for their respective interests to be addressed, those who exercise power in a particular group may well see the virtue of collaborating with those who have power in a different group. For example, the poor in one group may in time find that they have more in common with the poor in other groups than with the wealthy in their own ethnic or national groups. In brief, to begin to understand the complexity and interrelationship between the different arenas of identity, needs, and interests within a particular situation can be a liberating process—one that can lead to the formation of new relationships that can become a basis for addressing more complex and stubborn concerns.

Group relations are inevitably dynamic; they evolve over time. The discovery of common ground between opposing groups can be advanced by groups revisiting and reassessing the origins of their differences—perhaps recalling earlier alliances that may have existed between them. This level of potential understanding between groups can be enhanced and sometimes initiated by enabling protagonists to discover that, despite identity differences, they share certain basic needs and interests.

Simply stated, from beginning to end, peacemaking involves enabling communities to discover, understand, and acknowledge common ground. It is also about persuading key people within the different communities to use their influence to draw others into this common ground. Essentially, it is within this sphere that misperceptions and stereotypes begin to give way to realistic and more positive perceptions of others. The analyses of successful peace initiatives all suggest that encounters and open communications between different groups can change relationships for the better and enable the building of civic trust between opposing groups.

Roelf Meyer, Ramaphosa's counterpart in the South African negotiations notes: "Once we began to trust the intent of one another to find a solution to the conflict we faced, we were in a position to tackle the more difficult concerns. In fact, as the level of confidence grew around these issues, we were prepared to leave several issues to be sorted out after the political settlement." Have they been sorted out? "Not as fully as they should have. At the same time, however, having begun to trust one another in the face of threatening conflagration we were ready to settle—recognizing that a number of issues, not least economic issues, could only be resolved after the political settlement. Time was also against us and we needed to settle." Was this, in retrospect, the correct thing to do? "Probably, yes. It was the only option. We had extensive and difficult debates on property ownership and economic transformation but were determined not to get stuck on these concerns in a manner that would have delayed if not prevented the settlement and the violence would have intensified. The compromise was the economic clauses that are part of the interim [1994] and final [1996] constitutions. We recognized that affirmative action, black economic empowerment, and skills training would need to be part of the transformation process. This was the realistic way of addressing decades of economic depravation."[24]

Supportive Engagement

The underlying principle for peace building involves what Harold Saunders has aptly defined as "a cumulative, multilevel and open-ended process of continuous interaction over time, engaging significant clusters of citizens in and out of government and the relationships they form to solve public problems . . . either within or between communities or countries."[25] Václav Havel suggests that for this level of political engagement to be entrenched in society, more than the changing of political policy and structures is needed. It necessitates a commitment to what he calls "prepolitical" events and processes that encourage individuals and communities through critical thought processes and debate to resist the imposition of specious ideologies that mask the hypocrisies that are so easily carried over from one government to the next—while recognizing that this level of change takes time and hard work.[26]

This requires that change agents understand and, where appropriate, work toward modifying formal educational structures and interventions into communities (often through existing second-tier leadership structures) as well as promote open debate around social and other issues. It has to do with finding ways to alert people to their basic rights and enabling them to develop the self-confidence to give expression to their rights, concerns, and need to be taken seriously. This includes the rediscovery of what Paulo Friere called the "pedagogy of the oppressed," emphasizing the importance of informal and popular education through dialogue, community participation, and skills development that encourages and enables people to articulate their needs and proposed solutions to problems in engaging those responsible for policy development and good governance. Too often, we promote the structures and machinery of democracy without giving people the most basic skills needed to use these structures.

A seminar on the promotion of democracy among rural women in Sierra Leone identified seven priorities in the promotion of prepolitical skills and activities: identifying basic needs, prioritizing the most urgent needs, organizing one's thoughts before speaking, being able to speak in a logical and ordered manner, being able to think about and respond to counterpropositions, and having the capacity to reformulate a proposal in the light of critique and debate. At the beginning of the seminar, a young woman said she knew what she wanted to say to the elders in her community but did not know *how* to say it. She needed the support of those around her. "I don't have the confidence to tell the government officials in Freetown that they are talking nonsense," another participant noted. At the end of the seminar, the same woman said that the group she had worked with during the two days had given her the confidence to believe that the insights she had into the needs of her community constituted a body of knowledge that the leaders from Freetown simply did not have. "I realized that what I had to say about child soldiers was important and so I said it with a level of conviction that I never knew was within me."[27]

Political impact cannot be achieved in a single seminar. Restoration, political reconciliation, and peace building are by definition recurring processes that need constant attention through debate and other forms of statecraft. Above all, space is needed where divergent views and perceptions can be articulated without fear of revenge or reprisal. Societies that seek to merge all individuality, all corporate differences, and the energies of all national groups into one common enterprise in some utopian sense threaten the very fabric of democratic participation. A state that seeks to neutralize, exclude, absorb, or expel those whose national, ethnic, or tribal origins differ from that of a ruling majority or minority ultimately courts conflict. Differently put, robust debate and political inclusion constitute the lifeblood of a democratic process. Correctly channeled, they provide a necessary corrective to the temptation to force all dissident voices into conformity.

For there to be meaningful engagement between different groups in society, there needs to be a level of relationship building that constitutes a decided shift away from a notion of political power that imposes compliancy and conformity. Recognizing that coercion, even force, is sometimes needed, the bullying of weaker groups in asymmetrical situations is at the very least insufficient for the promotion of lasting peace. At times it is counterproductive.

In some situations the nonuse of force is the most powerful instrument of nation building. Nomhle Nkumbi-Ndopu sees what she defines as a "normative male tactic of muscle-flexing" in one form or another used to silence opponents as unproductive of sustainable results. "When we have power, it is easier to decide to use it than *not* to— . . . Not to use power [coercive force]," she concludes, "is something we do not do naturally—we have to learn it." Responding to Nkumbi-Ndopu's comments, Martin Kalungu-Banda observes: "Mandela has worked hard on how *not* to use power like a boss. Where he could punish, he tried to understand the position of the one at fault. He practiced restraint when he could have used power to settle scores with those who had treated him and his colleagues as if they did not matter. When he was in such a strong position that he could push others to comply, he preferred to consult, persuade, and even plead in order to settle matters. Instead of intimidating people with his power, he chose to bargain and quite often to forgo the short-term 'sweet victory.'"[28] Mandela did, of course, use his authority when needed. He could be immense in using moral authority when he regarded this as necessary. "Never forget his roots go back to chiefs and Thembu royalty. What makes him different is how he used his authority, as well as his willingness to shake hands after a conflict. Throughout his presidency, he was ready to draw his adversaries into future developments. He is not a bitter man. He does not bear grudges. This is the source of his greatness," suggests Jakes Gerwel, director-general in Mandela's office during his presidential years.

The kind of inclusivity seen in recent South African politics has often been ascribed to an underlying African sense of *ubuntu*, meaning that a person can only realize his or her humanity through other people. Clearly *ubuntu* has in some ways lost currency in contemporary society because of the cheap and opportunistic manner in which it has been used, not least in South Africa, to create a sense of emotional well-being without addressing the economic sharing and social inclusivity that are central to it. Without the recovery of such holism, *ubuntu* is reduced to little more than a romantic idea of generations past. Politics requires strong leadership—consultative leadership within the bonds of democracy and a realistic understanding of *ubuntu*. This is discussed further in chapter 5.

Transitional Justice

The formation of a new national identity that includes the space for multiple group identities is always a project in the making. This makes transition an exercise involving both invitation and challenge. The invitation is for those hitherto excluded as well as those who formed the epicenter of inclusion and privilege to participate in the new nation. The challenge is to overcome exclusive notions of race, culture, identity, class, and social privilege.

A limitation and oversight of the transitional justice debate is often its failure to address transformation concerns in an inclusive manner. By focusing on the standard and equally important issues of prosecution, amnesty, reparation, and related concerns, transitional initiatives sometimes fail to give sufficient attention to material concerns. Left for later are the issues of land distribution, impediments to the empowering of excluded sectors of society, structural economic inequality, and cultural and subjective concerns grounded in issues of identity, language, ethnicity, race, and other forms of social privilege. And when neglected, these issues have the capacity to derail the settlement.

Adam Habib provides an important critique of contemporary models of transitional justice, and more specifically the South African transition, with regard to economic redistribution. He contends that the exclusion of socioeconomic issues from the agenda often eases a breakthrough in negotiations from authoritarian rule to the beginning of democracy. The danger is that this often undermines long-term prospects for democratic consolidation.[29] He reminds us that the demand for economic justice is much more than an irritant to political reconciliation.

The failure to redress economic injustice in most deeply divided societies invariably returns to haunt the political terrain. In Zimbabwe the failure to adequately address the land question has returned to bedevil that nation. In South Africa the failure of the negotiation process to adequately address the economic disparities of the past is challenging the nation's negotiated settlement with new vigor. In Rwanda an underlying tension between Hutu and Tutsi, grounded in economic and political privilege, still waits to play itself out.[30]

A businessperson recently suggested that all we need to do in South Africa is create jobs and control crime. Reconciliation will easily follow. "Just grow the economy," he suggested. Acknowledging the utmost importance of economic growth in the reconciliation equation, my rejoinder was that a milieu favorable to economic growth, no less than reconciliation itself, requires that we respect one another despite status or location in life and that we entrench this in our everyday dealing with contentious and other concerns. In particular, all sectors of the community need to participate fully in the nation-building process. This means ensuring a public square that is conducive to the participation of all the communities whose cultures and identities need to be reflected in the ethos of the nation.

It is this need—for recognition, acceptance, and belonging—that links issues of identity so closely to economic growth and inclusion. It is this that persuaded those engaged in the South African negotiated settlement to recognize that the white South Africans who controlled the economy need to be drawn into the new political dispensation—and that the most effective way to do so was to enable them to experience the kind of belonging and well-being that provided a vested interest in the future of the nation. It is equally important that black entrepreneurs be drawn into the center of the economy through broad-based black economic empowerment. It is even more important to ensure that the poor, who can realistically only look longingly at the privilege of those (both black and white) who benefit from the wealth of the nation, have reason to believe that their material needs and aspirations can be met within the emerging economy.

Where victims are asked to suspend their economic demands, at least until after the political transition, this does not happen. Often victims are denied the right to see perpetrators prosecuted because, for example, a transitional amnesty clause needs to be been included in the political settlement. The danger is that when economic challenges are returned to later, they are invariably not confronted with the same sense of political urgency that was demanded at the time of transition—not least because by this time the new political elite have usually already begun to share in the economic benefits of the nation.

This point was vividly portrayed during a visit to Brazil in 1994 shortly after South Africa's first democratic elections. Speaking in Curitiba at a seminar on political change, I responded to a question as to whether the poor majority in South Africa would be better off after ten years under the new ANC government. I spoke of the massive voter turnout in the elections being an indication that the vote of the poor would ensure that the new government gave priority to their needs. In response an animated student, flexing his Marxist muscles, suggested that the democratic transition in South Africa would in time give way to what he called the "domination of the new ruling class." He insisted that the poor would lose interest in politics: "In Rio de Janeiro the poor play volley ball on the beach; in Curitiba we play soccer or simply stay at home. The novelty of the vote will soon wear off in South Africa." Arguing that it is not enough merely to have the scaffolding or machinery of democracy, he asked, "Would the poor in South Africa be allowed to use the new democratic space they have acquired to attain the kind of economic relief they need?" Suggesting that power and privilege are rarely if ever voluntarily surrendered, he concluded that South Africa, like any other country in transition, would "either get stuck in economic disparity or face a second revolution."[31]

Economic exclusion and material deprivation cannot be compensated for by "soccer on the beach." Patience and national unity in time give way to impatience and social unrest in the face of the grim reality of continuing social exclusion, although the language of exclusion changes in postindependent states. For example, Robert Mugabe with justification speaks about the impact of colonialism, but at the same time drives the poor out of the country's major cities in Operation Murambatsvina (the government-sanctioned destruction of informal housing and businesses), forcing them to languish and sometimes die in resettlement camps. Others long for days gone by. As a young girl, Tina van Malderen moved in 1951 with her parents to Bukavu in the eastern part of the Congo, where her father worked for the Belgian administration. She still speaks of the "happy" state of black Congolese in those colonial days. "We loved our blacks. . . . When they had children, we gave them presents." When reminded that the Belgians colonized the Congo in a program of slavery and tyranny that killed 13 million people in what has been called the first holocaust of the twentieth century, she conceded, "Well, maybe on the plantations they were a little rude to them."[32]

A dependency syndrome driven by fear of retaliation and the internalization of exclusion sometimes leads to those who are excluded and oppressed to fail to offer any form of meaningful resistance. "One who makes himself into a worm cannot complain when people step on him," suggested Immanuel Kant. In asymmetrical situations, where the root cause of conflict is located as much in the unequal relationship as it is in other specific causes, awareness raising and the conscientizing of the oppressed are indispensable in addressing conflict. Without a heightened awareness that allows both the hidden and less obvious causes as well as more obvious sources of conflict to be addressed, peace can only be a possibility or temporary.

Sustaining Peace

John Darby and Roger MacGinty suggest six such hurdles to be overcome in the pursuit of shared peace. They apply significantly to situations of an asymmetrical kind where the possibility of lingering if not overtly expressed conflict needs careful monitoring and response.[33]

The first is that most political settlements and cease-fires collapse in the first few months. This calls for special attention to be given to the initial nervousness that is inevitably present when former enemies begin to work together. In any attempt to share power, the temptation of the "power holders" is to resort to violence in the face of a crisis while the "power seekers" often keep their options open to return to violence if a political settlement does not work out. Trust building takes time and needs to be worked at constantly to ensure that differences are addressed politically rather than by resorting to the kind of unilateral action that leads to renewed violence, which is so often the case when power holders and power seekers stare one another down in confrontation. Mechanisms to deal with conflicts must be put in place and both sides of the conflict must be sensitive to the needs of opposing parties.

The second factor is that a lasting agreement is impossible to attain if it fails to include those who have the power to undermine it. Examples abound: The Mai-Mai and Banyamulenge in the Kivu provinces of the Democratic Republic of the Congo constitute an ethnic challenge with which Joseph Kabila's government is obliged to deal. His reluctance to include the recognized leaders of these communities in the postelection peace-building process has resulted in continuing violence in the area. In Rwanda the exclusion of recognized Hutu leadership from the political process continues to raise concerns about the nation-building process undertaken by Paul Kagame's government. In Burundi the government of the Conseil National Pour la Défense de la Démocratie / Forces pour la Défense de la Démocratie under the leadership of Pierre Nkurunziza has failed to draw the FNL into the new dispensation, to its own peril.

At the same time, it is important to ensure that a recalcitrant group that refuses to join a broader settlement is not allowed to hold the peace process to ransom. Apollinaire Gahungu, an aide to former Burundian president Pierre Boyoya, spoke of the "uncompromising pressure" that Mandela exerted on Boyoya in the talks leading to the Arusha Agreement in 2002: "Mandela scolded and charmed Boyoya and then went into the press conference, put his arm around Boyoya and complimented him on his statesman-like approach by agreeing to participate in the peace endeavor in Burundi. I learned that day that it takes both a carrot and stick to make peace. It demands the inclusion of as broad a coalition as possible. It takes a special kind of leadership for this to happen."

The third factor is that agreements must include militants, including those resistant to the settlement. Those who have the greatest power to make peace are those who control the violence. To exclude them is to place them in a position to derail the settlement from the outside. The temptation within political groupings is to exclude those militants who are likely to make consensus finding difficult. It is again, however, a question of not allowing a settlement to be held to ransom for what are often extreme demands that only a few are holding out for while ensuring that as many as possible of those sympathetic to the views of the militants are drawn into the settlement. Peacemaking is as much about conflict management as it is about getting everyone to agree on all issues, recognizing that if the first stages of the settlement can be sustained, the possibility of resolving outstanding issues can only increase—provided that trust building continues to be actively promoted.

The fourth factor is that leaders of the groups involved in the conflict should be left to bring their own people into the agreement. Not all leaders are capable of doing this, and it is important that those that are be given the political space in which to do so, without interference from opposing groups. This calls for understanding and tolerance on all sides while leaders endeavor to persuade their followers to join the peace process. Again, it is a question of all parties needing to discern the level of provocation and dissent a settlement can tolerate.

The fifth factor involves the disarmament, demobilization, and the reintegration of soldiers into society. This requires that soldiers and others be compensated for their loss of influence (and sometimes jobs) resulting from the settlement. Prudence demands that soldiers from all militia groups be integrated into the new national army or, alternatively, into civilian life. Clearly this brings with it a range of difficulties and challenges. The agencies with the skills to address these difficult situations need to be drawn into the settlement process as soon as possible. In the immediate wake of the Burundian elections in 2005, a senior government official argued with justification that one of the biggest challenges facing his country was the lack of resources and infrastructure to absorb the many former rebel soldiers and party officials into the army and the civil service: "We need to give them something constructive to do."

The sixth factor is that a peace accord is only the first step toward sustainable peace. The work that follows can be more demanding than the terms of the settlement itself. Conversely, for negotiators to wait until all problems are resolved before asking leaders to sign the agreement could result in the collapse of the process. Timing is important. Mandela sensed this in the Burundian settlement. Criticized by some for "imposing a settlement" on the Burundians, his action may well have prevented a new round of all-out warfare.

It is the sixth factor that identifies what is potentially the most difficult question to assess in a time of transition: What can be resolved at the time of transition and what can wait until later? It is tempting to avoid the most contentious factors in a conflict and to prioritize the views and proposals of moderates in the pursuit of peace. However, it is important to include militants—primarily because they are the ones who usually stand firm on the most contentious issues, but also because they are capable of derailing a settlement. History also suggests that where the difficult issues are postponed they are often neglected, returning later to haunt a settlement.

In *The March of Folly* Barbara Tuchman surveys thirty centuries of history, stretching from the fall of Troy to America's catastrophic involvement in Vietnam. She observes that the most likely response of nations facing disruption is to seek armed superiority in order to deal with the conflict. The folly is that such superiority can rarely be sustained.[34] A dispassionate assessment of the conflict, which all too often emerges as a "lantern on the stern," suggests that self-interest can often best be served by a commitment of energy, skills, and resources in the pursuit of a modus vivendi.

Drawing on the sages of the centuries, Tuchman reduces the primary source of political folly to lust for unrestrained power: Tacitus saw it as "the most flagrant of all passions"; Plato thought that the soul of humanity is unable to resist the temptation of arbitrary power, concluding that there is "no one who will not under such circumstances become filled with folly, the worst of diseases"; Lord Acton's dictum that "power corrupts and total power corrupts totally" continues to imprint itself on the politics of conflict.

Václav Havel's essay in memory of Jan Patočka at the height of the Polish resistance to totalitarianism in 1978 captures the essence of the dissent aroused by the ruthless defense of power: "This specter [dissent] has not appeared out of thin air. It is a natural and inevitable consequence of the present historical phase of the system it is haunting. It was born at a time when this system, for a thousand reasons, could no longer base itself on the unadulterated, brutal and arbitrary application of power, eliminating all expressions of nonconformity."[35]

The challenge is to enable nations and communities to develop ways of engagement that allow for nonconformity, dissent, open debate, and orderly political change when necessary. The reluctance of nations to do just this is what Tuchman defines as the "sheer stupidity" and "folly" that brings chaos to all concerned.

Plato identified the "sacred golden core of reason" as the possible source of peace, but he acknowledged that his fellow beings were anchored in the life of feelings and were manipulated by desires, fears, and passion. It is the realization that people are more than rational beings that necessitates an approach that addresses emotions, fears, and desires as well as reason. The engagement of an opponent is an art that calls for the sensitivity of those who have learned to promote peace where peace is no more than a distant possibility. It is *their* wisdom—the wisdom of those whose ability is often a by-product of sheer necessity in the face of threatening destruction—which is sought in chapter 3. This "road less traveled" calls for political reconciliation to be recognized as an essential ingredient of political realism.

3

FROM ENCOUNTER
TO SETTLEMENT

It is a very difficult thing to enter into dialogue with someone who has
no respect for you as a person, being quite happy to see you dead. And
yet without renewed dialogue, you cannot put an end to the suspicion
that perpetuates the conflict. In the immediate wake of the genocide
our priority was to stop the killing. This required armed intervention,
although we soon realized this was not enough. It required a willingness
to engage one another in dialogue.

—Aloisea Inyumba, former head of the National Unity and
Reconciliation Commission, Kigali, September 2006

The quest for political reconciliation in the face of threatened chaos and destruction presupposes a willingness to engage one's enemy in negotiation, dialogue, and the development of such measures that are required for there to be
sustainable peace. Whatever model of conflict management, resolution, or transformation is adopted for this to happen, three interrelated processes need to
be nurtured and developed for the wisdom of peace building to take root and
grow. The first is a willingness to explore the possibility of the cessation of
hostilities. The second involves mutual acceptance of criteria for resolving conflicts through negotiation. The third concerns agreement on a course designed
to ensure lasting peace. Each step involves different processes and different
levels of trust, engagement, and cooperation.

Conflicts differ in context and substance. They are driven by different
mobilizing factors that need to be carefully analyzed and understood when
developing effective peacemaking and peace-building strategies. There are,
however, certain common dimensions to most conflicts and peacemaking endeavors. William Zartman argues that internal conflicts begin with the breakdown of "normal politics" and that conflict interventions are aimed at facilitating

a process that allows the conflict to shift from violence back to politics.[1] Peter Wallensteen argues that civil wars are about the distribution of power and that conflict resolution involves interventions aimed at giving "reasonable social and political space to all groups in society."[2] Terrence Lyons focuses on demilitarization as a key variable in a peace process, arguing that where armed groups are able to transform themselves into political parties as a basis for pursuing their objectives, the possibility of sustainable peace is increased.[3] Where groups are unable to do so, the peace process is threatened. As such, peace turns on whether incentives for disarmament are seen to outweigh the incentives to continue an armed conflict.[4]

Thomas Ohlson's essay "Understanding Causes of War and Peace," based on a study of intrastate conflicts, contributes significantly to the discussion on how to enable groups to move from armed engagement to the beginning of a political process.[5] In brief, he suggests that there are essentially three incentives for people to take up arms: They have *reasons* in the form of grievances and goals, they have *resources* in the form of capacities and opportunities, and they have *resolve* because they see no alternative to violence. Building on these incentives, Ohlson argues that the possibility of peace is enhanced in a situation where there is a *mutually hurting stalemate* that can lead to the possibility of negotiations and a change in conflict behavior, where there are *mutually enticing opportunities* that emerge from negotiations that begin to generate intraparty trust and growing confidence in a peace process, and where there are *mutually obtained rewards* that can lead to the gradual implementation of normal politics.

The common thread that runs through any attempt to move beyond conflict is a willingness by former enemies and adversaries to engage one another in dialogue and negotiation—what Zartman calls "normal politics." Peace in whatever form, whether the cessation of fighting imposed through armed intervention, a mutually agreed upon cease-fire, or the planning and development of sustainable peace—invariably involves some form of dialogue and negotiation. The obvious ingredients of this process include the simple but crucial categories of engaging the other, ways of talking and listening, dialogue, imagination, and action—ingredients that are often overlooked by scholars studying conflict intervention and peace.

Clearly it takes more than having these ingredients in place to resolve a conflict. They are, however, constituent of a process within which interlocutors can get to the point of agreeing on what constitutes sincere engagement as well as on the necessary focus needed for serious dialogue and honest negotiations to take place. A key ingredient of this process is captured in Michel Foucault's understanding of authentic, free, and fearless speech in civic dialogue. He argues that it needs necessarily to include the burden to disagree and to speak the truth even at the cost of challenging the possible engagement with the other. Probing the nature of the relationship between the speaker and what he or she says, he favors "dialogue through questions and answers," within which the "common logos" of the city is pursued. This presupposes a sense of belonging and being a good citizen, which the disruptive orator does not have. "Who is able to tell the truth?" he asks. "What are the moral, ethical, and the spiritual conditions which entitle someone to present himself as, and to be considered a truth-teller? . . . What are the consequences of telling the truth?"[6] The capacity of the city to hear and respond to the truth is facilitated within a context of belonging and civic trust. The cost of retaliation, possible exclusion, and punishment is, conversely, an inherent part of the vulnerability with which the honest speaker exercises his or her responsibility as a citizen, even within an established democracy.[7] For Foucault, the right to free speech and the obligation to participate in political debate need to be continually fought for and responsibly pursued.

Honest dialogue of this kind is the opposite of what is, not without cause, often dismissed as being part of a "dialogue industry." Authentic speech creates a space within which opponents engage in honest critique and disagreement, as a basis for establishing processes and goals that they judge to be authentic and worth pursuing. Candidly pursued, this level of talk can be a wellspring of crucial forms of intervention and action. This is particularly necessary on the African continent, where the complexities of conflict almost invariably include the intertwining of ethnic, resource, and geographical factors. In brief, unless the proposed solutions to conflicts address these complexities and are locally owned and internalized by grassroots communities and their leaders, the projected peace is unlikely to endure.

Reconciliation, in the modest sense of being willing to engage an opponent in dialogue, joint decision making, civic respect, and self-criticism, although time consuming, is ultimately the most effective way of promoting sustainable peace.

The interrelated themes of *encounter and engagement*, and *exploration and dialogue*, along with *visioning and enactment* that are explored below draw essentially on experiences and insights gained in intrastate conflicts in Africa, although they may well have relevance for interstate conflicts as well. They suggest areas of reflection that are applicable to individuals, communities, and nations in both conflict and postconflict situations. At best, the themes provide a potential holistic movement toward a reconciling process that can only be initiated or partially fulfilled in the immediate to short-term future. Progress is dependent on growing trust between opponents as the first hesitant steps toward resolving disputes and, beyond that, to long-term peace building.

Encounter and Engagement

For any peace or reconciliation process to be advanced, the *encounter* between disputants needs necessarily to be one of sincerity and integrity. The nature and extent of the relationships that exist between disputants may, however, be of varying kinds. They can be anywhere on a scale ranging from outright mistrust of the other to tentative steps toward rapprochement and eventual deeper levels of mutual trust. What is important is an acknowledgment of the level of engagement that exists between adversaries.

Mac Maharaj, a leading participant in the South African negotiation process between 1990 and 1994, argues that the integrity of the process itself was more important than the trust that eventually developed between negotiators from the African National Congress (ANC) and the former government: "What got us through difficult moments in the negotiations was the integrity of a process and the balanced structures we agreed to put in place. We all knew what the rules were and we all knew they were being applied evenhandedly." He explains:

> There was a simple formula consisting of three boxes into which we placed issues as they arose—issues on which we agreed, those on which we disagreed and those where there was partial agreement. Slowly we moved issues into the agreement box—agreeing that we would be able to reassess all the "agreed" issues again before finalizing the process. In this way we were able to keep the process going. That was the secret of our success. The more we agreed on issues the easier it was to handle the more contentious issues which we began to see within the context of the broader agreements. The trust that existed was trust in the process. Whatever relationships emerged between negotiators were primarily within the framework of the actual negotiations. Although a few professional relationships that emerged were carried over into social relations or personal friendships, this level of relationship is simply not necessary in a serious negotiation process.[8]

Implicit in Maharaj's observation is the importance of professional respect and interaction among negotiators. Any deeper relationship that may emerge from the process can presumably be of assistance, provided that it does not interfere with the integrity of the decision making. The fact is, however, that the context within which the negotiations are held has both a direct and indirect impact on the process. It is more conducive to peace if it is of a cordial and empathetic nature rather than of a cold and indifferent kind.

The Zulu greeting *sawubona* literally means a lot more than a passing "hello." It means, "I see you" in the sense of recognizing and acknowledging who someone is and the context within which he or she operates. *Nayabonana* is the reciprocal "we see one another." A Methodist Biblewoman living in a rural area of KwaZulu-Natal, sensing one morning that for me *sawubona* was little more than a formal greeting, decided to challenge me. She explained: "The word *sawubona* reminds me to stop, to look at you, to see you, and to acknowledge you anew each time we meet, before we deal with the business of the day." I carry her words with me. Traditionally the greeting would be followed by inquiries about one's family, home, and village. In brief, one is encountered within the context of one's community and basic needs. This forestalls the danger of reducing the person encountered to a mere instrument to be used in a transaction. It opens the possibility of an emerging relationship that enables new acquaintances, business participants, and disputants to understand each other's needs and objectives as a basis from which to engage one another in an attempt to reach a mutually satisfying resolution to a conflict. It endeavors to see beyond the mask we project and that others impose on us.

The French philosopher Emmanuel Lévinas suggests that if we truly look someone in the eye, we are never again able to look away from that person.[9] The persons involved in this exchange may well disagree on issues and may even fight about them. However, once the encounter is there, there is a basis from which to engage one another as human beings with identities and needs. "A face breaks up a system," he tells us, and we encounter a person as someone who bleeds, laughs, cries, hurts, and, given the opportunity, is often prepared to settle for a fair deal.

Encounters of this kind enable us to move beyond habitually imposed assumptions, opening possibilities for a different kind of relationship between enemies or strangers. We begin to see our opponents, and by implication the problems we face, in a different way.

When asked how victims of atrocities can establish any kind of working relationship with a torturer or executioner, Lévinas replied that one who threatens or abuses a neighbor "no longer has a face."[10] Decades earlier, Jean-Paul Sartre, using a similar idiom, wrote of human aggression manifesting itself in the will to stare one another down, to dominate and destroy the other.[11] The way out, he suggested, is for opponents to find a goal that serves both their objectives. It is here, he argued, that the humanity of the other can be retrieved or established. In Lévinas's words, "the face" of the opponent reemerges. Sometimes it emerges for the first time—in cautious and tentative form.

The link between what Maharaj spoke of as a reliable structure and process aimed at a particular set of goals and the emergence of personal respect and trust through nascent relationships is important. It takes more than emotive relations to solve problems. There needs to be a structure in place aimed at addressing problems and reaching specific goals. However, relationships built on what is often a tough problem-solving basis can become a platform for taking a negotiation process onto a higher level that involves greater risk and uncertainty.

The incentive to encounter and engage an enemy or adversary and to commit to the rules of a process usually arises when those locked in a deadly conflict realize that the only alternative to a mutually destructive stalemate or battle is to find one another in common pursuit and to agree on the rules for getting there. It is to recognize the rights and to accept the humanity of one's adversary in return for similar recognition from him or her. Roelf Meyer, the chief negotiator in the 1990s for the former South African government, argues that politics, especially in the time of conflict, focuses on self-interest, with little thought being given to the interests and needs of others:

> It is usually only when the implications of a conflict of interests stare us in the face and we realize that neither side can impose their interests on the other that we begin to recognize the need to accommodate one another. When you look over the abyss, you realize just how much you and your enemy need one another. You begin to realize you need to talk. . . . This realization is one of the most important lessons I take away with me from the negotiations between the former government and the ANC in the 1994 settlement. After years of alienation and the fear of an escalating civil war staring us in the face, we began to see the necessity of accommodating one another. It was once we began to realize that we both needed to honor our commitments to one another that a measure of trust began to develop between us.[12]

Cyril Ramaphosa, the chief ANC negotiator and Meyer's counterpart, concurs: "A failure to find trust had destroyed thousands of people in tens of decades of fighting. . . . It was clear that a political settlement simply had to be found and a way of building trust became essential. . . . We knew that in order to build trust we would need courage. We also had no alternative."[13]

The earliest and most fragile notion of engagement often begins with no more than a pragmatic realization that an enemy cannot be defeated and therefore needs to be accommodated in order to avoid further debilitating conflict and eventual conflagration. In Burundi, this resulted in the Arusha Peace and Reconciliation Agreement in 2000. In the Democratic Republic of the Congo (DRC), a crucial turning point was the signing of a power-sharing deal in Pretoria on December 16, 2002, as the culmination of the Sun City Talks earlier that year. In Sudan, the Comprehensive Peace Agreement signed in January 2005 gave expression to a commitment by President Omar al-Bashir and John Garang, leader of the Sudan People's Liberation Movement at the time, to establish an interim government.

Encounters and relationship building need to go beyond any sense of cozy togetherness that threatens straight talk. There are risks involved. Sometimes such encounters fail to result in a viable solution. Often they break down and need to be rebuilt. Conflicts, standoffs, false posturing, and demands are part of most settlements. If correctly managed via established processes and structures, however, failures, successes, and hard bargaining can become a basis for building trust and the beginning of a political settlement.

The first signs of rapprochement in the South African situation were made manifest in several nervous and yet calculated social contacts that some dismissed as spurious. Thabo Mbeki had dinner in New York in 1986 with Pieter de Lange, the leader of the exclusivist white Afrikaner Broederbond. Other off-the-record talks were held in venues across the world. Between sessions at the historic Mount Fleur Scenario Planning seminar in 1991, Trevor Manuel, the present South African minister of finance, walked in the Stellenbosch Mountains with Derek Keyes, the minister of finance at the time. These talks all contributed to building trust and enabling the kind of encounter that created a milieu within which a settlement could happen. "Whiskey, a few beers, a decent meal, and in my case a pipe of tobacco all helped oil the wheels of the much-talked-about talks about talks," the late Steve Tswete observed. Reflecting on the process leading to the South African settlement, he added, "They discovered that we did not have horns and we realized that they could be courteous, even genteel. A measure of trust began to emerge, and with this the recognition of the humanity of the other. This was essential for serious talks to happen."

Serious encounters call for honesty and robust engagement. But before getting to this point, the conditions for negotiations need to be put in place. In the South African situation such encounters were captured in the Harare Declaration in 1989. Regarded as nonnegotiable by the ANC, they were accepted as such by the government of the day. The conditions included lifting the state of emergency, ending restrictions on political activities, legalizing all political organizations, releasing political prisoners, and the cessation of all political executions. It was only after these demands were met in January 1990 that serious talks got under way.

Some theorists insist that trust is not a requirement for the resolution of conflict, contending that it is enough to be problem solvers. This might be so in less volatile circumstances. The problem, however, is that in highly conflictual situations "tame problems" soon escalate into "deadly conflicts." Meaningful encounters emerge between adversaries when sufficient common interest is seen to exist between them to warrant a measure of respect, trust, and cooperative problem solving.

Hannah Arendt writes a tantalizing sentence in her study of imperialism in *The Origins of Totalitarianism*: "It seems that a man who is nothing but a man [someone living in isolation from others], has lost the very qualities which make it possible for others to treat him as a fellow man."[14] She suggests that a human being has rights only in relation to other human beings. To the extent that someone ignores or violates the rights of another, the promise and potential of a relationship between individuals, and indeed the creation of a caring and respectful community, is undermined. Put differently, to the extent that I fail to acknowledge another human being by turning away from a potential relationship with that person, I undermine the possibility of being taken seriously by that person and of my own rights being acknowledged. Reflecting on Arendt's sentence, the French postmodernist Jean-François Lyotard writes: "To banish the stranger is to banish the community, and you banish yourself from the community thereby." He argues that human rights are inherently reciprocal, linking rights and duties. This duality is what helps a society not to collapse into totalitarianism. Citizens have a right to speak, they have an obligation to speak, and they need to allow others to speak. He further argues that it is through engagement of this kind that a person realizes his or her full capacity and promise as a human being. A human being "does not precede but results from interlocution."[15] This is a big statement. It finds renascence in a later chapter on *ubuntu* and is an idea that is central to this book. It grounds the importance of "encounter and engagement" as much in self-fulfillment and self-interest as it does in an ethical commitment to others. It also provides a realistic basis for peacemaking.

Aloisea Inyumba, who had worked tirelessly as head of the Rwandan National Unity and Reconciliation Commission, spoke of the complexity of promoting meaningful encounter and common pursuits between former enemies:

> Our biggest challenge was to convince genocidaires and their victims that the solution to Rwanda's problems could not be settled with knives and machetes. Once people on both sides began to face up to this reality and began to understand that we were not asking them to forgive one another—a demand that was virtually impossible for most Rwandans to consider—a sense of relief emerged and a space opened within which to begin to explore ways of engaging one another in the pursuit of mutually beneficial objectives. These issues included the important question of how Rwandans could jointly begin to create a different kind of future.[16]

This Rwandan recognition of the need to engage the enemy is also seen in the South African situation. Shortly after Mandela's release from prison, he met with General Constand Viljoen, then commander-in-chief of the South African army. "If you want to go to war," Mandela told Viljoen, "I must be honest with you and admit that we cannot stand up to you on the battlefield. We don't have the resources. It will be a long and bitter struggle, many people will die and the country may be reduced to ashes. But you must remember two things. You cannot win because of our numbers; you cannot kill us all. And you cannot win because of the international community. They will rally to our support and they will stand with us."[17] Viljoen was drawn into the settlement process and later played a crucial role in drawing conservative Afrikaners into the election process. Not all antagonists show the pragmatism of Viljoen. Some prefer ashes to survival. The choice between the two is contextually bound. It involves time and place. Both require a discerning eye and an analytical mind. If the moment is correctly discerned and the response to it is appropriate, it can be a turning point that opens up new vistas, preparing the way for positive change.

I was invited to speak in Rwanda in 1996 by the Rwandan Ministry of Justice, two years after the genocide in that country and the South African transition to democracy in 1994. My brief was to talk about reconciliation in South Africa. After I had spoken at a public meeting, a man clearly carrying the scars of the genocide stood up and politely said, "Please don't ask us to reconcile. We are still burying our dead and looking for justice. Reconciliation may come later. For some of us it will never come. Right now we are angry. We need time to mourn." Choosing the moment for rapprochement demands social sensitivity. It is often a serendipitous moment with different political, theoretical, cultural, and emotional tensions coming together in an emerging synergy. The kaleidoscope clicks, and engagement happens. Such an engagement involves more than a meeting. It involves the realization that one's enemy is part of the solution. One's enemy becomes part of a shared future existence. This makes politics possible in the sense of an open-ended forum for the honest exchange of ideas in careful talk and deep listening.

The place and choreography of encounters and engagement can be as important as the timing. Ramaphosa speaks of the importance of choosing Groote Schuur, the historic Cape Town residence of South African presidents, for the "coming home of political exiles."[18] "The ambiance of the place made us feel we had to behave well and reach a settlement," Joe Slovo, the head of the South African Communist Party, noted at the time.[19]

In situations where division tears at the soul of a nation, there is no realistic alternative to honest encounters, talking long and hard into the night, and listening carefully to stories that give expression to the needs and aspirations of one's opponents. There is also no fixed route to this kind of encounter. However, the process can be facilitated by

- giving trust another chance—being open to the possibility of trusting an adversary, realizing that the alternative is further estrangement and an escalation of violence;

- understanding why the encounter is necessary and clarifying the problem(s) at hand;
- seeking to discover and engage the "person" behind the adversary;
- endeavoring to understand the perceptions and needs of opponents or adversaries;
- discerning the right time, space, and location for an encounter;
- acknowledging that sustainable peace is shared peace—it cannot be imposed on an unwilling party;
- signaling a desire to find a shared solution to the cause(s) of conflict; and
- establishing processes and structures that promote trust building.

Exploration and Dialogue

During a particularly tense event in 2004, when a cross-section of Sudanese people were brought together prior to the comprehensive peace settlement signed in that country in January 2005, a Dinka elder noted that "political reconciliation begins when enemies are prepared to sit under the same tree and talk." This serves as a basis for dealing with deep-seated conflict or what he called "an endemic will to destroy." "To sit face to face with an enemy and talk honestly provides a sense of the complexity of the problems involved. It requires sensitivity and a willingness to try and understand your enemy's hopes and fears. When your enemy in a similar manner begins to understand your concerns and aspirations, things begin to happen."

Maurice Charland writes of the importance of constitutive rhetoric in political encounters, arguing that communities are constituted in discourse.[20] In open exchange, they expose themselves to the possibility of social reconstruction. For him, constitutive political rhetoric invites a person or community into conversation in a manner that opens a space within which they and others can begin to reassess social identities in relation to others. In contrast to political rhetoric as diatribe, constitutive rhetoric is a participatory and formative process. It is an invitation to dialogue. It provides a "narrative space" in which to sojourn, recognizing that the occupants of that space can continue to become other than what they are at any given time. This opens a possibility for opponents to move jointly toward resolving their differences.

Conversely, confrontational rhetoric, whether in the form of reactionary diatribe or revolutionary ideology, tends to do little more than fan the fire of conflict. "I wish that politicians and their spin doctors would simply keep quiet," a participant in the South African peace initiative explained in a crisis moment when negotiations collapsed. "We knew at the time that the problems we faced could be overcome if only the protagonists would stop being so damned suspicious of one another. Their words led to further words, accusations, and counteraccusations. They were not solving problems. They were making them worse. Our task was to find words that would bring us together." It has been estimated that Roelf Meyer and Cyril Ramaphosa met more than fifty times during the breakdown in the South African negotiations. "We both rethought our positions and found words to take us forward," Meyer recalls.

Talk

Former South African president Nelson Mandela spoke of the importance of using words carefully in conflictual situations. Speaking on the HIV/AIDS crisis in South Africa, he observed: "It is not my custom to use words lightly. If twenty-seven years in prison have done anything to us, it taught us to use the silence of solitude to make us understand how precious words are and how real speech is in its impact upon the way people live or die."[21]

In Dinka custom, knowledge is "*Nginy e we*," which Francis Deng translates as "knowing the words." It means both accumulating information and custom and finding the appropriate form of communication and persuasion. "This thing called words," writes Deng, "is what is keeping the world in order."[22] We effectively shape and direct the world through the words we speak. Elsewhere, he writes of the use of words at peace conferences where words, including ritualistic words, can be "fighting words" but can also be used "to restore harmony and relationships." He cites a traditional chief as saying, "A man defeated by strength of power comes back. . . . But a man defeated with words does not return."[23]

Words are central to work of the *abashingantahe* in Burundi.[24] Explaining the centrality of speech as "an enhancing factor" of the *abashingantahe* as an institution (*ishirahamwe*), Domitien Nizigiyimana captures the importance of language in a poem:

> The language is all,
> It cuts, skins
> It shapes, it modulates
> It disturbs, makes mad
> It cures or kills on the spot
> It amplifies/reduces according to the weight
> It excites or quietens the soul[25]

For Nizigiyimana, words are the essence of encounter and dialogue. We need to find the right words to reach beyond the noise of mere talk. Words, he tells us, need to be weighed; they need to be truthful and sincere.

In contrast, in the South African struggle, words had lost their legitimacy and meaning. The government refused to talk to those whom they saw as anarchists, terrorists, the Antichrist, and communists, dismissing talk of peace as a ruse for the escalation of conflict and war. Conversely, the liberation movements dismissed the government as the incarnation of evil, fascism, and dictatorial rule. The only word that many within the liberation movements felt they wanted to say to the apartheid government had already been said in different places and forums over several years. It was "resign and allow democratic elections to happen." And the government had, with equal regularity, responded with an unequivocal "no." Within this context, words were weapons. "Peace" no longer meant peace. For the apartheid regime, it was a rallying call to destroy resistance. "Socialism" was used as a truncheon to bludgeon the poor. Liberation movements, in turn, used the word "capitalism" to refer to a monolithic system, designed and executed to exploit the poor. The word "reconciliation" was in some circles seen to be the equivalent of surrender. Words became missiles of attack rather than vehicles of communication.

Language needed to be redeemed for the possibility of peace to emerge. Words had to be unfettered. A new level of communication was needed to get beyond that impasse. "We were all looking for words to take us forward while knowing that there was still a huge gap to be bridged between us," Meyer said.[26]

In 1989 in an important address titled "A Word about Words," Václav Havel, former president of the Czech Republic, discussed the power of words to change the world for both good and evil.[27] He argued that when "beautiful words such as 'peace'" are used injudiciously, they need to have their true meaning restored so that they can assist in the pursuit of democratic debate. Perhaps it is only within the context of encounters and engagement that the humanity of others can be acknowledged and the legitimacy of words can be restored and used in the pursuit of truth and honesty.

John Paul Lederach speaks of the importance of such turning points that connect people. Within a mutually harmful situation, they effectively change the political milieu, enabling a new level of talk that releases the "moral imagination" and enables those locked in conflict to begin to see new options for peace.

Creativity and imagination, the artist giving birth to something new, proposes to us avenues of inquiry and ideas about change that require us to think about how we know the world, how we are in the world, and, most important, what in the world is possible. What we find time and again in these turning points and moments where something moves beyond the grip of violence is the vision and belief that the future *is not* the slave of the past and the birth of something new is possible.[28]

Yet turning points are rarely isolated events. A series of turning points are necessary. They need to be repeatedly negotiated and renegotiated. "The TRC

[Truth and Reconciliation Commission] process was an important turning point for South Africans—but only a starting point," observed Desmond Tutu at a conference marking the tenth anniversary of the first public hearings of the South African TRC. He continued:

> We need to keep working at reconciliation. The problem is that many perpetrators as well as victims and survivors of the past, plus many who simply stood silently by when atrocities occurred, have not responded to the challenges of the present in the best possible way. Maybe we are still all too traumatized. We are in many ways still strangers to one another. We have got to get to know and to trust one another. We need to tell one another about our hurts and our fears. We need to heal one another's wounds. We need to listen to one another's stories. This can open a space within which to address the economic and other woes that our people face. If reconciliation does not lead to people contributing in some way to transformation and the improvement of the lives of all South Africans it will, with some justification, be dismissed as a factitious thing to be ignored.[29]

Antjie Krog speaks of the importance for those who have suffered being able to shift from a prelinguistic state, within which they are overwhelmed by the extent of the suffering, to the point where they can begin to control the suffering. A "particular memory at last captured in words can no longer haunt you, push you around, bewilder you, because you have taken control of it—you can move it where you want to."[30] Yet talk is not easy. Often sufferings are so deep that they cannot be expressed in words. Victims of posttraumatic stress need to feel safe and to build relations of trust before they can speak.

Protesting against the silence of victims, Itumeleng Mosala provoked a measure of concern among many at the TRC's tenth anniversary conference when he suggested that South Africans ought to have achieved freedom first and held a TRC later, stressing that freedom precedes truth telling. "We need to be free in order to speak," he insisted. He argued that freedom involves more than the attainment of political democracy and indicated that a lot of truth still needs to be disclosed, not least by those who suffered most.[31] Clearly, truth telling is never an isolated event. It takes time for those who have been traumatized by abuse, silenced by years of autocratic rule, and forced to internalize their pain to begin to deal with their past.

Memory and truth disclosure are always incomplete. It is this incompleteness that cries out in different ways to be heard. Raw memory, painful struggle, defeat, and even victory are often buried in silence. Fear, anger, and confusion are embedded in that silence. Sometimes there is also hope. Truth rarely leaps forth. It needs to be dug out!

It is here that poetry, music, theater, and myth can perhaps contribute more to healing than any attempt to explain in some rigid forensic way "who did what to whom" can do. Truth in some contexts dawns spontaneously, intuitively, and unconsciously. The records of first-generation testimony to gross violations of human rights that include words both spoken and hidden await the interpolation of artists, poets, musicians, and storytellers. They need to be recaptured, retold, and freed from the tyranny of silence and obscurity. This said, the silence is a cry from the heart that perhaps can never be captured or fully understood—not even by the person who harbors the silence. And yet the wounds of nations cry out for their meaning to be heard.

The novelist and poet Ursula Le Guin tells us: "The story—from *Rumpel-stiltskin* to *War and Peace*—is one of the basic tools invented by the human mind for the purpose of understanding. There have been great societies that did not use the wheel, but there have been no societies that did not tell stories."[32] "Listen to the stories people tell, the folktales they remember, and the songs they sing, and you will discover something about them that words spoken in other ways will never reveal," a San elder observed in a storytelling session in the Kalahari in the Northern Cape Province of South Africa. Stories are the way most people remember the past and anticipate the future. Stories form part of our capacity to recall, to predict, to plan, to explain, and to hope. The cognitive scientist Roger Schank in fact concludes "humans are not ideally set up to understand logic; they are set up to understand stories."[33] Traditional societies in Africa, the Americas, and elsewhere all instinctively tell stories. Native Americans have story circles; remote communities in Burundi, the DRC, Sierra Leone, and elsewhere deal with their trauma and conflict through testimony and storytelling. These traditional ways of knowing and relating draw together emotional, intuitive, intellectual, and spiritual experiences in a holistic manner that provides what has been called a "narrative medicine." Words spoken with integrity can heal.

Conversely, not all stories are true or necessarily healing. Havel warns that "the distrust of words is less harmful than unwarranted trust in them." He counsels us to "keep a weather eye out for any insidious germs of arrogance in words that are seemingly humble."[34] The self, in both deceit and honesty, is expressed in story as perhaps nowhere else. The stories people choose to tell often reveal an unsolicited depth that no carefully constructed narrative can do. Storytelling captures human frailty and vulnerability as well as the strength of people who risk themselves in pursuit of goals and ideals. It is a way of enabling those who are excluded in totalitarian regimes, by those who provide canonical solutions from an international perspective and by the strongman politics of Africa, to find voice in addressing the challenges of their time.

Adam Kahane, reflecting on his experiences in several high-conflict situations around the world, provides a number of suggestions for talking and storytelling.[35] I draw on his insights:

- Speak up. Say what you are feeling and state your concerns and needs in as quiet and polite a way as possible.
- Be honest and sincere.
- Speak about your changing views and perceptions when these occur.
- Try to tell a story that captures the emotional energy of what you want to say.
- Pay attention to how you are talking. Body language is important, as are tone of voice and eye contact.
- Do a self-audit of your assumptions, anxieties, fears, hopes, and expectations—all of which can have an impact on those you hope to influence.
- Be prepared to say "I don't know" while exploring possible answers to tough questions. It can open the way for joint problem solving.
- Speak not only to the "nice guys" but also to those who are most difficult on the other side.
- Talk with an eye on how your words are being responded to. Be aware of changes in an emerging relationship.

Simple rules are difficult to implement. Fair-minded words, spoken in empathy, are important. They affirm the worth of the other person, even when you disagree with him or her. *How* we say things is as important as *what* we say. But *what* we say is vitally important. It is crucial to get to the real problems. Speaking exposes who we are. "The first rule of peacemaking is to identify the snake oil salesmen," a tough political strategist involved in the DRC peace settlement observed after a break in a planning session prior to the City Sun peace talks. "It is more important to speak to the honest, rude hardliners than those who are ready to enjoy your hospitality and speak sweet words."

To talk with integrity to the problem at hand, it is also necessary to listen. This is what makes "time out" periods so important in negotiating and learning sessions. Those engaged in serious talks need time to think and to reflect on what has been said so that options for the way ahead can emerge.

Listening

If talking with sincerity involves declaring who we are, listening involves an empathetic attempt to discover the deepest needs and concerns of others. This necessitates an understanding not only of their stated needs and demands but also of their unspoken needs. A wise teacher of conflict resolution once observed that "a person cannot do two things at once, if one of those things is listening." Listening demands our total presence, engagement, and patience as we struggle to come to terms with our feelings while receiving stories and the recounting of memories. To listen is to enter into the being of the one telling the story, endeavoring to see and hear from that person's perspective. It is only through this kind of active and careful *listening* that the depths of what is being said can be *heard* and *understood*. We need to listen to the total story, and in so doing open ourselves to hearing the smallest detail of what is being said and what is sometimes left unsaid.

Listening is not a facility that comes naturally to politicians and others engaged in competitive debate. When we are silent and pretending to listen, it is often to rehearse rebuttals and prepare rejoinders. At times when an exchange is with established adversaries, we easily become jaded. We claim to know what an adversary is saying before he or she speaks, assuming we have heard it all before. For communication to happen, there needs to be empathetic listening and understanding, recognizing that to understand is not necessarily to condone or support. Understanding, however, can open a space within which to negotiate a shared solution to a problem and, in so doing, reach beyond the standoff.

José Chipenda, a veteran political activist in Angola, spoke on leadership skills needed for peacemaking in Africa. Addressing a seminar for political activists and peace workers on the African continent, he insisted that "the primary requirement is a capacity to listen, ensuring that the nuances behind the words are heard and understood." He asked his audience to listen to the silence in the room. "Just listen," he said as the prolonged silence intensified. "We have forgotten to hear the dove cooing and bird calling. Africa has many big talkers. We all have something to say. There are fewer listeners around. There are too many words and ideas turning around in our minds that impede our ability to listen. To be able to speak we must listen and if we listen deeply and hear clearly we will better be able to speak in a manner that will enable others to hear what we are saying." He referred to the great leaders of Africa—Jomo Kenyatta, Julius Nyerere, Leopold Senghor, and Nelson Mandela—all men who showed a capacity to listen. He reflected on the fact that Nelson Mandela listened for twenty-seven years while in prison. "These were wasted years, but also a time for listening. He opened himself and listened rather than allowed himself to be trapped in bitterness and resentment."[36] We sometimes need to withdraw to listen not merely to words that are spoken but to the spirit of life itself—what Germans like to call the zeitgeist or the spirit of the time. To listen and then speak consciously into the spirit of the times—with a deeper sense of the challenges and thinking of the time—is often the difference between words going unheard and words evoking a response.

In Jinja, at the source of the Nile River on Lake Victoria, I used Otto Scharmer's four levels of listening in a series of meetings that drew together people from several neighboring countries.[37] Scharmer suggests that the most superficial level of listening involves "downloading" or listening from within the bounds of one's own story or credibility structure. We listen in order to confirm our own views, failing to make any serious attempt to understand what falls outside of that. This most superficial level involves angry listening, closed listening, indeed nonlistening. The second level of listening involves what Scharmer calls "debate-listening." We listen to both sides of the argument, mentally recording the two sides of the discussion, without engaging in the debate. A third level of listening involves "reflective dialogue." We try to understand. We listen with empathy. We begin to understand but refrain from responding. We fail to take the debate forward. A fourth level of listening involves what Scharmer calls "generative listening," within which we listen not only to understand what is within us and within others but also to enter into the conversation itself. We draw on and endeavor to go beyond the arguments of the different participants in the discussion. The conversation becomes more than a sum of the parts contributed by the participants. The dialogue itself becomes the wisest participant, taking the dialogue to a new level of understanding and problem solving.

"This is a bit like the confluence of the White and Blue Niles in Khartoum," Yacoub Yohannes, a young man from Sudan, dramatically suggested. He spoke of the different chemical components and the colors of the two Niles, each with different points of origin and identity. "The two rivers flow side by side for a distance," he noted. "They seem to clash and then synthesize—the two currents merge into a surge of water within which neither current dominates." All analogies have their limitations, and Yohannes's had its. Amid laughter, however, his analogy worked for his audience. It led to a discussion of generative listening, stressing the importance of finding synergy between opposing views. It opens the possibility of taking the debate forward. It is the beginning of dialogue in the full sense of the word. We let go of our preconceived ideas, allowing the different currents to merge and the thrust of the river to take us into new territory.

Listening within the context of peacemaking also needs to include a defensive dimension. We need to identify the lies and the lying. John Paul Lederach talks of "constructive pessimism" as an important dimension of constructive listening, functioning as an early-warning mechanism within the exchange of words. Its task is to ensure that the words spoken are an authentic harbinger of what is promised. Words are ambiguous. They have universal meanings as well as parochial meanings. In conflictual situations they often carry a plethora of ideological nuances and mental stereotypes that have an impact on communication. These need to be challenged and exposed. For this to happen, language often needs to be purged and cleansed, which makes careful listening an imperative. It suggests that linguistic analysis skills have an important role to play in political talk. We need to consult local lexicons to make sure that what we think we are hearing is in fact what is being said.

Careful listening is a skill that complements sincere talk. There cannot be one without the other. To talk sincerely, it is necessary to listen carefully. To listen carefully, it is necessary to talk thoughtfully and to use words that facilitate a similar response. This involves

- active listening,
- silence and thoughtfulness,
- suspending preconceived ideas,
- identifying prejudices that interrupt the listening process,
- listening for unspoken words behind the jargon and parochial language,
- commitment to hear and discover nuances and new insights,
- entering into the perceptions and ideas of those one engages,
- discerning patterns of thought and emotion that give birth to new possibilities, and
- envisioning new options for cooperation and shared decision making.

Integrated talk and listening, designed and structured to promote a level of engagement, is the precursor to dialogue and the exploring of new options for addressing the quarrels and problems that thrust societies into violent conflict.

Dialogue

Visions and ideas that take adversaries and former enemies beyond impasses and violence invariably emerge through shared encounters and engagements. These involve a commitment to talk to one another and to listen in a manner that frees participants from preconceived ideas and prejudices, opening a space where both honest disagreement and agreement can emerge.

The *Oxford Concise Dictionary* defines dialogue as "a discussion intended to explore a subject or to resolve a problem." This suggests a partnership and a willingness to explore solutions to difficult questions. It involves breaking out of preestablished mental models with a view to opening ourselves to possibilities not yet seen or articulated. Drawing on an ancient Chinese philosophy, Adam Kahane speaks of talk and listening as the *yin* and *yang*, which constitute the two primal opposing but complementary forces found in everything, ranging from nature and society to individual identities. They capture the essence of sound communication.

Preconceived ideas, even well-thought-through proposals, rarely emerge as fully formulated solutions. It is through the energy generated in dialogue, emerging ideas, tweaking of proposals, and listening with an open and honest ear that the way forward can emerge. Visions usually need reshaping. Courses of action need correction. The final form of the solution is more than any one mind can offer. The Dinka elder referred to earlier spoke of the need to "wait for the answer to come to us." Challenged by some in the group who argued that they had already waited too long for a solution to the Sudanese conflict, he responded: "Fight on, be impatient, demand change, but don't rush. Be open to the unexpected. Keep your eyes and ears open. Be ready to respond when the future is offered to you." He spoke of missed opportunities in Sudan and other parts of Africa: "The future does not tarry. It offers itself to us as a fleeting moment. We need to grasp it before we lose it." It is about seizing the moment.

The question in postconflict situations is often not precisely *what* needs to be done in some idealistic sense. Sincere and committed participants who have encountered and engaged one another, talked to one another, listened deeply, and committed themselves to continuing open dialogue and joint decision making usually come to a point of agreement on the broad characteristics of what the future ought *more or less* to incorporate. Commonly these include basic human rights, the rule of law, economic growth, job creation, and poverty relief. The pressing question is *how* to get there. This requires what has been referred to above as a "cumulative, multilevel, open-ended" political process of opponents engaging one another in a constructive manner. It involves the need to kindle a willingness to find sufficient common ground to deal with the challenges that divide a nation.

It is not an easy task for deeply divided societies to learn (or relearn) to engage one another in dialogue after generations of stereotyping, castigation, and confrontation. It calls for a new level of encounter and new or renewed words; it calls for the creation of new mental maps, the projection of new possibilities, and a desire to understand what one's opponents are saying. This level of dialogue holds the potential for a national consensus to emerge on how to address issues that threaten and have the capacity to destroy the gains already achieved when agreeing to talk.

The need to speak and the willingness to listen are often silenced by what are experienced as endemic forms of poverty, deprivation, and despair. A society in conflict is frequently prevented from engaging in the kind of rational dialogue being asked for by the unending inner roar of pain, anger, and fear that people experience. Simply put, this suggests that unjust material and social conditions need to be redressed *before* meaningful dialogue can take place. And yet, it is argued here, that encounter and dialogue are necessary to unleash the commitment that is necessary to enable this to happen. Talk has many levels. It is a process that needs to reach beyond silence, beyond empty words, beyond initial fears and anger to a generative level that produces the kind of corrective action that enjoys the support of silenced victims who are too traumatized to speak.

Democracy is about finding a modus operandi within which to speak and be heard when managing and finding solutions to problems that societies encounter. Democracy involves conversation. What is being argued for here is a relationship-centric approach to addressing concerns, especially the kinds of taxing problems that transitional societies face, recognizing that the way in which a nation addresses its problems is as important as the solutions it produces. Unless there is a level of peaceful coexistence among former warring parties, the chances of resolving material and other priorities are negligible. The African adage tells us that "when elephants fight, it is the grass that suffers." There needs to be a commitment to peace and coexistence for grass to be restored, and this recovery takes time. This requires substantive democracy that goes beyond a notion of democracy that is ultimately little more than party rule or elected oligarchy. A key ingredient to this brand of democracy is participatory development. This recognizes the essential right of those involved and those most directly affected by a particular problem to themselves decide on the nature of the compromise that may be needed to ensure peace and coexistence.

Dialogue, conversely, can become a comfort zone within which newly emerged good feelings with old enemies become an end in themselves and a substitute for action, policy change, and material transformation. Fearful that the kind of action needed may result in a relapse into past acrimony, negotiators can drift into an implicit agreement to postpone tough decisions. Eager to preserve the newfound détente, they often defer difficult decisions—sometimes indefinitely. As suggested above, this is why transitional justice initiatives are in danger of not dealing with crucial issues that later come back to haunt the settlement.

Sustainable peace building and political reconstruction is necessarily a process. It involves more than a grand, isolated celebration of peace. Endurance, patience, and continuing dialogue are needed to produce a process that enables participants to reach beyond counterproductive confrontation to engagement, dialogue, and shared problem solving. Also, it needs to address the tough and controversial challenges facing a transitional process by putting in place the necessary structures and policies that enable this to be achieved.

Dialogue and exploration happen differently in different contexts, yet there are underlying principles that are common to the process. These include:

- a willingness to encounter new ideas within a dialogue;
- immersing oneself in a dialogue with a view to grasping both the detail and the totality of the discussion and possible solutions;
- concentration, observation, openness, and alertness to the possibility of ideas that hold the key to a new future;
- imagination and a willingness to risk oneself in exploring new ideas and solutions;

- a capacity to sense possible solutions to the enduring differences and conflicts;
- a willingness to explore possible solutions by committing oneself to a shared process of taking participants to a new level of articulation and understanding; and
- a commitment to participatory decision making.

Vision and Enactment

Even the most inclusive and creative dialogues often reach a point where the interests of opposing parties are such that a settlement seems unlikely. For the deadlock to be broken, options and positions on both sides need to be broadened. It is here that a new sense of moral imagination is required. It is about seeing conflict positively.

The exploration of a new kind of future is called for—one within which the shackles of past hurts and offenses can be laid aside to allow new options for addressing problems to emerge. The past is not forgotten, even as the future is not held to ransom to that past. It is a case of asking adversaries to move forward, redressing the causes of past conflict—to the extent that this is possible—while ensuring that the forces that constitute the causes of this conflict are managed if not removed in order to minimize future conflict. This difficult task is a key dimension to political reconciliation, which is discussed in chapter 6.

The histories of conflict in many parts of the world, including the African continent, show that it is possible to imagine things differently. In diverse ways and difficult circumstances, the Hutus and Tutsis in Burundi and Rwanda are exploring options for coexistence that have ended the genocides and open warfare in their respective countries, although clearly the success or otherwise of these options will ultimately be judged on the basis of whether they ensure lasting peace. South Africans turned away from a predicted bloodbath to reach a political settlement intended to draw former adversaries into a common society within which the ravages of apartheid could be overcome. Again, time will tell to what extent this transition is sustainable. It is important to recognize that in all three situations other options came out of the realization that the only alternative was ongoing and escalating strife.

Sustainable peace building usually demands a creative alternative to—and sometimes a radical departure from—the tried and tested options put forward by those who have been party to the conflict and who have failed to produce mutually acceptable solutions for ending it. There is a demand for a new horizon to emerge. This means that there must be a willingness to reach beyond the glib solutions that at times disguise and entrench the status quo or necessitate that all the concessions come from one side. It calls for a willingness to question all the assumptions that underlie the encounters and dialogues that have already taken place.

The creation of a new horizon needs honest analysis of the prevailing situation and acknowledgment that the existing proposals are not capable of breaking the deadlock. Of particular importance, in most instances, it further requires the recognition that any attempt to move forward will probably be hindered rather than assisted by any proposal that is risk free, complete, and not open to challenge or even rebuttal. The "solution" is more likely to emerge from an ongoing willingness to engage one another with the problem by drawing on the richness of diverse views expressed in anger and frustration as well as in an attempt to hear and understand the aspirations, fears, and realistic demands of everyone concerned. It involves what Otto Scharmer defines as "generative listening," or dialogue that enables a process to be taken beyond the different arguments or proposals of those participating in the discussion.

The new horizon is invariably more than the sum of the parts contributed by the participants. The dialogue itself becomes the wisest participant. Visionary proposals are a consequence of ongoing encounters and permanent movement. Every encounter in which participants seriously engage changes both the participants and the nature of their arguments. In a free and engaging society, all is becoming. There is no permanent encampment. Deep conflicts are rarely solved on an isolated basis. They need to be tackled one step at a time.

It is worth recalling a poignant moment in ecumenical history that gave new life to the neglected ethical notion of "middle axioms." It came as a result of the intervention of J. H. Oldham and John Bennett at the Oxford Conference on Life and Work in 1937, which ultimately contributed to the birth of the World Council of Churches in 1948. The attempt was to promote social renewal and world peace on the eve of World War II. It failed in its immediate objective to prevent war, but it provided a helpful understanding of the challenges of social and political renewal. Bennett described the axioms as "not binding for all time" but rather as "provisional definitions" or "the next steps" that a particular generation could reasonably take in pursuit of the society aspired to.[38] Such axioms need to have concrete content so as to persuade those demanding more that some attempt is being made to address their demands. The axioms need to enjoy as wide a consensus as possible to create an environment that would make their implementation possible, while stressing that they are not an end in themselves. Middle axioms are "evolving principles" that constantly need to be reshaped in the light of aspirational goals through democratic participation grounded in a realistic understanding of *what is needed* and *what is possible*. A cautious, single-step vision can be as important in finding a long-term resolution to a problem as the bigger, more inclusive solutions that we celebrate. Every "big solution" can be broken down into several smaller breakthroughs and often into hesitant fearful steps that preceded it. New horizons involve uncertainty and risk. Where there is a measure of trust, based on good process and the honoring of previous commitments, the possibility of moving forward yet again becomes just a little easier.

Articulating the vision inherent in a new horizon is never easy. To be authentic, the vision needs also to move beyond words into delivery. The participants need to be rewarded for the progress they have made. The primary reward is the settlement itself, the cessation of war, and/or the first steps toward political or communal stability. More, however, is needed. For example, political prisoners need to be released; the poor need to receive access to land; and the wealthy need assurances that they will not be deprived of their homes, income, or pensions. Tangible sunrise and sunset clauses play an important role in peace settlements. It is equally clear that all aspirations cannot immediately be met without destroying the necessary balance between the demands made by adversaries. The most difficult task, thus, is to ensure that the aspirations do not fall off the national agenda.

The South African Interim Constitution (1993) and the ("final") 1996 Constitution emerged from a negotiation process that brought together people from all sides in a country where inequality was legally entrenched. Political inclusivity, at least in the sense of extending the franchise to all South Africans, was immediately addressed. The yawning material gap between the rich and the poor, however, could only be addressed by including in the Constitution a range of socioeconomic rights such as access to basic education, housing, health care, sufficient food, clean water, social security, and land. These rights could not be met either immediately or in the short term, primarily because of the lack of available resources, but the intent was to ensure that the state aspire to meet these provisions. To this end, the Constitution obliges the state "to take reasonable legislative and other measures" to realize these rights. The Constitution further provides for the Human Rights Commission to monitor this process so as to assess what measures are being taken towards realizing these rights. In brief, the commitment to socioeconomic rights provides an incentive for the poor and dispossessed to claim these rights. The Constitutional Court, in turn, holds out the option for citizens to take the state to court where constitutional obligations are not seen to be pursued adequately.[39]

The pursuit of these and related economic rights and demands are, at the same time, pursued by a number of legislative and policy initiatives, such as broad-based black economic empowerment, affirmative action, and skills training aimed at the formerly disadvantaged sections of the community. To cite a single example, the Promotion of Equality and the Prevention of Unfair Discrimination Act 4 of 2000 seeks to promote equality and counter unfair discrimination on the grounds of "race, gender or disability."

Excessive expectations can be as dangerous as the failure to create any expectations. Nothing destroys the vision of a nation quite as much a failure to deliver on promises made. The challenge facing any government of reconstruction in a postconflict situation is how to ensure delivery on promises, constitutional and other, without destroying a fragile democracy that is dependent on the participation of former warring parties.

In a letter to a friend, Thomas Jefferson wrote that he did not advocate frequent changes to constitutions, laws, and policy. Yet he stressed that law is an active, living, human process that "involves society's whole being, including its dreams, passions and ultimate concerns." He suggested that "as we become more developed, more enlightened, . . . with the change of circumstances, institutions must advance also to keep pace with the times. . . . We might as well require a man to wear still a coat which fitted him when a boy, as [expect] civilized society to remain ever under the regimen of barbarous ancestors." In less dramatic language, in progressive societies, the progress of yesterday can be the equivalent of reactionary politics today.

Seeking to transcend positivistic notions of law and wanting to address the need for a transcendent dimension to lawmaking and policy implementation, Harold Berman suggests that "law, through its stability limits the future, while a sense of the holy [is needed] to challenge all existing social structures."[40] In the words of the existentialist (and atheistic) philosopher Max Horkheimer: "No matter how skilful lawmaking and politics, it is in the last analysis mere business." Lawmaking, like nation building, he tells us, needs to be challenged by a what he calls a "theological moment" and a "sense of the more" to fulfill its role in society.[41] Paul Ricoeur speaks of the "poetics of existence" as an influence on politics and law that would be wrong to ignore.[42] What is seen to be impossible today needs to be challenged and critiqued by pursuing the ideals entrenched in constitutional law and demanded by those who form part of the body politic. This dialectic between present reality and the pursuit of higher ideals is returned to in chapter 7, where the relationship between the politics of reconciliation and forgiveness is considered.

Encounters, words spoken and heard, along with dialogue and vision, need to attain flesh in individual relations. We need examples of people rising to the national challenge. A rather dramatic moment in an encounter between perpetrators of gross violations of human rights during the apartheid years and returning soldiers who fought in the armies of the liberation movement illustrates the point. I listened to the story of a colonel in the South African security forces, guilty by his own account of numerous brutal acts of torture and killing. He spoke with restraint of an incident when he responded to a bomb alert in the Carlton Hotel in Johannesburg. The first to arrive on the scene, he found a woman holding what he described as the partially severed head of a child onto an emasculated torso. "I swore that day that I would avenge the death of the child and the trauma of that mother. It was the only way I knew how to cope with my situation." After telling his story, a woman whose son had joined the Azanian

People's Liberation Army touched him lightly on his arm, without speaking. Out of sheer desperation and despair, her son had taken up arms in rebellion against the South African state. When the session came to a close, the colonel thanked the woman for touching him. He resolved to commit himself to educating her grandchild, acknowledging, however, that "to help her educate her grandchild is not enough." Asked whether his story could be used, he said he did not want his identity to be disclosed. "As a soldier I find controversy, outward emotion and sympathy difficult. My vocation is simply 'to do,'" he observed. "I have done evil things. I must also try to do good. I could have applied for amnesty [referring to the amnesty provision of the South African TRC], but was not prepared to face the public emotion it would produce. I try to make amends in other ways." The woman listened. "All I can say is that my grandchild needs an education," she said. Individual deeds and actions are important, but nation building demands more. Transformation necessitates aspirational goals and values, plus policy, strategy, and words of inspiration to motivate people at different levels of society to turn these goals and values into practice. For the persons involved, this is a new horizon.

To envision and to translate vision into action entails

- risk, imagination, and courage;
- reaching beyond the conflict at hand to the source(s) of the conflict;
- exploring alternative options for moving beyond the conflict;
- knowing that imaginative alternatives usually involve more than the sum of an existing conversation;
- realizing that the implementation of an alternative plan involves risk;
- accepting that a journey toward an alternative solution involves taking a single step at a time;
- projecting beyond such first steps toward aspirational goals that may not be attainable immediately;
- thinking a new thought; and
- planning a different kind of future.

To return to an earlier discussion, national and individual renewal calls for a political process that is "cumulative, multileveled and open-ended" and allows for "continuous interaction over time, engaging significant clusters of citizens in and out of government and the relationships they form to solve public problems across permeable borders, either within or between communities or countries."[43] Above all, it requires that we address the demands and needs of those who feel excluded from, or alienated by, the relationships that constitute a working political process. Failure to address these needs and/or to deliver on them carries the capacity to undo the process that enabled opposing parties to face the causes of a conflict in a peaceful and constructive manner rather than through violent conflict or war. This can throw a nation back into the cauldron from which it seeks to escape. Talk, listening, and dialogue are not enough. They must provide constructive solutions to the prevailing problems.

The South African TRC is considered in chapter 4 as a case study—not as a model to be replicated in other countries but rather as a heuristic tool with which to explore options to facilitate political transition from the old to the new. It is considered primarily as an example of what the promotion of a national conversation entails: encounters, talking, listening, and dialogue in pursuit of a different kind of future.

My intent is to move beyond the parley of both those who romanticize the work of the TRC and those who often in the name of liberalism, morality, and the rights of victims castigate the TRC for what it sought to do. My intent is not to provide a scorecard of the TRC's successes and failures. It is rather to reflect on the extensive debate to which the TRC has given rise, recognizing that there is an important sense in which "the stream has risen above its source" in that the post-TRC debate is as important as the TRC event itself.

"The TRC has caught the world's imagination on possibilities of peaceful change in a manner that perhaps no other political intervention has managed in recent history," suggests Desmond Tutu.[44] Why this appeal? I suggest it has to do not primarily with the detail surrounding amnesty, reconciliation, or reparations and related concerns but with the incentive it gave South Africans to begin to engage one another in national conversation.

This was a difficult conversation that was always going to be partial and incomplete. Emily Dickinson once wrote that "the truth must dazzle gradually, . . . or the entire world would be blind." The nation was traumatized. Few South Africans who had lived through the apartheid years had not been psychosocially damaged. Individuals had suffered and communities had been shattered. Many could not speak. The public glare of the TRC was often too severe, and exposure was too harsh, for a sense of safety and trust to emerge where deeply damaged people could share their pain. The mandate of the TRC was also narrow. Thus, it was prevented from reaching into the depths of the malady that traumatized the nation. It was, however, able to break the silence on the past, give rise to an official acknowledgment of past gross violations of human rights, and initiate a conversation that could subsequently be taken forward in different ways and at different levels of society. It is to this conversation that we now turn.

4

NATIONAL CONVERSATION IN SOUTH AFRICA

There is no realistic alternative to talking to your enemy. It may not give you precisely what you want or even what you think is necessary for there to be peace. The only prerequisite is honesty by those engaging in conversation. There can simply be no lasting peace without the give and take of serious talk. Honest conversation is the womb that holds the possibility of enduring peace. . . . In South Africa and other countries that have faced the kind of conflict we did, unrestrained conversation is essential. It is an essential part of nation-building. It often includes angry words. That's okay.

—Desmond Mpilo Tutu, Cape Town, December 2006

The nature and extent of the national conversation generated by the South African Truth and Reconciliation Commission (TRC) is often overshadowed by interest in the amnesty offered to perpetrators, the extent of the truth provided by perpetrators, and the nature of reparations paid to victims of gross violations of human rights. This results in more ink from pen and printer being expended on questions of impunity, prosecutions, and amnesty than on either truth, which probably comes second in the contest, or reconciliation, which is at the bottom of the pile.

President Nelson Mandela, on receiving the TRC report in 1998, suggested that the chapter on the "Causes, Motives, and Perspectives of Perpetrators" might be among the most important in the entire report. He indicated that unless a social, political, and economic plan that enjoyed the support of as many as possible of those who had brought the country to the brink of collapse was put in place, the conflict was likely to recur in one form or another. He stressed that "South Africans need to engage in national dialogue as a basis for giving birth to a new country."[1]

Paul Collier's reference to the "conflict trap" into which societies so often slide in the wake of a civil war deserves serious consideration: "[The] typical country reaching the end of a civil war faces around a 44 percent risk of returning to conflict within five years. One reason for this high risk is that the same factors that caused the initial war are usually still present. If before a war a country had low average income, rural areas well endowed with natural resources, a hostile neighbour, and a large diaspora, after the war it is still likely to have these characteristics."[2]

For the underlying causes of past conflict and the potential triggers of future conflict to be realistically addressed, there needs to be a minimum level of reconciliation involving serious social and political engagement. This calls for serious conversation aimed at relationship building and mutual understanding. Without such serious debate and joint decision making by former enemies and adversaries, the possibility of escaping ongoing conflict is significantly reduced.

This presupposes a broad and inclusive approach to transitional justice and peace building that affirms both the need to hold perpetrators accountable for gross violations of human rights and the creation of a stable society based on human rights, the affirmation of human dignity, and the unfolding of democratic governance. The South African quest to attain these goals is succinctly captured in the words of Mac Maharaj, a senior African National Congress (ANC) participant in the process leading to the establishment of the TRC who suffered deeply at the hands of the apartheid regime: "We have taken the concept of justice in its broadest sense," he observed, "and found a formulation that meets the peculiar and specific element of restorative justice, while limiting retribution to public exposure and shame to be faced by the perpetrators, whose names and deeds will be made known."[3]

Expanding the Transitional Justice Debate

At the heart of the transitional justice debate is the pertinent question: Transition to what?[4] Political analysts and proponents of peace building and of transitional justice recognize that for peace to be sustainable after hostilities cease, a number of major political, social, economic, and legal steps are required: The root causes of the conflict need to be identified, and a structure needs to be put in place to minimize the recurrence of similar conflicts. This means that a minimum level of communication and reconciliation must be established between former enemies.

The danger of a transitional process that prioritizes the prosecution of perpetrators, and takes an unqualified judicial approach to reparations and related legal concerns without building or rebuilding relationships between former enemies and adversaries, is that the nation focuses primarily on the past and neglects the future. The depolarization of society fails to emerge, and conditions conducive to the kind of national conversation needed for a different kind of society are not established. This process must necessarily include the painful, in-depth grappling with the past as a basis for understanding and correcting the socioeconomic, political, and structural causes of conflict as well as psychological, spiritual, cultural, and identity-related factors.

In brief, for a nation to be reconstructed and transformed, more is needed than prosecutions, tribunals, national courts, the International Criminal Court, or amnesties when dealing with past offences. Sustained and authentic national conversation of the kind discussed in chapter 3 is necessary for effective transformation to occur.

This level of conversation is more than what any time-bound TRC can achieve. If correctly designed and carefully instituted, however, a TRC can initiate the kind of honesty and engagement that contributes to a social contract robust enough to put policies and programs in place. The conversation needs to include as many people as possible as a basis for generating policies that seek both to redress past wrongs and to minimize the reoccurrence of past abuses. It involves a debate that must necessarily address the contested task of prioritizing what can immediately be accomplished, and the setting up of a carefully managed national agenda on issues that can only be resolved later. Immediate priorities include the cessation of hostilities, the setting up of democratic institutions, and the affirmation of basic human rights. Other needs, not least socioeconomic rights, take longer to be realized. If the latter are not appropriately pursued and realized in at least a modest sense within a reasonable period of time, this can only have a negative impact on the peace process.

The South African Conversation

The work of the South African TRC has been variously described as theater, tragedy, epic storytelling, liturgy, and drama. In one form or another, it was a national conversation. It was about words spoken—there to be heard, begging for response, waiting for action. It was an invitation to citizens to talk as a basis for generating a new or additional vehicle for democratic participation.

Good conversation, whether in theater, storytelling, or debate, has a way of focusing the mind. It generates ideas. It unleashes new energies. At times it shocks. It silences. The railway line ends. The road stops. We are confronted with a new frontier. We experience a "what now?" kind of response that has the capacity for the creation of something new.

The TRC conversation gave rise to several such moments, breaking the public and official silence on the past. This happened at three different levels: the public conversation, the TRC hearings, and the intracommission conversation.

Public conversation on the TRC was often extremely heated—but it was an important part of the national conversation. Afrikaans-language newspapers were largely relentless in their condemnation of the TRC, believing that it was engaging in a witch hunt against white Afrikaners and the former government. English-language news media as well as black-based newspapers gave a more balanced overview, although here too controversy raged—for example, around the public hearings involving Winnie Madikizela Mandela, the killing of Chris Hani, and other high-profile people and events. The extent of the national debate in relation to the work of the TRC was huge. Few if any South Africans failed to have an opinion on the TRC. Most important, the silence on the past was being broken.

Some TRC hearings were iconic. They captured the pathos of a commission that carried the astounding responsibility to reconcile a nation. The first hearing, held in East London, reminded the nation of the intense struggle in South Africa between blacks and whites in the Eastern Cape, the frontier of early encounters between colonists and Xhosa communities, and the home of Nelson Mandela and other ANC leaders. The Eastern Cape also saw the beginnings of the breakaway Pan-Africanist Congress (PAC) and the Black Consciousness Movement under Steve Biko, and it was the geographical location of the Transkei and Ciskei "independent" homelands. The hearing covered the detention and death of Biko, the assassination of the Cradock Four, the death of the Pepco Three, the massacre at Bisho, and similar events. The emotion was intense. In her book *Country of My Skull*, Antjie Krog captures the sense of the occasion: "For me, [Nomonde Calata's] crying is the beginning of the Truth Commission—the signature tune, the definitive moment, the ultimate sound of what the process is about. She was wearing this vivid orange-red dress, and she threw herself backwards and that sound—that sound it will haunt me for ever and ever. . . . So maybe this is what the Commission is all about—finding words for the cry of Nomonde Calata."[5] It was a cry that cut through the stunned silence of an audience that listened as she told the story of the death of her husband, Fort Calata, and of his comrades Mathew Goniwe, Sparrow Mkonto, and Sicelo Mhlauli. In an equally telling moment at a Cape Town amnesty hearing, Jeff Benzien demonstrated the "wet-bag" torture method on Tony Yengeni, which was used to break the resolve of many hardened activists. Broadcast to the nation on radio and television, and filling the front pages of the nation's newspapers, these and other less dramatic but equally revealing moments spoke to individual and community needs.

Intracommission conversation on the task of the TRC was intense and not always amicable. The tensions inherent to the South African conflict manifested themselves in the attitudes of commissioners and staff. Issues of race, identity, social class, and political persuasion had an impact on the TRC's work, contributing to a tension that underpinned its inability to reach a consensus on either the nature of reconciliation or the relationship between truth finding and reconciliation. There were those who equated reconciliation with interpersonal reconciliation and forgiveness. This position was promoted primarily through the passionate and persuasive voice of Desmond Tutu, chairperson of the TRC, but also in certain instances by the Human Rights Violations Committee. A second group argued that it was inappropriate for a state-sponsored commission to promote interpersonal forgiveness. This group advocated the promotion of a national framework for coexistence and civility within which individual healing and forgiveness could eventually take place. The third group had a still more limited view on the role of the TRC. It wanted to focus exclusively on truth finding, arguing that this would provide a basis both for future coexistence and for reconciliation.

Through the structures of the TRC, conversation between perpetrators and victims of gross violations of human rights was varied and multilayered. Perpetrators denied and blamed, and some confessed. Most are likely to take their memories and unspoken words with them to the grave. Victims remembered. Many chose without success to forget. Most bystanders denied and looked the other way. Some endeavored to be part of the new order. The nation continues its conversation in a struggle of remembering against forgetting. Silence persists and conversation beckons, perhaps inevitably so, if Yael Danieli is correct in attesting to the inability of many individuals and communities to speak about their trauma: "They can find no words to narrate the trauma story and create a meaningful dialogue around it."[6] This silence eats like a cancer. It renders victims unable to "move on" or to grasp the opportunity to repair or restore their lives. It is this that raises the question of the importance of symbol, ritual, and cultural resonance in dealing with the past—a discussion taken up in chapter 6.

The hearings for perpetrators and victims were structured differently, and yet both conversations shaped the identity of the South African TRC. Philippe Salazar suggests that perpetrator testimony was in the genre of the tragic. The voices of victims constituted an epic tale.[7] In the case of the former, a distance was maintained between the person of the perpetrator and his (rarely "her") staged voice as narrator or actor. Perpetrators spoke through lawyers. Often perpetrators said little more than a standard oath, carefully scripted and cautiously uttered. Where there was personal testimony, it was rehearsed to comply with the requirements of the legislation governing the TRC. Amnesty applicants needed to be heard as "perpetrators of integrity."[8] It was required that testimony reflected a political motive for committing a gross violation of human rights, narrowly defined in the mandate of the TRC as "killing, torture, abduction or severe ill-treatment." Where applicants did not show that they were politically motivated, they failed to receive amnesty. They were not required to show remorse—and most failed to do so. When remorse was expressed, this too could be scripted.

Perpetrators spoke to multilayered audiences. The primary audience was the amnesty panel consisting of judges and lawyers. Indirectly, perpetrators also addressed family members and friends, former colleagues, the media, and, in some instances, victims and survivors. This posed the question as to precisely who was on the stage addressing which audience at any one time. When interviewed by researchers two years after appearing before the TRC, several successful and unsuccessful amnesty applicants expressed regret that they had not felt free (often because of pressure from their lawyers) to make the kind of disclosure that in retrospect some felt they ought to have made.

"I never told *my* story. There was a gap between what I wanted to say and what I said," a high-ranking former military officer observed. "If I said too much, I could have endangered former colleagues. I did not want to embarrass my family. I simply wanted to put the past behind me. The easiest way was to play by the rules of the game. I felt I would be damned if I said too much, and I knew I was damned for not saying enough." Another referred to the sensationalism that often surrounded the amnesty hearings: "I am a soldier. Soldiers don't cry. They do their job and take the consequences. My day of judgment lies ahead when I meet my God." Some perpetrators responded remorsefully and as best they could in their amnesty applications and subsequent attempts to contribute to the healing of their victims. Most seemed callously to use the amnesty law to get away with as much as possible.[9] This said, no process—retributive or restorative—can compel perpetrators to show remorse or to tell the unequivocal truth as they saw it or to make restitution.

The TRC could do no more than open a space where both perpetrators and victims had the opportunity to deal honestly with their past, recognizing that the space given for perpetrators to do so was more controlled than the space afforded victims. If the amnesty hearings, in the words of one amnesty applicant, were "overjudicial," the intent of the TRC was to facilitate victim hearings in a psychologically and socially supportive manner—although it did not always succeed in doing so. There was no cross-examination of victims. The intent was to have commissioners listen attentively with a view to enabling victims to deal with their suffering in a cathartic and honest manner. They were encouraged to speak without reserve. In the words of the TRC report, the "subjective truth" was encouraged and accepted by the TRC as part of an inclusive process of truth recovery. Tears were frequently shed by victims who testified, by members of the public before whom they testified, by television and radio audiences who looked on, and at times by commissioners themselves—not least Tutu, who chaired the proceedings. It is this that made visible the essential difference between the TRC victims' hearings and court proceedings. Judges do not cry. This genre of storytelling and testimony is part of the national memory. The question is how deep it reached and what level of response it evoked beyond the victims and those closest to them.

The victims and survivors responded differently to the TRC hearings. Some found solace and catharsis. Others felt their wounds were reopened and left unattended. The TRC often failed to follow up on requests and promises made by commissioners. The state, in turn, was slow to recognize or honor the victims through appropriate forms of reparation and in related ways. Some politicians scoffed at what they saw as unnecessary public hysterics. The attempts by the TRC to "heal" a nation torn apart by decades of violence and death were caricatured in cartoons and explored through the theater and the visual arts. Maurice Charland talks of the importance of the "impiety of politics" in dealing with the ambiguities and tragedies of history.[10] "To mock and to ridicule the attempts of the TRC to heal was part of the healing process," he suggests.

Trauma is rarely resolved or overcome in a single cathartic moment. It returns to haunt and plague the victim, requiring time and deep reflection to heal, influenced by the social milieu within which the victim finds him or herself. This has resulted in heated debate between those who argue that the TRC victims' hearings enabled individuals who appeared before it to overcome their trauma and those who argue that the hearings simply raised painful memories that were left unresolved. At best the TRC hearings could only be part of a longer healing process.

The benefit of the hearings was more at the political level. The nation was confronted with a body of testimony that few could ever ignore or simply dismiss as untrue. This helped South Africans begin to challenge the systemic denial that characterizes so many situations of violence, abuse, crimes against humanity, and genocide in other parts of the world.

A Double Critique

The purpose of dealing with the past in a restorative way ultimately, of course, involves more than verbalizing memory as an end in itself. It is primarily an exercise in looking back in order to reach forward. The major challenge facing restorative initiatives in a postconflict situation is to ensure that the initiatives open the way to future conflict prevention, which embraces economic transformation and restores political engagement between those torn apart by conflict. Shortly before his death in 2001, Govan Mbeki, the veteran ANC leader and father of President Thabo Mbeki, spoke of the need to balance "having and belonging" in the nation-building process in South Africa and elsewhere on the African continent. "For political renewal to endure, the economy needs to be restructured in such a way that the poor and socially excluded begin to share in the benefits of the nation's wealth," he insisted. "People—all people, both black and white, Hutu and Tutsi, Shona and Ndebele—need to feel they are part of a new nation. Those who do not feel welcome or at home in their respective countries will not work for the common good. They can also cause considerable trouble."[11] The need to accomplish both having and belonging, which is a difficult task that takes time, is discussed again in chapter 7.

To begin to deal adequately with "having and belonging," the nature and the causes of an oppressive past need to be defined and placed firmly on the national agenda. Failure to do so could result in an alliance of elites drawn from all sides of the conflict, with the poor continuing to be excluded and alienated. Alternatively, as is the case in some countries, former victors and victims could simply exchange places. Some have made the TRC the whipping boy for failing to address this challenge in South Africa. The question is whether it was politically opportune or indeed possible to do so in the immediate wake of a conflict that had a capacity to destroy any possibility of peace.

This acknowledged, the most telling critiques of the South African TRC, and the ones that capture Govan Mbeki's insights, are those of Wole Soyinka and Mahmood Mamdani. Both authors—conscious of the fragility of new democracies emerging from oppressive regimes where those on opposing sides of a deadly conflict must ultimately learn to live together—show an understanding of the need to find an alternative to Nuremberg-type trials as well as impunity. And, at the same time, both regard the mandate of the TRC as having failed to adequately address the underlying depths of the South African malady. Both further imply that this level of exploration is still possible—although increasingly more difficult to realize.

Soyinka asks the probing question: How far dare a nation go in seeking to accommodate both victims and perpetrators of past abuse?[12] Affirming the need for a purgation of the past through truth telling and acknowledgment, Soyinka is critical of the South African amnesty process, primarily because it allowed perpetrators to be absolved not only of criminality but also of responsibility. His concern is to move beyond the "hazy zone of remorse" to "a social formula that would minister to the wrongs of dispossession on the one hand, chasten those who deviate from humane communal order on the other, [and] serve as a criterion for the future conduct of that society, even in times of stress—and *only then*, heal."[13]

In brief, his plea is for reconciliation and healing to be grounded in appropriate forms of reparations and the affirmation of the rule of law, arguing that the roots of apartheid oppression went deeper than the torture, abduction, killing, and severe ill treatment that constituted the TRC's definition of gross violations of human rights. Recognizing that apartheid was grounded in material deprivation, social humiliation, naked racism, and dehumanization, Soyinka says reparations need to include material restitution as well as the need to redeem victims from what he defines as a "slave condition" that undermines the humanity of the oppressed. Victims need to divest themselves of the internalized perception of being a lesser species of humanity. This imposes a sense of obligation and responsibility on both perpetrators and beneficiaries to engage with, understand, and respond to the needs of the victims of apartheid. It also requires victims to "seize and alter their [own] destiny."

Mahmood Mamdani's critique of the South African TRC is similar to that of Soyinka.[14] His concern is essentially that the TRC reduces the definition of injustice from the "injustice of apartheid," which involved the dehumanization of the majority of the population through the degradation of apartheid, to a narrower one. He sees the defining character of the South African struggle not as a conflict between a "fractured political elite" of perpetrators and victims, as described in the TRC legislation, but as one among all the apartheid system's beneficiaries and victims. With justification, he suggests that Bantu education and forced removals entrenched generations of black South Africans in a national gulag that needs to be confronted in order for justice and reconciliation to become a reality: "The violence of apartheid was aimed less at individuals than at entire communities, and entire population groups. . . . The point is that the Latin American analogy [from which the South African TRC drew its inspiration] obscured the colonial nature of the South African context: the link between conquest and dispossession, between racialized power and racialized privilege. In a word, it obscured the link between perpetrator and beneficiary."[15]

Locating apartheid within the history of European colonialism in which the native majority needed to be subjugated in order to maximize the privilege of beneficiaries, Mamdani's argument is that truth is not enough to ensure reconciliation. This, he argues, can only be realized through systematic socioeconomic reform, which he defines as "a form of justice other than punishment." Without opposing prosecutions, which may well be part of the justice he seeks, he prioritizes restitution and structural change. He simultaneously stresses the importance of acknowledgment and apology, insisting that these go beyond the formal "deep regret" about apartheid expressed by former president F. W. de Klerk, which he contrasts with the postwar apology of the German leader, Willie Brandt, who went on his knees in the former Warsaw ghetto.

The lacuna in the critique of the South African transition by Soyinka and Mamdani is its failure to give sufficient attention to the complexities involved in the need to both broaden and deepen the national conversation as a basis for a shift in the national mindset—something anticipated, although not fully realized, through the TRC. This level of engagement among victims, perpetrators, benefactors, and bystanders required to realize the kind of justice that Soyinka and Mamdani so eloquently demand in turn requires an integration of political incentives, modes of economic repair, and social transformation that scholars, activists, political leaders, and citizens need to address at a level that has not yet been realized.

The former government, its supporters, and others on whom apartheid bestowed its privileges were not ready to apologize or make the kind of social and economic changes required at the time of the TRC—and arguably are still not ready to do so. Democratic politics and debate in South Africa must continue to wrestle with how to respond to the kind of past that refuses to go away. Despite the fact that many perpetrators and benefactors were victims of a state ideology that drew bystanders and would-be decent people into its clutches, individuals were not entirely without resources to resist this level of propaganda.[16] Daniel Goldhagen's argument in *Hitler's Willing Executioners* that Germans were under the "grip of a cognitive model" or "monolithic conversation" so powerful that few were able to escape its impact goes a long way to explaining the hideous anti-Semitic behavior of otherwise seemingly decent people.[17] The reality is that some did act at great personal cost against dominant ideologies—in Germany, South Africa, and elsewhere. The limitation of the South African TRC was that it did not have the mandate, the time, or perhaps the will to address the underlying problems of racism and privilege that underpinned the gross violations of human rights that it sought to uncover.[18]

The question is how to get those who supported and benefited from a system to commit themselves to work for the restitution and integration of the victims and survivors of a repulsive past? It can only be through continued engagement and democratic debate. Nelson Mandela's answer is that this needs to be accomplished gently and in a conciliatory manner. In his state of the nation speech, delivered two weeks after his inauguration as president on May 10, 1994, he declared that in engaging the past, South Africans "must be constrained . . . regardless of the accumulated effect of our historical burdens, seizing the time to define for ourselves what we want to make of our shared destiny." According to him, this would need to include the granting of amnesty to perpetrators of the most horrible crimes:

> In this context, I also need to point out that the Government will not delay unduly with regard to attending to the vexed and unresolved issue of an amnesty for criminal activities carried out in furtherance of political objectives. We will attend to this matter in a balanced and dignified way. The nation must come to terms with its past in a spirit of oneness and forgiveness and proceed to build the future on the basis of repairing and healing. . . . In the meantime, summoning the full authority of the position we represent, we call on all concerned not to take any steps that might, in any way, impede or compromise the processes of reconciliation that the impending legislation will address.[19]

The double critique of the TRC involving "having" and "belonging" stands. There is, however, also a sense in which the TRC could do no more than initiate a conversation, for others to take further.

Back to the Beginning

The TRC was born in the fragility of the earliest days of the South African democracy and needs to be considered within the context of this tenuous beginning in order to be adequately understood and assessed. The national conversation was hesitant and constrained. It was also volatile and dangerous.[20]

Shortly before the first democratic elections in April 1994, General Constand Viljoen, the former chief of the South African Defence Force, walked out of the Afrikaner right-wing Freedom Front Party, committing himself to "building and maintaining the armed potential for the more militant Afrikaner Volksfront." He warned that the nation was on the brink of war. However, he soon became disillusioned with the ill discipline and violent tactics of the Volksfront and returned to a leadership position in the Freedom Front. After a series of behind-the-scenes meetings with the ANC and others, he persuaded his party to participate in the pending elections. In a later submission to Parliament's Joint Committee on Justice, he applauded Mandela's "spirit of reconciliation" but warned that what would satisfy the constituency of the ANC on reconciliation would have the opposite effect on the Afrikaner constituency, arguing that the transition had failed to produce a shared vision for the nation. There were skirmishes and threats of insurrection. In Bophuthatswana—a Bantustan given "independence" by the apartheid government in 1977—an uprising known as the Battle of Bop involved the armed forces of the Bophuthatswana Defence Force, troops of the Afrikaner Weerstandsbeweging, and the Volksfront. The South African Army was ordered to intervene, and Bophuthatswana was stripped of its independence.

There was also the bizarre invasion of the World Trade Center, where the constitutional negotiations known as Codesa were being held. Eugène Terre'Blanche, head of the Afrikaner Weerstandsbeweging, led his followers into the hall on horseback, but this too came to nothing—except for the embarrassment of those in charge of security. Ultimately, however, there was no resolute armed confrontation, and Viljoen later said that he knew of no serious coup plans at any point of the transition. However, the antics of those threatening revolt were enough to alarm the ANC leadership waiting in the wings to assume power.

Responding to these concerns, President Mandela stressed that "the majority party must show understanding . . . to ensure the confidence of minority parties . . . and see to it that their views are fully accommodated."[21] Dullah Omar, the minister of justice at the time, responding to the criticism of Amnesty

International and other human rights' groups that the amnesty clause in the TRC legislation threatened the integrity of international human rights' law, stated: "We are building a future for South Africans [and as] there is conflict between what the international community is saying and what is in the interests of the people of South Africa then I think that we will have to live with that kind of conflict."[22] The die was cast. The TRC was to be what Johnny de Lange, an architect of the TRC legislation and later deputy minister of justice, called a "model in the middle."[23]

The rapprochement reached between the former government and the ANC in the multiparty Codesa talks was not readily embraced by some both inside and outside the TRC who wanted it to deal with the broader crimes of apartheid. The daily burdens of those who, for example, suffered under forced removals, Bantu education, and related apartheid crimes were implicit in all that the TRC did. And yet for a range of reasons—including political compromise, the need to be seen to be reconciling the nation, and what Kader Asmal called the "liberal procedures of transition"[24]—the nuts and bolts of apartheid policy and practice were not adequately addressed by the TRC. This, ultimately, also had an impact on the extent to which the TRC was able and/or prepared to demand deeper levels of truth from alleged perpetrators, including officials of the former state. The focus was on "killing, abductions, torture, and severe ill treatment," not on apartheid policy and the racist ideology that gave rise to these crimes.

The TRC was discrete in its handling of some of those who refused to appear before it. For example, the head of the Inkatha Freedom Party, Mangosuthu Buthelezi, was not subpoenaed when he refused to appear before the TRC a second time. In the case against former president P. W. Botha, Tutu visited him at his retirement home in the Wilderness in an attempt to persuade him to appear before the TRC. Having refused, Botha agreed to respond to the TRC's questions in writing through his lawyers. This turned out to be a circuitous tome that failed to provide the information sought, and he refused to participate in what he described as a "witch hunt" and a "circus." He was subpoenaed in the George Magistrate's Court, which found him guilty of contravening Section 39(e)(i) and Sections 134 and 29 of the Promotion of National Unity and Reconciliation Act. He was sentenced to a fine of R 10,000 or twelve months' imprisonment, plus a further twelve months' imprisonment suspended for five years on the condition that he did not contravene any provisions of the act again. His lawyers lodged an immediate appeal, which was upheld on technical grounds—and he ironically expressed appreciation for South Africa's judiciary. The TRC, after intense debate, decided not to take the matter further.

The closest the TRC came to addressing the realities of apartheid policy as a whole was in the political party and institutional hearings. Many opportunities to uncover the depths of responsibility and hurt that characterized apartheid were missed in these hearings. At the same time, they did open spaces for truth recovery that still wait to be explored.

In the political party hearings, former president F. W. de Klerk, on behalf of the National Party and former government, expressed a formal regret for the hurt caused by apartheid, but he failed to show the passion and conviction that either the TRC or the public was looking for. He insisted that apartheid had gone wrong, perhaps horribly wrong, while stressing that he had no knowledge of the atrocities committed by the security forces. Questioned by the TRC, he indicated that he was "not prepared to accept responsibility for the criminal actions of a handful of operatives of the security forces of which [his] party was not aware and which would never have been condoned."[25] When individuals and organizations both inside and outside the country earlier drew his attention to the gross violations of human rights committed by the security forces and related agencies, he appointed several commissioners to look into the accusations but failed to demonstrate the kind of commitment to get to the bottom of these accusations that the TRC and many beyond its structures were seeking.

Contrary to de Klerk, his deputy minister of law and order, Leon Wessels, observed: "It was not that we did not know; we didn't want to know. We didn't talk about it; we whispered it in the corridors of parliament. . . . I cannot condone these violent unlawful acts, but nor can I condemn the persons; I cannot disown them. We were on the same side and fought for the same cause. . . . I cannot disown any of those men and women who were on our side." Acknowledging the positive role played by de Klerk in the political transition, Wessels stated: "I simply believe it is a pity that there is not a collective political and moral acceptance of responsibility forthcoming from the quarters from which I emanate. Apartheid was a terrible mistake that blighted our land. South Africans did not listen to the laughing and the crying of one another. I am sorry that I have been so hard of hearing for such a long time." In acting on his commitment to put his own involvement in the apartheid system behind him, Wessels today serves as a member of the South African Human Rights Commission.[26]

A less-publicized submission to the TRC came from the "liberal" Democratic Party (DP) as the official opposition party in the apartheid parliament. The members of the DP, which was closely aligned with big business, initially declined to appear before the TRC at all but later agreed to do so. The various DP representatives spoke of their role in monitoring and witnessing the "human rights abuses and construction of the edifice of apartheid" and "a programme of Afrikaner domination . . . [that was] central to the promoting of white interest, depriving blacks, coloureds and Indians of their basic human rights."[27] Distancing themselves and the English-speaking community from what they saw as an Afrikaner-imposed ideology, they referred to their role in opposing the "repression of individual liberties," pointing out that they had warned that government policy would "inevitably lead to ever more violence and counter-violence." They stated that in their attempt to promote peaceful change they had been fed false information by the government. At the same time, they made no reference to their complicity as an opposition party in an all-white Parliament, or the difficult choice they had to make in this regard. They portrayed no sense of white privilege or selfish gain that lay at the root of an evil and dehumanizing system. Closely aligned to business, they opposed economic sanctions and the commitment of the black majority to render the apartheid government dysfunctional. Indeed, Douglas Gibson, a senior member of the Democratic Alliance (DA), to which the DP had evolved, would some years later criticize a civil society initiative calling on whites simply to acknowledge that they benefited from apartheid, insisting that as a white person he had attained no benefits from the apartheid system. In the words of a respected newspaper editor, the DA needed to "shed its image as a right-wing party of white fat cats" who benefited from the privileges of apartheid. The DA made no attempt to persuade or enable whites to acknowledge culpability for accepting the benefits of apartheid or to take responsibility for any form of reparation.

The submission of the ANC was both more candid and extensive than the submissions made by other parties. It included, for example, disclosure on deaths and torture in the ANC detention camps. Although critics saw the level of disclosure in the ANC's submission as partial and inadequate, the TRC's findings on the ANC, as published in the TRC's final report, were significantly shaped by the ANC's own submission. Despite this, the ANC resorted to court action in an unsuccessful attempt to stop the release of the final report on the eve of it being handed to President Mandela on September 26, 1998. The fact that this was done before the ANC was given sight of the report suggests that a member of the TRC had leaked an earlier, unedited, less-discrete version of it to the ANC, which heightened the already-tense relations between the ANC and the TRC.

Despite the insights into the political machinations gained through the TRC's political party hearings, the lack of candor by politicians resulted in a lost opportunity to plumb the depths of the past in a more complete manner.

The special institutional hearings that included business and labor, faith communities, the health sector, media, prisons, the military, and the legal fraternity, as well as special hearings on children, youth, and women, were as tentative as those on the political parties. They failed to acknowledge or disclose the extent of institutional complicity in the functioning of apartheid. The former security police spy, Craig Williamson, illustrated this in seeking to justify or mitigate his crimes in his declaration to a TRC hearing in Cape Town in October 1997:

It is not only the task of the members of the Security Forces to examine themselves and their deeds. It is for every member of the society we served to do so. Our weapons, ammunition, uniforms, vehicles, radios and other equipment were all developed and provided by industry. Our finances and banking were done by bankers who even gave us covert credit cards for covert operations. Our Chaplains prayed for our victory and our universities educated us in war. Our propaganda was carried by the media and our political masters were voted back into power time after time with ever increasing majorities.[28]

More so than in the other hearings, it was perhaps the legal fraternity hearing that illustrated the TRC's restrained approach to discerning the malady of the past. In this hearing—in much the same way as people in business, journalists, and members of the medical and health fraternities expressed regret in their hearings that they had not done as much as they should have to uphold the moral and professional expectations of their professions in the apartheid years—many judges and lawyers echoed their words while insisting they were merely "doing their job" within the restraints of what the law permitted. Members of the Black Lawyer's Association, Lawyers for Human Rights, the Legal Resources Centre, and the National Association of Democratic Lawyers and others, conversely, were highly critical of the legal community and the judiciary. The judges initially refused to appear before the TRC at all, arguing that this would call into question their independence and open the way for them to be called to account for their behavior in future situations. Commissioner Yasmin Sooka insisted that the judges be subpoenaed but lost out to the majority of commissioners, who felt this would be interpreted as a hostile act by the TRC in what was already an unsympathetic environment in government circles. The compromise was a number of voluntary written submissions by several senior judges, including Justice L. W. F. Ackermann (judge of the Constitutional Court), Justice Arthur Chaskalson (president of the Constitutional Court), and Justice M. M. Corbett (chief justice of the Supreme Court). These were augmented by submissions from a range of legal scholars and others.

Justice Albie Sachs, commenting on the TRC report, commended the TRC for its serious reflection "on how evil behaviour is condoned and spreads itself and [it's reflection] on what institutional mechanisms . . . are necessary to prevent its reappearance." But he asked "Did it go far enough? What restrained it?" "Business, where were you? Business was making money, business was cooperating directly with the security forces, supplying explosives, trucks, and information. The press, where were you? There were some brave newspapers and wonderful journalists, but by and large the press was racist in its structure and fearful in its thinking. The legal profession, the judges, where were you? We judges, old and new, had hard debates in our ranks. The strongest view was that the judiciary had contributed substantially to injustice by enforcing racist laws and showing an unacceptable lack of vigilance in the face of accusations, torture, and abuse."[29]

By committing itself to a TRC, South Africa went further than most nations in dealing with its past. However, its work, and more particularly the work of the nation in this regard, is still unfinished. The underlying motivations and causes of the apartheid malady and the culpability and responsibility of the many who benefited from apartheid run deep. Not all whites were guilty of gross violations of human rights. Some whites protested against apartheid—but all in one way or another benefited from white privilege. They, together with those blacks who collaborated with their apartheid masters, were drawn into an ideology that imposed exclusion and abuse by way of fear and violence.

The question is how to get people to acknowledge complicity. The demand for truth continues—raising its head in times of conflict. Sleeping dogs do not lie quietly. In time they smell a forgotten bone that they seek to uncover. Memories slumber but do not sleep.

The point has already been made. Extensive conversation is necessary for the past to be managed if not redeemed. The uncovering of the past could never have been concluded in an isolated event. The plethora of books, autobiographies, interviews, and indeed the current deep conflict within government and political circles can be seen as a de facto continuation of the TRC. At the same time, the indications are that the disclosure and counterdisclosure that is taking place will engender a level of bitterness that the TRC intended to ameliorate if not avoid. Truth in different guises and versions insists on coming out in the ongoing national debate, and this is likely to continue for the foreseeable future.

The strained conversation of the TRC process was an important step in the public debate, but the hard work of lasting reconciliation needs still to be tackled with a renewed sense of truth telling and the building of a caring society—one that looks beyond past divisions in pursuit of unity rather than division, harmony rather than contention, integrity rather than corruption, and civil and constructive debate rather than confrontation and abuse—as a basis for creating an opportunity for subjective and material transformation and renewal.

Unfinished Conversation

Central to the South African transition is an unfinished conversation that raises all the questions pertinent to the international transitional justice debate. Here, I mention four pertinent concerns that brood at the heart of the unfinished South African transition: perpetrator engagement, reparations and rectification, prosecutions and accountability, and truth telling and clarification.

Perpetrator Engagement

The late chief justice Ismael Mohammed spoke of the South African transition as an "agonising balance," designed to enable both victims and perpetrators to cross the historic bridge from the past into the future.[30] The invitation, as understood by Mohammed, was for all South Africans to share in the nation-building process without undue restraint.

The victor's justice that imposes retribution, whether in a no-nonsense revolutionary sense or in a liberal democratic form, has the capacity to turn former perpetrators and beneficiaries into victims. Sometimes it unleashes a new wave of terror, as witnessed in a range of African countries from Sudan to Zimbabwe. If the victor's justice had been imposed in South Africa, the democratic government elected in 1994 might not only have lost the moral high ground but might have found itself drawn into a new round of warfare. The victor's justice could have precipitated a level of partition and disintegration as seen in the former Yugoslavia or in the Indian-Pakistani separation that continues to generate conflict almost sixty years later.

An alternative to the victor's justice in a transitional situation as volatile as was South Africa's in 1994 demands an inspired if inherently compromised response. Retributive justice, in the sense of an impartial system that metes out justice on the basis of everyone getting their just deserts, needs to be weighed against restorative justice, which focuses on healing and the renewal or creation of community relations.

The most controversial aspect of the South African restorative justice process was to allow perpetrators, some of whom had committed heinous crimes, to receive amnesty in return for acknowledging those crimes and for making full disclosure of them. This meant that at least some perpetrators and all those who benefited from apartheid would be free to share in the new society. They would not be required to pay reparations, undertake community service, or face ceremonial purification of any kind. There was a realization that whites and other benefactors were here to stay. They needed to be drawn into society, excused for past crimes, and allowed to keep the material benefits they had acquired during the apartheid years. The intent was to create space where all who had the necessary skills and resources could contribute to building a new society.

To what extent has this happened? The economy has grown, black empowerment is in place, and affirmative action has placed many formerly disadvantaged people in important and lucrative positions. At the same time, many remain without life's most basic needs. Transformation and rectification are incomplete, and if this situation persists it could have dire consequences for South Africa's future stability.

Reparations and Rectification

I use the notion of rectification in an attempt to capture the breadth of restoration required for victims and survivors.[31] It involves recognition that comes in different ways. Compensation, reparation, restoration, apology, law suits, and punishment are all important ingredients that can contribute to the realization of rectifying justice. It is, however, the social and political context of rectification that determines, for instance, how much punitive justice or compensation is possible and how much is wise to impose. Donald Shriver suggests that "vengeance however understandable from the perspective of victims ultimately kills politics, if by politics we mean negotiations between groups that permit people to realize their mutual interests without destroying those very interests in acts of violence."[32] In a democratic order, he suggests, a responsible citizen is required to vote for someone else's interests in addition to his or her own and ultimately the interests of the nation as a whole.

To provide more than an imaginary, artificial, or hoped-for stability and rectification, both the *material* and *subjective* needs of victims and survivors of an oppressive past must be prioritized. In South Africa the newly elected democratic government's decision in this regard was to initiate a truth-telling process through the TRC, to play down the need for retribution, and to focus the nation on building a strong economy. It asked the poor to be patient. "You cannot give away what you do not have," are the frequent words of Trevor Manuel, the South African minister of finance. But how long will the poor be patient? Clearly not enough is being done to include the dispossessed in the new dispensation.

Subjective needs are equally difficult to meet and deeply intertwined with material needs. In the words of the TRC mandate, this requires the "restoration of the human dignity" of victims. This involves acknowledgment of the suffering endured, recognition of the price that was paid, and the inclusion of victims and survivors in their own restoration, in that of the communities of which they are a part, and in the nation as a whole. Nyameka Goniwe, whose husband Mathew was killed by the security police in 1985, puts it this way:

> The TRC helped me to recognize that I have human rights and that those who violated my rights would under normal circumstances be prosecuted. I accept that this was not possible in our situation and so I go along with the amnesty process—and yet it is perhaps only those who have been as deeply violated as I have who are able to understand the deep sense of personal depravation and sense of helplessness I

experience. I need to almost daily regain my loss of dignity and self-confidence. The recognition I have received in society has helped but there is still a horrible sense of worthlessness that continues to raise its horrible head as I attempt to rebuild my life and that of my children. Maybe it will always be there because certain things can never be restored or put right. I sometimes think a sincere apology from the persons who destroyed my life by killing Mathew would help me. But so far I have refused to meet them. I simply don't know how sincere their apology will be. It is so difficult for me to trust them. I am not prepared to risk a simple "I am sorry." I need a sense of heartfelt sorrow and grief and a genuine attempt by Mathew's killers to put right what they destroyed in our lives. Right now I simply want to be left alone, so that I can try to heal myself.[33]

The South African TRC is a process that continues to intrigue, bewilder, and anger all who ponder the meaning of rectifying justice in situations of political transition. The essential goodwill that existed in the early stage of the transition between those who benefited from and those who suffered at the hands of apartheid has not resulted in a willingness to add economic and material restoration to the political transition that whites conceded.

Frustrated by the failure of this to happen more than a decade into democratic rule in South Africa, some ask whether trials would not have been a better option for ushering in a new society. "At least I would not have to see my torturer living a comfortable life while I continue to be excluded from the society I helped see born in 1994," Sipho Tshabalala, an angry township resident, shouted at a conference audience in Cape Town.[34] It is in the interests of beneficiaries of the old order and those who have succeeded economically from the new to ensure that Tshabalala and the poor have reason to feel that the new order will meet their most basic needs and aspirations.

Prosecutions and Accountability

Would Tshabalala be less angry had his torturer been prosecuted? Does prosecution bring closure? Do most victims want prosecutions? What more than prosecution is needed? These questions continue to haunt the transitional justice debate.

The jury is still out on whether victims in the South African situation feel that they have a sufficient base on which to build their human and civic worth. The priority at the time was to bring an end to apartheid. A survey conducted in the wake of the TRC, which ended its work in 1998, showed that black South Africans saw truth, acknowledgment, apology, and an opportunity for victims to relate their stories of suffering in public as important alternatives to both retribution and monetary compensation.[35] The survey showed that 65 percent of blacks conceded that amnesty for perpetrators was a price that needed to be paid in return for disclosure of the truth about the past and a peaceful transition to democratic rule, whereas only 18 percent of white South Africans saw it as such! Interestingly, 73 percent of whites surveyed concluded that apartheid was a crime against humanity!

Thembi Simelane-Nkadimeng has spent twenty-three years trying to find out what happened to her sister, Nokuthula, who was abducted by the security police and has not been seen since. Speaking at a public symposium on the tenth anniversary of the TRC, she said: "I am favoring prosecutions now because it is the only option I have, but if I had an option to sit down and talk [with Nokuthula's abductors] I would choose that."[36] Victims often resort to prosecutions as much out of an effort to gain access to the truth as out of a desire for retribution. The much-publicized prosecution of former minister of law and order Adriaan Vlok, former commissioner of police Johan van der Merwe, and former police officers Christoffel Smith, Gert Otto, and Johannes Van Staden, which eventually occurred in August 2007 (nine years after the formal closing of the TRC), failed to reveal this level of truth and has consequently failed to bring closure to their cases. After a fifty-minute court appearance in which no evidence was led against them, Vlok and van der Merwe each received a ten-year sentence suspended for five years, and the three officers received a five-year sentence also suspended for five years.

The advent of the International Criminal Court (ICC), which postdated the South African transition, has intensified the demand for prosecutions, although the demands of the ICC have also evoked an ambiguous response. The Office of the United Nations High Commissioner for Refugees (UNHCR) in Uganda captures this in a February 2007 publication titled *Options for Accountability for Reconciliation in Uganda*.[37] It reaffirms the position of the ICC that "those responsible for the most serious crimes be held accountable in accordance with international norms and principles" and that "there can be no amnesty for serious crimes, such as war crimes, crimes against humanity, genocide and gross violations of human rights." The publication also recognizes that "accountability and justice do not begin and end with prosecution and punishment, but include a variety of other measures aimed at ensuring that victims' needs are properly addressed so that society as a whole can come to terms with what previously divided it and fuelled the conflict." The "other measures" cited in the document include truth and reconciliation commissions, other historical clarification bodies, and traditional reconciliation practices—recognizing that there is a need to know the truth about past atrocities in order for reconciliation and healing to take place. Stressing that these initiatives cannot be a substitute for formal judicial process in the case of perpetrators of serious crimes as defined under international law, the UNHCR in Uganda sees these as complementary options capable of promoting transitional justice, and it recommends that a national consultative process be set in motion to gather views on appropriate forms of accountability and reconciliation. These are important ideas that have become part of the Juba Meetings between the Ugandan government and the Lord's Resistance Army, as discussed further in chapter 6.

There are ultimately three considerations that need attention with regard to prosecutions and accountability. Perpetrators need to be held accountable as required by the Rome Treaty and the ICC. There needs to be political stability for justice and political reconciliation to be achieved. The penalties imposed on perpetrators found guilty of crimes must be determined in relation to both the need for justice and political stability and the willingness of those found guilty of a crime to contribute to the latter.

Truth Telling and Clarification

Timothy Garton Ash identifies three ways of dealing with past atrocities: trials, purges, and history lessons, arguing that it is the path involving history lessons that is the most promising.[38] Michael Marrus identifies the difficulties inherent in criminal trials, arguing that the process involved undermines the quest for a full historical account of the past. The duty of the court is to prosecute against a limited charge sheet.[39] The duty of the defense team is to produce an array of legal arguments designed to challenge and exclude from the court record some of the basic information used in persuasive story-telling and history writing. This is seen nowhere more clearly than in the trial of Saddam Hussein. He was convicted of crimes against humanity, for the killing and torture of 148 Shi'ite villagers in Dujail following a failed assassination attempt in 1982. He was sentenced to death and subsequently hanged. The courts did not address the more extensive record of his reign of terror. Questions about America and the West encouraging Hussein to invade Iran in 1980—an invasion that led to the deaths of 1.5 million people—were not posed. The supply of chemical weapons components, with which Saddam drenched Iran and the Kurds; the anarchy unleashed by American and British troops in the aftermath of what was described as a "mission accomplished"; and the use of Saddam's Abu Ghraib torture chambers by America torturers are not part of the court record.

Saddam is the first ruler to be found guilty and made to pay the ultimate price for his crimes against humanity. There was no impunity, at least not for him. Yet the truth behind his reign of terror remains untold. More is required than the trial that found him guilty. Hundreds of thousands of Iraqis, Iranians, Kurds, and people in the West still seek to know the causes, motives, and perspectives that are part of the monstrous crimes central to his rule. If truth has a capacity to heal, it must include this level of disclosure. Historians, journalists, and those who suffered most will wrestle with this challenge for decades to come. Saddam's trial has not brought closure for many people.

Writing on the International Criminal Tribunal for Rwanda being held in Arusha, Babu Ayindo sees the truth telling that emerges from dialogue as being at the heart of most "African traditional justice systems," which aim to reintegrate both the offender and the victim back into society. "There are questions to which the victim badly needs answers in the absence of which he will conjure up his own. For instance, the victim badly needs to know why particularly his wife, father, daughter, to mention a few, were maimed or killed." Turning his attention to the role of the courts, Ayindo's concern is that "at the end of the day, the success of the International Criminal Tribunal for Rwanda will be determined not by how much healing has taken place in the Central African nation, but on the number of prosecutions carried out."[40]

Trials are important and have a crucial role to play in dealing with the past, but *additional* means must be found to achieve the level of reconciliation that Africa needs to restore itself. I am suggesting that a broad-based, both formal and informal national conversation is one way. The quest for truth can be endless. It can also be unrelated to the immediate needs of those seeking to put a terrible past behind them. Truth seeking can become esoteric, academic, and unrelated to the immediate needs of those directly affected by past events. The concern of victims and those related to them is primarily at the level of clarification of events affecting their lives and those around them. They often do not want to know the kind of detail that scholars and others are demanding. Michael Ignatieff suggests that "all nations depend on forgetting: on forging myths of unity and identity that allow a society to forget its founding crimes, its hidden injuries and divisions, its unhealed wounds." He further suggests "it must [also] be true, for nations as it is for individuals, that we can stand only so much truth. But if too much truth is divisive, the question becomes: How much is enough?"[41] The medium of truth telling is also important, as are the tone, genre, and format. Art, theater, drama, music, and storytelling are slowly beginning to take the national conversation beyond discursive forms in several African countries.

Reconciliation and nation building take time. They have to do with finding different ways of promoting what Harold Saunders calls "a cumulative, multi-level and open-ended process of continuous interaction over time, engaging significant clusters of citizens in and out of government and the relationships they form to solve public problems, . . . either within or between communities or countries."[42] This is a process that could probably not have happened at the time of the South African TRC twelve years ago. Tensions were too high and the cost of failure is too great. The negotiators who sat at the table to make peace chose to postpone issues of economic restitution until later. In politics change comes through the assertion of power rather than simply through an

attempt to promote moral concern. This sense of power is beginning to manifest itself in South Africa through protests and resistance by those whose social
and economic situation has not been adequately addressed since the advent of
democracy.

Generative Conversation

The TRC was no more than a cautious beginning to explore the nature of
reconciliation. It could have reached deeper into the nation's memory by holding a sharper and more penetrating mirror before the nation, persuading it to
reflect with a more rigorous, penetrating gaze on the origins of what gave rise
to the gross human rights violations that it highlighted within the morass of
the past. Maybe it was too soon for this to happen. This is precisely why the
conversation needs to continue.

The South African TRC did not succeed in depolarizing the nation. In
the words of former president Thabo Mbeki, South Africa continues to consist
of two nations—a white one and a black one, a rich one and a poor one. Not
many former perpetrators chose to use the TRC as an opportunity to deal fully
with their past. Senior politicians and generals in the security forces refused to
take responsibility for the deeds of their foot soldiers. Most beneficiaries of
apartheid have refused to acknowledge the privileges that they have carried with
them into the present. The full extent of the apartheid infrastructure has not
been wholly faced by most white people; nor has the new government adequately
succeeded in changing the economic dimensions of these structures. State institutions have not been able to transform themselves adequately. Insufficient
attention has been given to the roots and the nature of racism. The redress of
poverty and human security remains a major challenge facing South Africa.
Without making any dire prediction of a popular revolutionary upsurge in the
short to medium terms, this entrenched inequality can only result in new forms
of struggle—what Neville Alexander calls "movements of desperation."[43] The
social and political discontent surrounding the election of Jacob Zuma as president of the ANC (he was later also elected president of South Africa) and the
subsequent resignation of Mbeki as South African president, rooted in jobless-
ness and economic alienation, are clear indications of this.

For generative conversations in postconflict situations to be effective, they
must result in new horizons of thought and action, as discussed in the previous
chapter. They must also make conflict prevention central to their programs of
socioeconomic and political reconstruction and transformation. It is here that
the peace-building debate in the broad sense of conflict resolution, conflict
transformation, and socioeconomic development contributes to the unfinished
business of a transitional justice agenda.

To return to the words of President Nelson Mandela on receiving the TRC report from Desmond Tutu in September 1998: "South Africans need to engage in national dialogue as a basis for giving birth to a new country." In continuity with Mandela's words, eight years later Tutu spoke of "honest conversation [as] the womb that holds the possibility of peace" (see the prologue to this volume). The grounding of this sentiment is captured in the African notion of *ubuntu*, which presupposes a sense of belonging or inclusivity within which people in conflict, who have different priorities and interests, can encounter one another with honesty and authenticity. *Ubuntu* is often dismissed as no more than an ideal that is beyond the grasp of a complex modern society. Certainly it is frequently exploited and romanticized by those who seek to benefit from its offer of belonging without responding to the sense of responsibility for the other that it presupposes. *Ubuntu* at the same time persists as a virtue that challenges the individualism and greed of many postconflict societies that struggle to rise above the social and political structures they vowed to overcome on what Chinua Achebe calls the first day of creation.[44] The next chapter addresses the vision and scope of *ubuntu* in a modern society in transition.

UBUNTU

Ubuntu is less romantic than is often thought. There is a bit of realpolitik in it. It is about drawing an adversary or a potential opponent into the community rather than leaving him outside where he is likely to cause trouble. Inclusively understood, the idea of *ubuntu* reaches across intra and intercommunity divisions, whether political, religious, or other. If on the other hand it is confined to the limitations of tribal or ethnic borders, it can be as vicious as any other nationalistic exclusivity. Inclusively understood, *ubuntu* means we cannot turn our backs on anyone who genuinely wants to be part of our community, provided that person is ready to accept the privileges as well as the responsibilities involved in being part of a family or community. *Ubuntu* in this sense places dialogue at the center of what it means to be fully human. It involves a future that seeks to rise above exclusion and alienation.

—Gabriel Setiloane, Maokeng, Free State Province, January 2004

Can one confront a former enemy or adversary in demanding one's rights and human dignity—being prepared to engage in the necessary conflict that is likely to occur—without destroying the humanity of the other? How does a person preserve his or her moral values and humanity in a situation of armed conflict? How does one restore ethical values that have been violated in war? These are questions that are central to the discussion on *ubuntu*. In situations of armed conflict and war, some fight for freedom. Others fight to suppress the freedom of others. For peace to prevail, they need to learn to live together.

Sindiwe Magona writes on township violence at the height of the South African struggle in her novel *Mother to Mother*. She describes the angry and violent Mxolisi as an "agent executing the long simmering desires of his race" and "the blind but sharpened arrow of the wrath of his race." Within this context, she tells us, "*ubuntu* took flight." She recalls the brutality of apartheid that gave rise to the brutality of a subjugated people who lost their own humanity in their resistance to evil:

Just as we kept on calling, insisted on calling, the people who did the necklacing [the practice of killing by placing a motorcar tire around a person's neck, filling it with petrol and setting it alight] "children," "students," and "comrades," we called a barbaric act the necklace, protecting our ears from a reality too gruesome to hear; clothing satanic deeds with innocent apparel. . . . Not many of our leaders came out and actually condemned the deed. Indeed there were those who actually applauded the method, the innovative manner of killing a human being, of doing away with those with whom one was in disagreement. They said it would lead to our freedom. However, to this day, I have never heard it said that even one of the oppressors was necklaced. I had not known that it was our own people who stood in the way of the freedom we all said we desired.[1]

Pondering the extent of crime and violence in South Africa ten years after the publication of her novel, Magona reminds us of the enduring impact of the loss of humanity: "The evil of apartheid created a climate within which young people resorted to desperate deeds and today we all suffer. We are all in it together, the creators of apartheid, those who fought against it and those who did nothing to stop it—the innocent, the guilty and the indifferent. We share a common humanity. This is the essence of what *ubuntu* teaches us. We are who we are in relation to those around us."[2]

Can a rediscovery of *ubuntu* realistically assist a people to heal themselves? How valid is the *ubuntu* ideal as a viable political ethic? To what extent is *ubuntu* little more than a nostalgic longing for a projected sense of precolonial cultural homogeneity and coexistence? Did it emerge as a colonial imposition designed to exclude African communities from colonial privilege? Given its origins in a preindustrial society, grounded in family, clan, and tribal belonging, can it be updated to address the complexities facing heterogeneous contemporary societies? Has *ubuntu* made South African and traditional African nations substantially more humane than other societies? What are the limitations and strengths of *ubuntu*? What, if anything, does *ubuntu* offer the modern state?

The underlying principle of *ubuntu* is that human existence is interconnected and communal. It emphasizes the virtue and potential contribution of every human being to the well-being of society. Though *ubuntu* is essentially South African, there is synergy between *ubuntu* and traditional values in other African countries. It is about the importance of human social cohesion and mutual fulfillment. Captured in the proverb *Umuntu ngumuntu ngabantu* (a person is a person through other people), *ubuntu* suggests that the realization of one's human potential can only be achieved through interaction with other people. To be out of harmony with another is harmful to the well-being and survival of the community as a whole. This means that to the extent that there is enmity between me and another, I am a lesser human being and so is the person alienated from me.

By implication, if a particular community is estranged from another, both communities suffer. "*Ubuntu* is a piece of homegrown African wisdom that the world would do well to make their own," Gabriel Setiloane, an old man who took pride in his deep Sotho-Tswana identity, told me in a long conversation in Maokeng, a dusty township outside Kroonstad in the Free State, a year before he died in early 2004. "Do I live according to the principles of *ubuntu?*" he asks. "The answer is: Not always. Ought I to do so? Yes, I would be a better person and so would others if I did. *Ubuntu*, like any ethnoethical ideal, reminds us who we ought to be. It can be defended in terms of the major religious and ethical ideals in the world, while providing a critique of the individualism that has made its way into most religious practices in the West."

The sociolinguist Buntu Mfenyana, using a Xhosa variation of the proverb *Ubuntu ungamntu ngabanye abantu*, says that in order to understand the meaning of *ubuntu*, the prefix *ubu-* must be separated from the root *-ntu*.

> *Ntu* is an ancestor who got human society going. He gave us our way of life as human beings. It is a communal way of life that says that society must run for the sake of all. This requires cooperation, sharing and charity. There should be no widows or orphans left alone—they all belong to someone. If a man does not have a cow, then give him a cow to milk. There should be no *ohlelelekileyo, a* deprived person. . . . *Ubu* refers to the abstract. So *ubuntu* is the quality of being human. It is the quality, or behaviour, of *ntu* society, that is, sharing, charitableness, and cooperation. It is this quality which distinguishes a human creature from an animal or a spirit. When you do something that is not humane then you are being like an animal.[3]

Sustainable peace involves more than the absence of rebellion and war. It requires justice, human fulfillment, mutual respect, peaceful coexistence, and the building of a caring society. *Ubuntu* suggests that this must necessarily be a *shared peace*, requiring more than the empathy and understanding of others. It involves self-realization by engaging the other as a source of self-enrichment and completion. It is an inward or spiritual sense of belonging and community that draws people toward a fullness of humanity through others.

The African Challenge

Romantic notions of *ubuntu* do little to address such questions. Mike Boon, for example, argues it is not something that an African chooses. "It simply exists.

It is moral and good. It is emotional and deep, and people simply act in a way they intuitively know to be right. It is not something one chooses, and it is accepted as a way of life."[4] This is not the case in contemporary society and may well never have been so. Africa is diverse in its traditional makeup and identity. Like other regions of the world, it is subjected to competing ideologies. *Ubuntu* needs to be seen and assessed within this complex, competitive, and ever-changing milieu—where strangers and former enemies encounter one another. Does *ubuntu* have a contribution to make to peace building beyond the African continent? Does it have significance for a continent that is so often divided against itself?

The South African author Zakes Mda suggests that "African identity" and the quest and talk of "African unity" is a recent phenomenon. Arabs at the turn of the Common Era used the word Afriquia for the northern part of what is today the African continent. The Romans, in turn, captured Carthage in 146 CE and soon extended their dominance from parts of modern Libya to Mauritania. They referred to the region as their African proconsular province. And yet, writes Mda, "Until about 100 years ago the inhabitants of the continent did not generally refer to themselves as Africans. . . . They recognized and celebrated various identities that were based on ethnicity, clan, family, gender and class. They at the same time recognized their human identity as their core identity. That is why they called themselves Abantu or Khoikhoi and other names that designate and validate their humanity in the various languages of the continent." Africa, suggests Mda, is "an identity in the making."[5] It recognizes the plurality of identities that make for a common humanity, although this propensity like so many other cultural values is often forgotten. It could, nevertheless, be a significant anthropological contribution that Africa makes to the global debate on coexistence and identity.

An obvious broader African example of inclusivity is seen in Swahili identity, which is a product largely of its Bantu and Arab or Persian roots, which evolved through a complex history. Other influences—anthropological, historical, and geographical—have in turn resulted in many within the broader Swahili collective preferring to use local regional identities like waA'mu and waMvita (from Lamu and Mombasa). Others opt to be identified with their lineage (external to uswahilini or Swahili territories) and prefer to be called waArabu and waShirazi (from Arabia and Persia).[6] What is true of the Swahili is of course true of a range of other African clans and ethnic groups. Africa and African identities, like identities in Europe and elsewhere, are less homogeneous than popular perception suggests. The roots of *ubuntu* in Southern Africa are varied, capturing the interaction between groups originating in Africa as well as those who have come to make Africa their home as a result of colonialism, the heritage of slavery, and other forms of mobility.

Ubuntu, which is seen and practiced in different ways and is often forgotten, has a potential for appropriation in those African circles that are suspicious of religious and secular ideologies that are seen to be part of Western and other forms of imperialism. "The thing [*ubuntu*] makes sense to us, even if we do not always practice it," Setiloane said. I argue that it is perhaps this that means *ubuntu* can be developed and expanded in relation to a range of contemporary challenges facing the modern state.

Ubuntu has been drawn on both romantically and more thoughtfully to develop communication and business skills. Some have drawn on it to expound what has been called an Afrocentric management approach in business.[7] Others emphasize its centrality to the 1993 Interim Constitution of the Republic of South Africa, recognizing that while it is not specifically mentioned in the final (1996) Constitution, a reading of several of the Constitutional Court's rulings indicate the extent of its influence on South African jurisprudence.

Justice Albie Sachs, in a South African Constitutional Court judgment, sees *ubuntu* as being central to the South African Constitution and Bill of Rights: "The spirit of *ubuntu*, part of the deep cultural heritage of the majority of the population, suffices the whole constitutional order. It combines individual rights with a communitarian philosophy. It is a unifying motif of the Bill of Rights, which is nothing if not a structured, institutionalised and operational declaration in our evolving new society of the need for human interdependence, respect and concern."[8]

The unanimous ruling of the South African Constitutional Court on the unconstitutionality of the death penalty is instructive in this regard.[9] Justice Arthur Chaskalson, for example, argues that in order "to be consistent with the value of *ubuntu* ours should be a society that wishes to prevent crime, . . . [not] to kill criminals simply to get even with them," contending that the death sentence offers no greater incentive to deterrence than imprisonment. Justice Pius Langa stresses the need to show "respect for the dignity of every person," arguing that a failure to do so will perpetuate a level of violence in which life is "cheap, almost worthless." Justice Ismael Mohamed writes, "The need for *ubuntu* expresses the ethos of an instinctive capacity for the enjoyment of love towards our fellow men and women; the reciprocity this generates in interaction within the collective community; the richness of the creative emotions which it engenders and the moral energies which it releases both in the givers and the society which they serve and are served by." In the words of Justice Yvonne Mokgoro, "Our new Constitution, unlike its dictatorial predecessor, is value-based. Among other things it guarantees the protection of basic human rights, including the right to life and human dignity, two basic values supported by the spirit of *ubuntu* and protected in Sections 9 and 10 respectively." She elsewhere stresses the need to ensure that *ubuntu* be more than a "vague spirit" pervading the Constitution. She argues that *ubuntu* as an ideal needs to be made explicit in actual legal decisions.[10] In brief, *ubuntu* as understood in the Constitutional Court case on the death penalty discerns a level of dignity and the right to life within even the most deprived of people. For Mokgoro, severe punishment is valid only to the extent that it both "deters and rehabilitates" the deviance of human nature. This, she states, is the *ubuntu* principle at work.

"Deters and rehabilitates" are concepts central to the transitional justice debate. The question is how to deal with perpetrators of gross violations of human rights in a manner that deters them and others from resorting to or continuing the practices of a society marred by human rights abuses. More than that, the question is how to contribute to their rehabilitation—enabling them to cross the historic bridge from the past into the future. *Ubuntu* speaks to this double need. It does so in contrast to a form of transitional justice driven by a Western focus on individual responsibility and retribution. It takes the other, including the perpetrators of gross violations of human rights, seriously enough to ask what it is that drives a perpetrator or benefactor to commit or tolerate the gross violations of human rights that bring a society to the point of uncompromising conflict. It further seeks ways of enabling perpetrators and benefactors of the old regime to contribute to the growth and development of the new order. It inquires about the nature and extent of what needs to be done by perpetrators and victims in order to restore a severed relationship that constitutes the very essence of humanity for victims, perpetrators, and benefactors alike.

Some are critical of *ubuntu*, viewing it as a restrictive custom that militates against an individual rising above his or her place within a community. Themba Sono sees the notion as "overwhelming, totalistic, even totalitarian. Group psychology, though parochially and narrowly based, . . . nonetheless pretends universality. This mentality, this psychology is stronger on belief than on reason; on sameness than on difference. Discursive rationality is overwhelmed by emotional identity, by the obsession to identify with, and the longing to conform. To agree is more important than to disagree; conformity is cherished more than innovation. Tradition is venerated, continuity revered, change feared and difference shunned. Heresies are not tolerated in such communities."[11]

Sono's concern is ultimately that *ubuntu* is a conservative if not reactionary tradition that undermines both individual and national development and progress. He sees it as undermining open democratic debate, bending the political ethos in favor of traditional beliefs, practices, and prejudices that are unable to meet the demands of contemporary society. Critically posed, the question is how to relate if not balance the appeal of traditional and modern demands.

Differently stated, the challenge facing contemporary states in Africa and elsewhere is how to imagine a new and different kind of society within which citizens rooted in different languages, cultures, and social backgrounds are able to contribute to the new order without restraint or hesitation. The need is to ensure that no single group, either by default or design, either dominates others or undermines the inclusivity of what constitutes a particular state. This requires a national ethos that awakens its people to their rightful sharing in the nation-building process. In Frantz Fanon's words, the need is "to compose the sentence which expresses the heart of the people and to become the mouthpiece of a new reality in action."[12] An individual political and social milieu needs necessarily to be open to what it means to be Afrikaner, Xhosa, Zulu, Hutu, Tutsi, African, Arab, Kurd, or Basque in relation to other ethnic groups. The structural implication of this requires creative forms of nation building.

As unpalatable as it was for many South Africans on all sides of the political divide, the national unity government formed in 1994 between the New National Party, the former political home of many white Afrikaans-speaking South Africans, and the African National Congress, requiring that the latter be the dominant partner, forced the nation to again face the implications of cultural inclusivity as captured in its own history and in the South African Constitution. The fact that the former president, F. W. de Klerk, led his party out of this government may yet prove to have been a grave mistake at the level of institutional reconciliation—making political debate in government on cultural inclusivity that much more difficult. This debate, which is too often left to a few intellectuals and those who feel most offended by a sense of exclusion, is one for which the structures are in place in South Africa: There is constitutional recognition of diversity, eleven official languages of equal status, and minority parties are represented in the national assembly on the basis of the smallest percentage of the national vote.

As discussed in chapter 3, the politics of inclusion requires honest exchange between enemies and strangers through *encounters and engagement*, *exploration*, and *dialogue*, accompanied by *visioning and enactment*. It is here that democratic participation and *ubuntu* find common ground.

Democratic Dissent

Václav Havel writes on the importance of dissent in his essay titled "The Power of the Powerless."[13] He tells the story of the manager of a fruit and vegetable store who places a notice in his window reading "Workers of the World Unite." "Why does he do it?" asks Havel. "What is he trying to communicate to the world? Is he genuinely enthusiastic about the idea of unity among the workers of the world? Is his enthusiasm so great that he feels an irrepressible impulse to acquaint the public with his ideals? Has he really given more than a moment's thought as to how such unification might occur and what it would mean?" Havel says the manager of the store does so because "the poster was delivered to our greengrocer from the enterprise headquarters along with the onions and carrots. He put it in the window simply because it has been done that way for years, because everyone does it, and because that is the way it has to be. . . . He does it because these things must be done if one is to get along in life. It is one of the thousands of details that guarantee him a relatively tranquil life, 'in harmony with society,' as they say."[14]

Havel suggests that, from the perspective of the greengrocer, it was easier to comply, whereas from the perspective of the state, the greengrocer made a small but important contribution to maintaining the status quo. The greengrocer's compliance gave the state the assurance that "all political life in the traditional sense has been eliminated." In the same essay, Havel is reproachful of those in Western society who exaggerate the importance of outspoken and critical individuals in posttotalitarian states yet fail to understand that in societies where open debate and inquiry have been suppressed, their impact is limited. He argues that open and critical learning and debate need to be entrenched in all aspects of life for there to be effective political debate. He writes of the importance of an open "prepolitical" sphere, which he sees as "the living humus from which genuine political change usually springs." Dissent takes different forms. It is grounded in a rejection of what Sono calls the "longing to conform" in a democratic society, as well as imposed forms of totalitarian thought and practice. It is born out of a willingness not to question the status quo. To the extent that *ubuntu* subdues the adventurous spirit (as suggested by Sono), it serves neither democracy nor communal healing. Conversely, where it affords dissidents and heretics the opportunity to be heard and responded to within the structures of society, it has the potential to renew society from within.

Ubuntu is grounded in historical continuity. It remembers past generations and ancestors, drawing on the memory of the lived experiences of success and failure. Like any ethical ideal, it must adapt in order to survive. It regards *conservation* as a prerequisite for a system to maintain itself. This is not to suggest, however, that it seeks either to escape the challenges of the present or to glorify what has been. At best, it avoids the tyranny of the present that holds out the illusion of immediate political and economic gratification by seeking to develop a richer and more reflective response to the challenges of the present and the demands of the future. To return to Setiloane:

> Africa has its fair share of revolutionaries who seek to turn the status quo on its head, assuming that they can recreate the first day of creation. The most effective leaders build on what is there and in Africa there is a long and proud history that needs to be mined for its riches and incorporated into the present. This, at best, is what the African renaissance is all about. This blending of past and present necessarily

takes time and "African time" is slow time. Sometimes too slow. But that's who we are. The wise ruler draws on the memory of his people, knowing that there are resources in that memory on which to mobilize his [her] people.

Ubuntu is an evolving spirit, existing between memory and an ability to create something new. Dirk Louw speaks of "restorative communication" being at the heart of *ubuntu*, affirming both the historicity of one's own community and that of others. "An *ubuntu* perception of the other is never fixed or rigidly closed, but adjustable or open-ended. It allows the other to be, to become."[15] Because *ubuntu* gives expression to self-realization through the other, the other needs to be respected and taken seriously. When this happens, the possibility of meaningful encounter and dialogue, as outlined in chapter 3, becomes a possibility. *Ubuntu* is about how to engage the other. It is about how to see and talk with neighbors and enemies. *Ubuntu* is an ethic for serious conversation. "To say it is nonsense because it is not practiced is a bit like saying Christianity, Islam, or Hinduism is nonsense because its moral values are rarely seen in its adherents," concludes Setiloane, who was an ordained Methodist minister and fierce critic of what he saw as the colonial heritage of his church.

Ubuntu is a process aimed at inclusive democracy. In contemporary society it requires that structures, institutions, and policies be put in place to allow people who may disagree on a range of issues to find a space within which to express their views, to engage one another, and to oppose the dominant ideas of the time where and when it is appropriate to do so.

Ubuntu and Transitional Justice

Though African in character and texture, the *ubuntu* sense of self-realization and social healing through engagement with others is not exceptional to Africa. It has resonance with a number of academic disciplines. The Italian feminist Adriana Cavarero, for example, develops her literary theory on storytelling around what she calls the "narratable self." Her thesis is that humans cannot but speak. They are compelled, however inadequately, to speak—knowing that there is always more to say. We are drawn into deeper conversation with others and ourselves, cementing relations with others and making ourselves fuller and more complete human beings by telling our stories and engaging the stories of others.[16] Deborah Posel writes of the constitutive role of the "inner monologues" within all of us that interact with a range of dialogues that we have within our family units, extending to schools and other "external sites of knowledge and expertise."[17] She suggests that the recourse to confession in the Truth and Reconciliation Commission (TRC) has, although "not necessarily in the manner intended or imagined by the TRC," given rise to what she calls a "politics of intimacy" that carries within it the rudiments of "a confessing society" that collides with the silence and secrecy of our past. She quotes Michel Foucault: "Confession has spread its effects far and wide: in the judicial system, in medicine, in pedagogy, in familial relations, in amorous relationships, in everyday life and in the most solemn rituals; crimes are confessed, sins are confessed, thoughts and desires are confessed, one's past and one's dreams are confessed, one's childhood is confessed. One's diseases and problems are confessed."[18]

Posel's argument is that secularized disciplines of confession have played a central part in the production of the modern self. The sharing of the inner self, "whether with a parent, friend, doctor, therapist or one's self," she argues, is "an integral part of the practice of self-knowledge" and "closely linked to the practice of taking good care of oneself."[19] This level of self-discovery and communication of oneself to others opens the door and invites others to reciprocate. Obviously not all types of confession necessarily lead to the healing of self and relations with others, and yet, taken seriously, the discovery of the mutuality of humanity and of speech, not least between former enemies, can constitute the basis of dealing with a violent and traumatizing past.

The synergy between traditional notions of *ubuntu* and the endeavor to scour the depths of human identity and community as discussed by Cavarero and Posel deserves further research. Their argument is that, realistically, no individual or community can ever claim to be fully realized or accomplished. To be human is to strive for more by engaging with others. This has important implications in situations of conflict resolution and negotiation. Where participants can be enabled to understand the significance of an open-ended sense of self and others, they are likely to be less rigid in affirming a "nonnegotiable bottom line," thus opening the way for a possible settlement.

Narnia Bohler-Müller identifies a range of spin-offs for issues of justice and the discerning of truth as well as for reconciliation and nation building that reside within *ubuntu*.[20] She sees it as opening the way for what she calls a "jurisprudence of care," within which the antecedents (what the TRC refers to as "causes, motives, and perspectives") that give rise to crime are taken into account. This takes the quest for justice beyond the level of abstract rules and rigid legal formulations to a richer understanding of truth discernment and justice.[21] It opens a space for the pursuit of a better and more just future by enabling victims, perpetrators, and the broader community to address the underlying causes that gave rise to past conflicts.

This jurisprudential approach allows those who are party to a conflict to deal with the complexity of political crimes in a manner that enables them to move beyond the "limited charge sheet" that concerns Michael Marrus and others, as discussed in chapter 4. Bohler-Müller recognizes the difficulties involved in allowing this kind of broader evidence or storytelling, which "captures the irreducible complexities of life," to be presented in courts. Values located in different contexts often clash, and stories can be used to rationalize and obscure factual detail that is pertinent to fair judgment. All this, she suggests, makes it "more difficult to do justice" as defined in Western notions of the rule of law. At the same time, it opens new avenues for uncovering insight, truth, and motivation—perhaps even a level of mitigation that requires a more nuanced judgment than what a court is able to deliver or that either victims or the public generally may be seeking.

In his novel *The Native Commissioner*, Shaun Johnson tells the story of a commissioner presiding over a court in Kentani in the rural Transkei. He is required to adjudicate a case involving the assault and attempted murder of Sikutuni Cengima. Accused number one is Tanase Ntabaka, a young man with an aura of authority. "He was tall, lithe and startlingly handsome, with broad features like a larger-than-life sculpture." He declined legal representation and admitted to having, together with his accomplices, severely beaten Sikutani. He had meant to kill him. And yet, in his own mind, he was not guilty—*"for reasons."* The commissioner had no option but to find him guilty. Sensing that there were community values and practices that Ntabaka was not ready to divulge, he handed down the lightest sentence the law permitted—which was six strokes with a cane. Before doing so, he asked Ntabaka whether he had anything he would like to say. Ntabaka at first hesitated before replying briefly. "My Lord," he said, "I understand that we will be found guilty of these beatings we have been talking about all these days and that we will be punished. This I understand. But I wish to ask this: *What has it to do with you, Sir?"* This question, in a nuanced form, is returned to in the next chapter, where the often-troubled relationship between international law and African customary law is addressed.

From that day on, the commissioner referred to this moment as "Ntabaka's Question." Ntabaka had earlier said that there were "reasons" for his action that he would not air in an alien court. Tradition and custom had bestowed on him the task to ensure peace. His leadership was challenged, and he had dealt with the challenge in what he regarded as a legitimate manner. The novel tells of the commissioner's deep uncertainty about his role as executor of the law in an apartheid state, yet he simultaneously felt that his wards were "not ready to govern" themselves. And still his uncertainty grew as a result of his encounter with Ntabaka. It "now gnawed at him like a constant and ravaging illness."[22] His court had been unable to understand the antecedents that gave rise to the assault or to take them into account. It had not brought closure to the conflict and would not prevent future conflicts of a similar kind. Natabaka was not able to tell his story—the court would not understand it. There was no meeting of Western and Xhosa traditional laws and beliefs. The details of Johnson's story aside, competing worldviews of Africa need to engage one another. This calls for the kind of considered talk, careful listening, and meaningful dialogue envisaged by people as diverse as Setiloane, Cavarero, and Posel.

The complexities of human rights abuse and violence in politically oppressive societies require perhaps more than a simple "guilty" or "not guilty" verdict. "All I really want is an opportunity to tell my story—to get it all off my chest," a military officer told me. "Maybe I should have gone to the TRC. I sometimes think I should have my day in court, even if found guilty. . . . No, I cannot go that far. My family will suffer and realistically who wants to go to prison? For me to talk would be to expose former colleagues, most of whom seem to have a stronger constitution than me—but perhaps they too lie awake some nights. I cannot open old wounds. So I live with my past. What else can I do?" The former intelligence officer spoke with me in a brief but intense discussion in a car park after I encountered him in a Cape Town supermarket. I had first met with him in the TRC eight years earlier. He had chosen not to apply for amnesty and is now writing a book for his daughter to read. "I am not going to publish the book, but I want someone to know my story—warts and all," he said.[23] Cavarero's "narratable self" suggests that we all have an innate need to tell our story. Richard Kearney suggests that "telling stories is as basic to human beings as eating. . . . [Stories] are what make our condition human."[24]

Ubuntu gives expression to this insight. It suggests that in engaging others we realize our own humanity and that healing truth is *human* truth. It is about *who* people are, not simply *what* they do. Speaking on court evidence and testimony, Bohler-Müller agues that a people-centered storytelling methodology enables us to reach beyond legal abstractions and institutional voices, allowing other voices to be heard that are often not heard in a conventional courtroom. These are the voices that Garton Ash suggests are better heard in "history lessons" rather than in trials and purges.[25] The need to hear the voices of victims and perpetrators is what motivates Martha Minow to identify the importance of truth commissions, while affirming the importance of organized (state) retribution as an exercise in taming, balancing, and recasting the personal animus involved in vengeance.[26] Prosecutions, she tells us, are "slow, partial and narrow," and it is this that underlines the importance of the "independent value of commissions investigating the larger patterns of atrocity and the complex lines of responsibility and complicity."[27]

Geoffrey Heald, drawing on Carl Rogers's therapeutic learning principles, suggests that for therapeutic learning to take place, people need to engage one another without front or facade.[28] This involves opening ourselves to learning more about ourselves and others. *Ubuntu* suggests that for this mutually restorative and self-fulfilling process to occur, individuals and groups need to move beyond confrontation. They need to open themselves to the possibility of new options for mutual fulfillment in order to move to what has been described as a win-win encounter. Differently stated, *ubuntu* suggests that sustainable peace can be realized through engaging one another. It is a basis for exploring the possibility of changing attitudes, allowing institutionally and historically predetermined boundaries to give way to new affinities and potential for a different kind of future.

Heald contrasts the Western thinking influenced by Cartesian logic with African *ubuntu* philosophy: the Cartesian logic captured in the idiom *Cogito ergo sum*, versus the restorative idiom *Estis ergo sum*—or *Umuntu ngumuntu ngabantu*. His contention is that the "argument idiom" generates self-reinforcing and self-perpetuating spirals of conflict that undermine the possibility of realizing a win-win situation. Heald quotes Edward de Bono's classic argument formulation:

> There is an idea that needs changing. There is an idea you believe to
> be wrong. There is a case, a claim, a point of view, or an activity, which
> you wish to oppose. So you set up to attack what is being presented.
> There is a thesis, and you bring forth an antithesis. From the ferment
> and clash of battle there is supposed to emerge the "synthesis" which
> combines the best of both. It would be absurd of me to say this never
> happens, but it very rarely happens. It is not hard to see why it rarely
> happens.[29]

One side wins and the other side is defeated, not least in deadly political conflicts where a great deal it at stake. A willingness to understand an enemy's viewpoint is often regarded as treachery, and if a settlement is reached as a result of one side capitulating to the other, it usually results in a grudging compromise and an abiding resentment. Successful negotiations, conversely, produce something new.

Speaking about the breakthrough in the South African negotiations, Roelf Meyer recalls:

> We started looking towards what we wanted [to create] . . . and stopped
> concentrating on what we wanted to retain. . . . The old paradigm was
> to retain power for a white minority. . . . The new paradigm changed
> that. It was not about retaining power, but about how to ensure equal
> rights for all, how to build a constitution and how to live that constitu-
> tion. It was because of that shift in consciousness amongst previous
> enemies that we were able to start to manage the negotiation process.
> There was a transformation in my own mind. I was ready to opt for a
> whole new paradigm.[30]

The South African settlement was premised, for a variety of reasons, on the need to find a win-win solution in a context where both sides had the capacity to destroy the nation while neither had the capacity to create peace without the cooperation of the other. Both sides realized that for peace to endure, a great deal of transforming and restorative work was required. This included the creation and restoration of fundamental human rights, economic well-being, social decency, and political freedom. The South African paradigm was one of restorative justice and *ubuntu* rather than retribution and individual or sector-based victory. Within this came moral compromises and a political understanding that continues to trouble many hard-liners and others on both sides. There is still a lot of political work to be done. The good news is that the settlement brought peace. If *ubuntu* teaches us anything, it is that for this peace to endure, the material, social, and subjective well-being of all interested parties needs to be addressed. To ignore this reality is to sow the seeds of individual and community discontent and conflict.

The philosophy of *ubuntu* does not stand alone in the world of ideas. Its resonance with the thinking of Bohler-Müller, Cavarero, Posel, and others makes this evident. *Ubuntu*'s affirmation of others further makes it a ready partner in dialogue with a range of other secular and religious discourses. It finds resonance in the communitarian traditions found in the ancient Arab, Greek, and Roman civilizations. It is there in the Vedic traditions, in ancient Buddhism, in the Taoist and in Confucian traditions, as well as in the Judaeo-Christian and Muslim faiths. It is affirmed in the teaching and practices of Aung San Suu Kyi in Myanmar/Burma and those of the Dalai Lama. It is developed in the Christian witness of Desmond Tutu. It lies at the heart of the South African constitutional process and in transitional mechanisms such as the TRC process and in the other statutory commissions that emerged from the transition.

Ruth Mompati, a veteran in the South African struggle, speaks proudly of what she calls her "double heritage": traditional African belief and Christianity. "My grandfather's family were Christians, but my grandmother's family saw no apparent reason to convert to the religion which the missionaries brought to the area. . . . Christianity had nothing to offer them which they did not already have." She traces her understanding of what it is to be human and the need to respect all those around her back to both her African and Christian roots. When I interviewed her, she chose to speak of the African tradition she learnt at her grandmother's knee:

> There I learnt that each of us is endowed with an inner energy. In Tswana we called it *seriti*. In Xhosa it is *isithunzi*. *Seriti* means dignity or personality, coming from the word *moruti*, which means shadow or shade. This force or presence within us has its origin in *modimo* or shade. Driven by this divine force, human beings who are awakened to this presence within them cannot rest until the divine dignity of humankind is manifest in the entire community around them. . . . To be human is to belong to the community as a whole. It is to take responsibility for the entire community.

Mompati insists that for her there is no contradiction between traditional African beliefs and Christianity, arguing that the one should feed off the other. What matters is "giving expression to the spirit of the divine within us." This is what makes the spirit of *ubuntu* so important. "It is about how we see and relate to others." Speaking on the South African negotiated settlement, she says, "We are free because we fought for our freedom, but there was also a deep ethical and spiritual dimension that gave our struggle a certain texture. It never degenerated into the kind of terror and unnecessary slaughter that sometimes characterizes an armed struggle for liberation."[31]

Tutu has probably done more than anyone to develop the synergy that exists between *ubuntu* and Christian belief, giving the notion credence in theological and faith-related circles. Persistent in his preaching and public presentations is a message that says "my humanity is caught up, inextricably bound up, in yours." He develops this thought in his book published shortly after the closure of the TRC: "Social harmony is for us the summum bonum, the greatest good. Anything that subverts, that undermines, this sought-after good is to be avoided like the plague. Anger, resentment, lust for revenge, even success through aggressive competitiveness, are corrosive of this good. To forgive is not just altruistic. It is the best form of self-interest. What dehumanizes you inexorably dehumanizes me."[32]

Tutu's words receive nods and sighs of understanding from many victims and oppressed people around the world. There are also those who have never known the reality of deep suffering who in their better moments long for the kind of society within which there is a deeper sense of community and social care. South Africans, both black and white, are acutely aware of the extent to which the "new South Africa" has fallen short of this ideal. *Ubuntu* is an ideal that South Africans and citizens of other countries who are seeking to extricate themselves from a terrible past would do well to consider, allowing it to challenge any sense of complacency in their nation-building endeavors.

Ubuntu, progressively understood and adapted to meet the challenges of modernity, offers a cultural incentive to promote a level of communal coexistence among individuals, clans, ethnic groups, and nations that lingers in the ethos and memory of a continent devastated by greed, conflict, and war. It provides an African proposal for resolving a global problem of moving from an abusive and tyrannical society to the beginnings of democratic rule and respect for human rights. It lies at the heart of a viable understanding of political reconciliation, without which shared positive peace is constantly undermined.

David Kennedy suggests the global human rights debate is "an overwhelmingly one-way street." He shows it to be "a product of a particular moment and place: "post-Enlightenment, rationalist, secular, Western, modern and capitalist."[33] Its neglect of the more diverse and regional experiences and conceptions of human emancipation (including other Western traditions) is at the heart of the problems experienced in Africa concerning the imposition of international human rights law. This, suggests Kennedy, raises serious questions of whether "international law" is indeed international at all. Africa offers complementary, if not alternative, options for dealing with acts of perpetration that Western-trained human rights activists cannot afford to ignore. It is to such traditional African values and modes of conflict resolution that we now turn.

TRADITIONAL AFRICAN RECONCILIATION PRACTICES

Everyone who wanted to speak did so. It was democracy in its purest form. There may have been a hierarchy of importance among speakers, but everyone was heard: chief and subject, warrior and medicine man, shopkeeper and farmer, landowner and labourer. People spoke without interruption and meetings lasted many hours. The foundation of self-government was that all men were free to voice their opinions and were equal in their value as citizens. . . . I was astonished by the vehemence—and candour—with which people criticised the regent. He was not above criticism—in fact, he was often the principal target of it. But no matter how serious the charge, the regent simply listened, showing no emotion at all. The meetings would continue until some kind of consensus was reached. They ended in unanimity or not at all. Unanimity, however, might be an agreement to disagree, to wait for a more propitious time to propose a solution. . . . Only at the end of the meeting, as the sun was setting, would the regent speak. His purpose was to sum up what was said and form some consensus among the diverse opinions. But no conclusion was forced on those who disagreed. If no agreement could be reached, another meeting would be held.

—Nelson Mandela, *Long Walk to Freedom*, recalling the proceedings of a traditional Thembu court

Modern democracies have neither the time nor the staying power of the Thembu court described by Nelson Mandela. Democracy as a marketplace of ideas in the sense of the ancient agora is, however, undermined when ideas are not heard and spoken about in times of conflict. This is where inclusive democracy and political reconciliation find common cause in what has been defined above as "multileveled, open-ended processes of continuous interaction that engage clusters of citizens in and out of government in resolving public problems."[1]

Traditional African courts and reconciliation practices, despite their limitations in terms of gender inclusion and legal procedures, give expression to the need for a high level of participation by victims and other citizens in decision making and conflict resolution.[2] It is this level of inclusivity rather than the precise forms of traditional courts that suggest they have an important contribution to make to postconflict restoration that proponents of international law would do well to take into account. They also draw on cultural and religious linkages between individuals, their families, clans, communities, and ancestors. Alien to a Western worldview, this interconnectedness is what provides a sense of belonging, responsibility, and purpose within African societies that reaches from the past into many facets of contemporary society.

This chapter defines a possible meeting place between international law and traditional African mechanisms for justice and reconciliation. It suggests that individuals and nations committed to sustainable justice and reconciliation, in the wake of deep conflict, cannot afford to either demonize or romanticize international justice and the International Criminal Court or traditional African mechanisms for justice and reconciliation. The proponents of the two approaches instead need to engage one another along the lines of *encounters*, as suggested in chapter 3. This is arguably the only constructive way in which to unpack the dialectic located at the interface between the emphasis of the international community on individual responsibility and the breakdown of the social milieu within which such violations occur that is central to the concerns of traditional African mechanisms.

This proposed encounter between international and local justice holds the potential to overcome the isolation of evil by criminalizing specific acts and particular individuals in a manner that allows accomplices and bystanders to escape responsibility for such deeds. It also addresses the need for all citizens to take responsibility for the creation of a more humane society. The legal training and skills development of those who are part of the structures required to advance these needs is clearly a necessity. The proposed encounters at the same time offer a way of overcoming the elevation of judges and lawyers at the cost of the broader community. They allow citizens to share in the decision on how to judge the past and what to do about the future.

The appeal of traditional African structures is the provision of spaces and milieus that are conducive to victims and perpetrators being able to break their silence on the past within a context that is culturally familiar and as socially secure as possible. In Rwanda, Uganda, and elsewhere, attempts are being made (with varying levels of success) to encourage people to deal with their anger, fears, and hope by actively promoting traditional-type initiatives to augment formal justice mechanisms. In other situations, Mozambique and Namibia among them, courts and truth commissions have been deliberately rejected. People have been left or encouraged to find their own ways of dealing with trauma and truth seeking. At the heart of each of these initiatives, however, is the recognition that there is the need for a space where the silence that so often follows major trauma and abuse can be overcome.

International transitional justice initiatives, which include United Nations agencies and international nongovernmental organizations, are increasingly recognizing the role of traditional reconciliation mechanisms in this regard. A 2005 UN report on combating impunity, for example, notes that programs rooted in community and national contexts are more likely than those imposed from outside "to secure sustainable justice for the future in accordance with international standards, domestic legal traditions and national aspirations."[3] A Policy Advisory Seminar on United Nations Mediation Experiences in Africa, in turn, concludes:

> In Africa, traditional cultural norms, mechanisms and systems for promoting reconciliation without permitting impunity, must be recognised. For example, among the Acholi of Northern Uganda, indigenous reconciliation processes involving truth telling; the demonstration of genuine remorse; the delivery of reparations; the request for forgiveness; and the granting of mercy; provide a system for reconciliation while seeking at the same time to ensure that perpetrators do not get away with impunity for human rights abuses. In this regard, local communities may have different views on reconciliation and restorative justice in contrast to Western legal systems that tend to place more emphasis on prosecution and retributive justice.[4]

The reality is, however, that retributive impulses promoted through international courts and tribunals invariably take precedence over traditional practices in most transitional situations. The traditional practices are simply not given the kind of support that could assist them to make a significant impact on the transition process—primarily because they do not meet the retributive requirements that shape international legal standards. It is this that persuades David Kennedy to write of international human rights as an one-way street, effectively being "criticism of the periphery by the center."[5] To counter the argument in Africa and other developing-world situations that reject some human rights values as "external interference," traffic needs to flow in both directions. As such, the exponents of international justice would do well to seek for areas of synergy between international law and the values of traditional African communities.[6] The exponents of traditional African mechanisms in turn need to address the priorities of international law that are applicable to the complexities of both the intrastate and interstate conflicts that plague the African continent.

Traditional African mechanisms for justice and reconciliation have not demonstrated an obvious capacity to meet the challenges of the contemporary conflicts they face.[7] Speaking of traditional structures in the Horn of Africa, Tarekegn Adebo points out that "these structures have in many instances over the years been discredited and marginalized by colonial authorities and missionaries as well as by postindependent governments. This has often resulted in the emergence of incompetent elders and leaders who are open to manipulation and corruption."[8] He also suggests that this does not distract from the fact that these institutions are still the carriers of certain traditional values and principles, for which people continue to show high regard. "It is these ideas and values, rather than the existing structures and elders that should be incorporated into the peace-building structures." He speaks of the need for people with legal and formal conflict-resolution training to be drawn into traditional courts as a way of rediscovering and enriching traditional African structures. He insists that "there is no reason to suggest that the historic value and integrity of traditional institutions cannot be rediscovered and applied or adjusted to meet the demands of international law." He further indicates that traditional reconciliation structures were in the past rarely authorized or equipped to deal with blood feuds or murder. In present-day Ethiopia this is still the case, with traditional structures being used to settle less serious crimes, while high-level crimes are referred to national courts. Similarly, in Rwanda the *gacaca* courts deal with crimes up to a certain level, with "category one" crimes being referred to formal courts.[9]

A willingness to adapt traditional practices in Rwanda, Sudan, Uganda, and elsewhere reminds us that tradition and culture are malleable and evolving realities. Lisa Schirch suggests that culture and ritual "bind loosely," tending to be changed by social forces as much as they change the existing social order.[10] There is clearly room for traditional forms of justice and established modern courts to complement one another in addressing issues of war crimes, rebellion, genocide, and other crimes that occur in situations of armed conflict and war. "Traditional reconciliation and healing mechanisms," Adebo argues,

> provide a sense of cultural resonance that gives truth seeking, perpetrator accountability, and peace building a level of accountability that no external agency can easily deliver. People facing political and cultural upheaval are enabled to experience a sense of belonging and continuity with the past as they grapple with demands from the international community for there to be accountability concerning past violations of human rights. Traditional mechanisms offer spaces within which people

can talk and share in the decision-making process in relation to the conflict they face. . . . Traditional mechanisms also legitimate changes in society as they themselves adjust to these changes.[11]

Clearly the extent of community trust in these organizations needs to be assessed and the importance of developing credible and able leadership needs to be acknowledged. Institutions often need to be updated to meet current needs and to be better resourced. What is clear, however, is that traditional reconciliation initiatives continue to be practiced across the continent. A first and important step, which goes well beyond the confines of this chapter, is the need to identify and audit traditional practices used to deal with conflict in different African countries, and to assess their relevance to specific African conflicts and the demands of international law.

The pages that follow provide no more than illustrative insights into some of these initiatives, without claiming that they are representative of all traditional reconciliation practices on the continent. Even a cursory overview suggests that there is a potential within these practices that proponents of formal justice procedures would do well to consider. Sierra Leone had both a truth commission and a special court, while traditional healing ceremonies were held independently of these structures in remote communities across the country, many of which were not aware of these initiatives. In Rwanda traditional *gacaca* courts have been formally adapted to meet the needs of those affected by the 1994 Rwandan genocide. Furthermore, the Rwandan National Unity and Reconciliation Commission has launched *ingando* meetings to enable people to talk about past and present conflicts and has introduced *ubusabane* events to draw people together through music and song festivals. In Burundi and elsewhere in the African Great Lakes region, the *abashingantahe* bring disputants and enemies together to resolve conflicts through ritual and related ways as part of peace-building initiatives.[12] The Agreement on Accountability and Reconciliation signed between the Government of Uganda and the Lord's Resistance Army (LRA) in Juba on June 29, 2007 (the Juba Agreement), in turn calls for recognition of traditional practices and rituals which, it declares, can "with the necessary modifications" play a central role in the proposed framework for accountability and reconciliation between government forces and the LRA.[13] In Mozambique there is no formal truth-seeking mechanism, but traditional ceremonies of healing and cleansing are taking place at the grassroots level.

Traditional practices vary from country to country, and at times within different parts of the same country. They often have no appeal beyond the confines of those communities that practice them. Irae Baptista Lundin, speaking on traditional practices in Mozambique, argues that "Magamba Spirit practices are essentially limited to specific communities who have their roots in the province of Sofala in Central Mozambique, with no appeal beyond these communities." She adds that the underlying principles of the Magamba Spirit movement are, however, "compatible with the broader restorative dimensions of an African sense of justice that favors restoration and reparation over retributive forms of justice practiced in other parts of Mozambique."[14] Bishop Dinis Salamao Sengulane goes further in suggesting that "punitive justice is foreign to Mozambique." Reflecting on the Mozambican experience, he observes: "Our culture and our religion, as well as the bitter civil war we fought, teaches us that it is counterproductive to look backward and seek revenge. We remember not in order to take revenge. We remember in order to strengthen our resolve to rise above the past in the creating a new future within which spiral of violence is broken."[15]

Despite the multiple different traditional practices in Africa, certain common threads run through these traditions. These include preverbal and nonverbal healing, and relationship building—entailing culture and ritual, the living dead, sacred space, reconciliation practices, community involvement, and adaptation.

Preverbal and Nonverbal Healing

Indigenous African healing and reconciliation practices provide both *preverbal* and *nonverbal* spaces as a pretext for rational debate and conversation to take place as a way of dealing with the violence and trauma of the past. Through ceremony and ritual, perpetrators and victims are encouraged to make an attitudinal and behavioral shift from a prelinguistic state to the point where they can begin to articulate their experiences in words and ritual. Perpetrators can begin to acknowledge how they violated human rights and victims can begin to deal with their suffering. When effective, it can provide solace for individuals and groups sharing in these practices—drawing adversaries into an experiential bond that provides a basis from which to make reparations and promote community reconciliation and healing.

The link between ritual and behavioral response is a contested field. Some scholars working on the relationship between ritual and peace building are, however, drawn to neurobiological research to explain that while the human brain directs human behavior, the opposite also occurs. Some suggest that ritual can have an impact on the physical structure of the brain, in much the same way that Western-based musicologists argue that music affects our brains in shaping our moods and responses to the daily challenges we face.[16]

Briefly stated, it is suggested that rituals, symbols, and ceremonies have an impact on different levels of human consciousness. In some situations they are said to facilitate new ways of thinking, allowing a person to respond more thoughtfully and with less spontaneous aggression to attack. Sarah Crawford-

Browne draws on this kind of research to show how postconflict societies that have earlier been traumatized are unable to put the trauma behind them. This results in them continuing to portray "high levels of arousal, distrust, entitlement, anger, aggression, irrational reactions, fear, guilt, shame, a distrust of authority, anxiety and patronage" in response to the challenges and opportunities that the "new" society offers.[17] For this cycle of aggression to be broken, she argues, people require a physical, emotional, and psychological "safe space" where they can deal with their past as a basis for rebuilding relationships.

Discussing the Mozambique situation, Alcinda Honwana writes that, contrary to Western therapeutic therapy, traditional African healing and protective rituals "do not involve verbal exteriorization of [past] experiences." She explains that "healing is achieved through nonverbal symbolic procedures, which are understood by those participating in them. . . . Recounting and remembering the traumatic experience would be like opening a door for the harmful spirits to penetrate the communities. Viewed from this perspective, the well-meaning attempts of psychotherapists to help local people deal with war trauma may in fact cause more harm than help."[18]

In war-torn situations when people have been taught violence and suffer trauma, active remembering of past atrocities and personal loss can indeed further traumatize the individuals concerned if inappropriately handled or where there is insufficient time for extensively counseling—which is frequently the case in many postwar situations. This is especially the case in developing countries, where counseling services are not readily available.

Traditional healing practices provide a potential alternative to individual counseling, while speaking to the cultural needs through group rituals described by Honwana and others. Seeing public ceremony and ritual as facilitative of communal healing, Richard Schechner argues that trauma and anxiety can be ameliorated through "repetition, rhythm, exaggeration, condensation, and simplification." Such practices "stimulate the brain into releasing endorphins directly into the bloodstream yielding the ritual's second benefit [which is] a relief from pain [and] a surfeit of pleasure."[19] It is suggested that Buddhist meditation, Christian chants, the fivefold daily prayers of Islam, liturgical prayers, incantations, drum beats, and rhythmic dance create "new pathways and biological connections between the various parts of the brain."[20] Marx may well be smiling to hear that both religion and opium have the capacity to calm or pacify people!

The impact of traditional African cultural practices on institutional religion, not least in rural and other isolated areas, happens widely in Africa. In modern times these traditions are often blended with Christian, Muslim, and other religious practices. A Lebanese activist, Freda Haddad, spoke of Eastern Orthodox Tewahido Church ritual in Ethiopia. She told of liturgical practices varying from one location to another, while giving expression to a common underlying belief system. Liturgy is adapted to fit the context within which it is practiced, and yet it remains in continuity with the historic Christian origins of "drinking the cup and breaking bread." People remember their past, and in so doing they are able to interpret their present suffering through the sacraments, as have generations before them. This, says Haddad, "empowers and enables us to go into the world to deal with the challenges we face."[21] She argues that it is the "medium of ritual" rather than the "rational content" of the words employed in the ritual that shape the lives of parishioners in both "survival and resistance." The willingness of people to explore and participate in this kind of ritual over an extended period of time is an indication of both the need and importance of dealing with the past.

The ways in which traditional African healing and reconciliation practices have an impact on society and are integrated in contextual forms of religion will continue to be debated among theologians and social scientists. What is interesting is the extent to which traditional ceremonies are increasingly considered as important components of transitional justice programs in African countries undergoing political change.

Speaking on the impact of Magamba Spirit healing ceremonies in Mozambique, Sengulane observed: "The success of indigenous healing ceremonies is that those who attend them generally do so with the intent and expectation that they will be healed, whereas many who come to church on a Sunday do so out of habit. They do not expect the problems they face to be resolved. They do not expect to leave the church transformed."[22] He went on to speak of specific healing services in his diocese conducted in collaboration with traditional leaders where people are relieved of their fears and sometimes healed: "The road to healing and reconciliation begins deep within the people themselves. The role of churches, indigenous healing ceremonies and indeed Western psychology is to enable people to reach into the recesses of their own lives as a way of accepting the offer of forgiveness, restitution, and transformation that people are often ready to make."

In brief, the dominant characteristic of ritual is its binding dimension. Schirch suggests that ritual "binds loosely."[23] It draws people into unity and yet it is open-ended, fluid, malleable, reflective, and inviting of response and action. Ritual and memorialization can be an escape from the contemporary world. By locating practitioners in an established tradition of activism, it can also heal, empower, and reintegrate victims and perpetrators back into society.

Relationship Building

Common among traditional structures for accomplishing relationship building are the notions of culture and ritual, the living dead, sacred space, reconciliation practices, community involvement, and adaptation.[24] Each provides space and opportunity to deal with conflict through dialogue, reflection, negotiation, and compensation.

Culture and Ritual

Not least in traditional communities, which are more homogeneous than modern societies, culture is all encompassing. Culture is "the action through which a people has created itself and keeps itself in existence."[25] Culture is the "ordinary" way in which we think and act. It is inherited and it is taught. It also evolves through encounters, storytelling, memory, and dialogue. Paradoxically, it is both imposed and chosen. It is given and changing and yet, especially in traditional societies where people face few alternatives outside the status quo, people feel most comfortable in conforming to the dominant culture. It is warm. It has a feeling of home. And when people are alienated by change and trauma, they instinctively take refuge in what home (despite its limitations) has to offer.

The use of traditional rituals in rural Uganda, especially in the war-ravaged regions of the northern part of the country, has been widely discussed in literature on peace building and options for traditional justice. These rituals are written into the Ugandan Amnesty Act and, as already shown, are central to the Juba Agreement concerning the need to find a balance between prosecutions and the use of traditional mechanisms in dealing with the conflict between the Ugandan government and the LRA in Northern Uganda.[26] The rituals and ceremonies are seen to provide culturally entrenched practices for cleansing of evil.[27] The Acholi refer to *kiir* (evil) as a form of possession or all-consuming psychological or spiritual condition that is at the heart of violence and other forms of antisocial behavior. Best known of these are the Nyouo Tong Gweno, Mato Oput, and Gomo Tong practices of the Acholi that illustrate the place of complex symbolic forms of ritual healing. Other ceremonies often attached to these rituals are the reconciliation rituals of Kayo Cuk Ailuc and Tonu ci Koka as well as the compensation ritual of Culo Kwor, which comes when an appropriate settlement is agreed upon.

The Nyouo Tong Gweno ritual marks the beginning of a reconciling process, practiced when receiving a returning soldier or when someone is abducted from the village. A raw egg is crushed underfoot in the belief that this allows the evil of violence and war to be transferred into the purity and innocence of the egg, thus enabling the combatant to be cleansed. A twig from the Opobo tree, traditionally used to make soap, is sometimes also employed as a cleansing agent and a *layibi*, a stick used for the opening of the granary, is sometimes used to symbolize the right of the returning person to eat with the community again.

The Mato Oput ritual marks the conclusion of a dispute. Its origin is attributed to two estranged brothers who fled from an approaching lion and were forced to take refuge in an Oput tree, where they then reconciled their differences. The ceremony begins after a council of elders has mediated between both the individuals or groups party to a conflict, as well as their families and clans. The mediation involves truth telling, a cooling-down period, and agreement on compensation and restoration. To mark the settlement, the conflicting parties partake of a drink made from the bitter roots of the Oput tree to wash away the evil, after which a goat is slaughtered and a ceremony of restoration is held.

Gomo Tong, which means the "bending of the spears," celebrates the cessation of hostilities and a willingness of warring parties to put aside their aggression in pursuit of peace. The celebration centers on opposing communities or clans bringing their weapons to a central place, where in response to ritual and prayers they are bent or destroyed, being rendered unusable as weapons.

The depth of meaning captured in such activities is difficult for outsiders to understand. "The overall sense of ceremony among aggrieved people who are seeking to turn away from violence is perhaps more important than a rational understanding of the different rituals within the ceremonies," Archbishop Ogulu Odama told religious leaders in Jinja at a meeting that explored the role of ritual in reconciling communities and nations. "This is not very different from the Christian sacraments of Baptism, the Eucharist, and divine unction [the anointing of the sick and dying]. Not all my parishioners grasp the full theological meaning of the sacraments," he argued.[28]

After the Ugandan government referred the situation to the International Criminal Court (ICC) in January 2004, the leaders of the Acholi people asked the ICC prosecutor to withdraw his arrest warrants and defer instead to traditional Acholi ceremonies of reconciliation and forgiveness.[29] A 2005 survey, however, suggests that the request did not represent the views of all victims, who were divided on the topics of justice, accountability, amnesty, and reconciliation.[30] The majority expressed the view that perpetrators of crimes should be prosecuted. The survey further showed that most supported amnesty. A further survey, released at the time of the Juba Peace talks between the Ugandan government and the LRA in September 2007, shows similar ambivalence in the responses to questions on forgiveness, reconciliation, and the reintegration of soldiers into communities. A total of 66 percent believed that LRA soldiers should be tried, while 55 percent of respondents said that the Uganda People's Defense Forces should also face trials and possible punishment.[31] Although most argued that the process ought to include some form of amnesty, 67 percent of respondents believed that the ICC should be involved in the settlement of the Northern Ugandan crisis. Approximately half of the respondents also saw traditional ceremonies as important mechanisms for the reintegration of perpetrators.[32]

Soldiers, displaced people, and abductees undoubtedly wish to go home. A return to their communities is also where the true measure of both justice and reconciliation is assessed—inevitably over an extended period of time. The purpose of cleansing ceremonies, engagement in communal rituals, welcoming home the dead as ancestors, demands for compensation, payment of reparations, dialogue, and reincorporation is to facilitate this homecoming. Justice of whatever kind: Punishment, censure, restoration, and reconciliation should ultimately address the need for families, communities, and clans to reestablish a sense of belonging.

The surveys cited above suggest that the Acholi are not opposed, on cultural or other grounds, to prosecutions. The sentiment of Odama is at the same time significant:

> All I can say is that I experience the healing capacity of Acholi rituals, ceremonies and traditions among my people. We want to explore this further and engage with government in enabling this process to be taken further. I am not suggesting these practices constitute some kind of Holy Grail. I am simply arguing that they need to be part of the greater peace-building initiatives in Uganda. Whatever the outcome of the work of the international community, Museveni's amnesty process, or a truth commission for that matter, when the dust settles ordinary folk, traditional Acholi people are going to need to find a way of reintegrating their communities and getting on with life. The traditional Acholi rituals can contribute to this process. This is how we have healed ourselves through the ages.[33]

Among South Sudanese ethnic groups consisting of the Nilotics, Nilohamites, Bantu, and other Sudanese, traditional authorities play a similarly important role in conflict transformation processes as that expressed by Bishop Ochalla, although terminology and rituals often vary.[34] The decentralized social structure of the Nuer has resulted in different rituals dealing with concerns relating to cattle husbandry and rustling, some with water concerns, feuds, and war, which together provide a sense of cohesion to Nuer society. The anthropologist Edward Evans-Pritchard referred to this diverse structure of the Nuer as "ordered anarchy."[35] Dinka society is more centralized, with disputes traditionally being settled at a central level.

In both Nuer and Dinka groups, however, the elders and chiefs by tradition mediate or adjudicate a conflict in consultation with the community. The South Sudanese Peace Commission suggests that this centralized structure contributes directly to the peace process by drawing communities together, while warning that if the traditional leaders are alienated they have the capacity to throw the country back into war.[36]

A conference organized by the New Sudan Council of Churches that drew together the Jie, Kachipo, Anyuk, Murle, Nuer, and Dinka ethnic groups in Bor in May 2000 saw traditional African religious practices and Christian rituals being performed simultaneously. Canon Clement Janda, former general secretary of the All-Africa Conference of Churches, said of the use of the white bull within this context that "it was . . . to seal the peace covenant" that emerged from the event. "We saw the affinity between African customs and missionary Christianity. It is as though an ancient spirit called us home, reminding us of the bond that binds."[37] At the conference, traditional leaders of the Nuba people, ethnographically consisting of groups and subgroups that are said "to speak as many different languages as the ninety-nine hills they occupy," were drawn together by their traditional leaders to resolve their differences. The role of traditional leaders was a key element in enabling feuding groups to find a common agenda and make peace.

Francis Deng, in a contextually rich assessment of conflict resolution in southern Sudan, identifies unity and harmony as the underlying cultural values of both Dinka and Nuer traditional conflict resolution. Traditionally, a chief is not a ruler in the Western sense but a spiritual leader whose power rests on divine enlightenment and wisdom. To reconcile people, the chief should be a model of virtue, righteousness, and, in Dinka terms, "a man with a cool heart," who must depend on persuasion and consensus building rather than on coercion and dictation.[38] Drawing on the insights of Evans-Pritchard, Deng identifies five deeply rooted cultural elements of dispute settlement among the Nuer, which he sees as similarly practiced among the Dinka. These are the general desire of disputants to resolve a conflict, the sanctity of the chief's person and the legitimacy of his role as mediator, the free and exhaustive discussion by everyone concerned that leads to an agreement, the feeling that a person can concede to the wisdom of the chief without losing face, and finally the losing party's recognition of the justice of the other side's case. Deng insisted on a meeting held in Cape Town that "to fail to understand this culture, which is grounded in a spiritual reality that binds the disputant to the divine through the chief, is to fail to tap into the wisdom of traditional dispute resolution. At heart, Africans are deeply spiritual people. To fail to draw on this reality is to fail to see the limitation of secular approaches to peacemaking. We need to find the link between international law, Western modes of conflict dispute, and African traditional spirituality."[39]

Other countries have their own rituals. In Liberia, a country torn apart by successive generations of conflict, coups, and civil war, the rule of law and any sense of government accountability had virtually disappeared by the latter part of the last century. William Tolbert III, son of the president of Liberia who was murdered in 1980, suggests "it was largely the traditional authorities, under attack by government forces, that provided some form of social cohesion and moral accountability to a devastated society." As we stood at his father's grave in Monrovia, he spoke of the "palaver hut" as a practice that brought people together to deal with disputes and facilitate community decision making under the guidance of elders and leaders. "Not least in the rural areas," he said, "the palaver hut continues to play an important role in dispute resolution. . . . Most Liberians understand this concept. It is a place to speak and to resolve differences."[40]

In the Democratic Republic of the Congo's Barza Intercommunautaire, or council of elders, functions in the North Kivu Province to bring disputants together—although, as Phil Clarke shows, this has been less successful than in recent years.[41] It requires acknowledgment of guilt, reparations, and ceremonies of purification. In Ethiopia and neighboring countries, there is Gadaa.[42] Yacob Arsano writes of the importance of the Gadaa system among Borana people in southern Ethiopia. Seen as a source of resistance and dissent, the system has survived attempts by successive Ethiopian governments to eliminate its rituals and practices.[43] Arsano suggests that without culturally sensitive forms of conflict resolution and social support, as provided by Gadaa, a sustainable peace is unlikely to prevail in Ethiopia:

> Gadaa and similar practices are vehicles that lend themselves to the resolution of conflict and the promotion of peace building in Ethiopia and across its borders. The problem is that they have not in recent times been given the space or the resources by successive oppressive governments to do so. Of course, these practices need to be adapted and developed. This is already happening. Gadaa, in one form or another, has survived the test of time and is unlikely to disappear in the near future. It needs to be drawn into the peace process by national and international advocates of peace-building.[44]

The use of traditional reconciliation practices in Africa, not least in rural areas that remain less influenced by Western notions of the rule of law, can only enrich peace-building endeavors.

"African people sometimes understand symbol and ritual better than words," Odama argues. "Symbol and ritual captures the ambiguity and sense of divine intervention that is part of the African healing process in a manner that words perhaps never will—not least words that form part of the lexicon of lawyers and politicians who fail to understand the African milieu within which they pursue their profession." The talk that happens in these ceremonies is aimed at healing and reconciliation. It is at the interface of this discussion between Africa and the West that both the global transitional justice debate and peace building in Africa can be enriched.

The Living Dead

In southern and eastern Sub-Saharan Africa in particular, the focus is primarily on an impersonal and yet accessible power that is present in material objects, natural processes, people, and communities, leading to encounters with spiritual power through the extended family, the clan, and elders of a community, suggesting that African consciousness spans three generations—the living dead, the living, and the living not yet born.[45] Ancestors need to be remembered by their families and community in order to exercise their influence and authority within the community. "We remember our ancestors. We live our lives based on the memories of the past and anticipate the future that must be realized through our children and grandchildren yet to be born," explained Gabriel Setiloane.[46]

Writing on the work of the Amani Trust in Matabeleland, established to work among survivors of the Matabeleland massacres in the late 1980s and other torture survivors, Shari Eppel identifies the limitations of Western-based counseling and other therapeutic interventions in Zimbabwe, primarily because they fail to understand this level of generational inclusivity. Noting that traditional Ndebele practices focus on the communal dimensions of existence that link individuals to their ancestors through social hierarchies, she recognizes the importance of *umbuyiso* ceremonies at the time of exhumations, burials, and tombstone unveilings. Through these ceremonies the spirit of the dead is received back into the community as an ancestor. This enables ancestors to fulfill their role in society in facilitating social restoration and the empowerment of the community. Eppel argues that this is evidenced by the extent to which such ceremonies have been restricted and in some instances banned by the Zimbabwean security forces. "This [empowerment]," she writes, "is the only palpable reason we have for exhuming in a country that currently offers impunity to perpetrators. At the moment there is no legal forensic potential for analyzing evidence from exhumations."[47]

In Mozambique the *magamba* spirits of war are appeased in ceremonies conducted by *magamba* healers, who reenact the civil war through symbols and dance by crawling on the ground, brandishing weapons, engaging in simulated fighting, and aggressively thrusting their bayonets in the air as if stabbing people. Often they smoke *nbanje* (cannabis) and drink alcohol to induce a sense of spirit possession, creating a milieu within which the survivors of war, who are themselves possessed by the hostile *magamba* spirits, can experience healing and peace. Through these rituals, war survivors are brought into contact with the spirit of a person killed in war whose spirit has been prevented from returning home as an ancestor because he or she had been denied funereal rights.

Victor Igreja describes the rituals as conjuring up spirits of the dead in the bodies of women whose relatives were allegedly involved in their killing.[48]

In these encounters accusations are made and reparations are demanded through the mediation of the *magamba* healers as a way of enabling a form of justice to be carried out. Symbolically and ritualistically, negotiations are entered into between the living community and the unappeased dead. The aim is to heal the possessed person and to enable the spirit of the dead to rest in peace.

Nokuzola Mdende, a practitioner of traditional African religion and a member of the South African Commission for the Rights of Cultural, Religious, and Linguistic Communities, is critical of the South African Truth and Reconciliation Commission for its failure to integrate the cleansing practices of traditional communities into its reconciliation work. She refers to the Ukukhupha Iqungu initiatives in Xhosa communities that seek to remove the urge or incentive within perpetrators to commit violence. This opens the way for individuals and clans involved in the violence to be reconciled. Ancestors are invoked to intervene in the feuds that caused the violence, and the community's elders are called on to acknowledge the wrongs perpetrated by their people and to commit themselves to restoration through reparation, symbolic handshaking, and animal sacrifices.

The common objective of all these practices—in Zimbabwe, Mozambique, South Africa, and elsewhere in Africa—is the restoration of relations between the living and the dead through acknowledgment, reparations, and reconciliation. "The ancestors need to be appeased for reconciliation to happen and our children to prosper," Mdende insists. "The veneration of ancestors in traditional communities provides a focus through which communities can be healed and relationships restored." Central to this process is engagement not only between individuals and communities involved in dispute but also with the "living dead," who are seen to be involved in the conflict as well as the restoration of peace in a community. The relationship between the living and the dead is complementary— each needs the other. In African tradition, a person dies when he or she is no longer remembered in the community. No ancestor wants to be forgotten. The living, conversely, need the presence of ancestors to promote their well-being in the community. No living person wants a displaced or alienated ancestor. The ceremonies are complex. The negotiations involved and restoration of relationships take time. "Healing is a difficult and costly process. We need to persevere and have patience. This is ultimately the only way in which the ravages of the past can be put behind us," suggests Mdende.[49]

Sacred Space

Place is important in ritual. A tree that provides shelter is often a sacred place for ritual practice. Frequently it is a historic tree that has been used through several generations for healing and reconciliation ceremonies.

Taban Sabum, living in the Upper Nile region of South Sudan, speaks of the adaptability of the ceremonies, recounting how the bark of trees in a sacred place sometimes is used to make a brew that washes away evil and restores relationships. This brew is poured onto the graves of ancestors and over the heads of those who have committed evil. He tells of seeing "tobacco being sprinkled, ashes rubbed on feet and hands, and elders spitting on the heads of people seeking a blessing in Kaduk, the home village of Riek Machar the Nuer leader." The sacrifice of an animal is invariably part of the ritual. The blood of a cow, a goat, or a chicken, depending on the wealth of the family, is used to symbolize the cleansing of evil, while the meat is used in celebration. Some rituals are confined to particular households and families. Others have a further reach. "We need to reknit the social and spiritual fabric that once bound us together as people, after more than thirty years of war that reached into every village and settlement," suggests James Kok Ruea, the founding chairperson of the South Sudan Peace Commission. "If we do not draw on the traditional practices of our people, we simply will not reach the majority of villagers who live in isolated *bomas* [villages] across the country."[50] If we fail to do that, peace will simply not take root and grow.

Reconciliation Practices

Inherent to the culture and ritual of traditional African reconciliation practices is relationship building. Such censure and restitution that may emerge from a settlement seeks to benefit not only the victims but also the victims' families, clans, and communities.

The removal of enmity between the groups and the restoration of cordial relationships involves extended negotiation processes. Elders preside at the ceremonies, sending mediators to engage in a traditional form of "shuttle diplomacy" between the two sides. "These are envoys and conflict managers in the modern sense of the word. The relationship building is less mysterious than what outsiders seem to realize," observed Odama. If well executed, he tells us, "the process leads to the emergence of a measure of trust and understanding between the two sides and when the time is ripe this leads to face to face meetings between the antagonists, followed by rituals and ceremonies that cement a settlement."

A person, eccentric in appearance and communication, introduced himself to me at a meeting in Kinshasa as "a priest, a lawyer, and a traditional healer" in North Kivu in the Democratic Republic of the Congo. A colorful and yet retiring person, he called himself Mpatanishi—from the Swahili word for peacemaker (*mpatanisha*). Blending traditional customs and contemporary practices in peace building and the pursuit of justice, he too spoke of traditional rituals being "less mystifying and more predictable" than is often realized. "A lot of negotiation and preparation goes into the process before it becomes public. We are not miracle workers. We are social workers, negotiators, and judges. This involves hard work. But, yes, we also draw on the wisdom and the charm of the ages captured in rituals and ceremonies. This brings a sense of legitimacy, gravitas, and mystique to what we do. It provides an opportunity for the community to be part of the decision-making process."[51]

The link between African reconciliation processes and contemporary forms of restorative justice is obvious. Both recognize that certain dimensions of justice are often lost within the institutional retributive judicial process. Without rejecting all punitive measures associated with retributive justice, restorative justice seeks to be more inclusive. At best it is a process whereby the parties to a conflict resolve to deal with the consequences of the conflict and its implications for the future in a collective manner. Both traditional African and modern forms of restorative justice prioritize the need to salvage and affirm the moral worth and dignity of everyone involved.

The centrality of restorative justice to traditional African reconciliation processes extends quite obviously to the *ubuntu* debate discussed in the previous chapter and reminds us of the extent to which justice and reconciliation are grounded in relationship building, as noted in discussing Bohler-Müller's concept of the "jurisprudence of care" in the last chapter.[52] It opens a space for the pursuit of a better and more just future by enabling victims, perpetrators, and the broader community to address the underlying causes that gave rise to past conflicts and to find ways of settling these issues in order to move on.

Community Involvement

John Paul Lederach's colorful account of the two cousins in Somalia—one an activist and the other a politician—reminds us that political leaders as well as the broader community need to be involved in holistic peace building if peace is to prevail.[53] To adapt the analogy, reconciliation needs leadership in the form of guidance and management from both national and community leaders. It also requires participation by the broader or grassroots community. Any pre-negotiation and tentative agreement reached between disputants needs to be brought into a public space where the community can share in the process.

Traditional African communities in earlier times were essentially homogeneous. They had hierarchical structures of decision making that are today challenged even in some remote communities. Women challenge stereotypically imposed roles of subservience, and young people are exposed to ideas and insights that were simply not part of earlier traditional communities. This raises questions concerning the extent to which traditional reconciliation practices can be adapted to less homogeneous communities. "The traditional ceremonies need to allow for dissenting voices and debate," a community worker engaged in conflict resolution in South Sudan noted. "Simple consensus is sometimes just not possible. . . . What is necessary is for dissidents to feel that their views are captured in the decision-making process. It also requires that the voices and concerns of women be included in any peace process."[54]

Traditional courts and structures are often criticized for being gender insensitive, although in some situations courts and ceremonies are presided over by women. Though this is the case in the *gacaca* courts in Rwanda, where 30 percent of the *inyangamugayo* (judges) are women, many women continue to find the process intimidating where issues of rape and sexual violence are involved.[55] In recent years women have become *Bashingantahe* in Burundi, and women exercise significant power among traditional matriarchal groups in parts of Mozambique, Ghana, Mali, and elsewhere on the continent. This said, Africa is predominantly a male-dominated society, which is reflected in most traditional judicial and governance structures.

For traditional reconciliation structures to maintain relevance, they need to ensure that reconciliation is inclusive. This necessarily means the demands and needs of women must be addressed. The battle for gender sensitivity and parity cannot be separated from the struggle for restoration and renewal in postconflict situations. "The gender issue is not going to be won overnight. It is also not going to disappear. Women are making their voices heard in this country. We were an indispensable part of the war effort and we need to be a part of the peace process," stated Beatrice Aber, the deputy chair of the South Sudan Peace Commission.[56]

Western proposals for the promotion of justice in countries struggling to overcome past oppression usually focus on the need to hold perpetrators accountable through the courts, tribunals, or perhaps a Truth and Reconciliation Commission. This point has been amply stressed in the pages above. The problem is that at the completion of this process, the structures and institutions of the former state, along with the civilian and political leaders, often remain either directly or indirectly in authority. Individuals and groups who were excluded from the former regime often continue to be excluded from decision-making processes in the new society, and insufficient attention is given to the institutional healing of communities. Even where a constitutional or legal framework for human rights is instituted, those who were excluded are unable to embrace the opportunities that the new dispensation offers them. The result is that asocial behavior and crime persist. Communication between those who disagree on important issues continues to be neglected, resulting in the settling of old scores through violence. Children entering newly established schools often resort to drugs and violent behavior, and political accountability gives way to corruption and favoritism.

A level of social cohesion and civic trust is required to meet the needs of alienated and traumatized communities. Traditional African reconciliation practices should be adapted to meet this need and be given the resources to do so.

Adaptation

Although clearly some traditional leaders resist all forms of adaptation and modification, many practitioners of traditional African reconciliation customs accept that practices need to be shaped and adapted to meet changing times and circumstances. They acknowledge that some cases should be referred to the courts for prosecution. A traditional leader in Bor in South Sudan explained: "Sometimes we introduce practices of Christianity, Islam, or Western ideas of conflict resolution. Most religious and cultural practices in Africa are somewhat synchronistic. We appropriate what works in pursuit of our overall aim which is to resolve conflicts in a restorative way, trying to reach a solution that both the victim of a crime or offence, and the perpetrator, as well as their families and clans can agree to." He spoke of prosecutions, community-imposed forms of punishment, psychosocial counseling, spiritual healing, conflict resolution, reparations, and community service, as well as public shame as options he required people to accept. "Discretion is a priority in our work, with the chief or elder having maximum discretion when resolving a conflict. No one would traditionally have questioned his ruling. Things have changed today, although chiefs and elders continue to exercise a lot of power, especially in isolated areas. Increasingly, the emphasis is, however, on consultation, mediation, and compromise."[57]

When the South Sudan Peace Commission drew up its strategic planning exercise and released its manifesto, it gave prominence to the role of traditional authorities and leaders in the promotion of "South-South" and "people-to-people" dialogue. James Kok Ruea spoke of the need for the Sudan People's Liberation Army (SPLA) and other military groups to meet with the "chiefs, kings, and queens" in order to express appreciation for the support of local communities in the war effort and to apologize for the suffering that the SPLA and other rebel groups had inflicted on them. "We need also to learn from [local communities] how best to mete out justice to the perpetrators responsible for the terrible things that happened to them. We need to draw on local customs and ceremonies to heal our communities. We need to be accountable to our own people, while taking into account the wisdom of international law."[58]

The adaptation of traditional reconciling structures to international judicial norms is a complex process, wrought with all the difficulties inherent to any negotiation process. As indicated above, the incorporation of traditional practices into the Juba talks between the Ugandan government and the LRA suggested an initial willingness by LRA rebels to use the opportunity to make peace. It has since, however, become apparent that Kony and his followers were seeking to use the talks to have ICC warrants against them withdrawn, without an obvious desire to make peace.

Questions abound. Can such traditional practices meet the demands and the needs of a contemporary society? Can traditional and culturally embedded practices be adapted to meet the demands of modern notions of the rule of law and the need for judicial transparency? A number of specific challenges in this regard are returned to in chapter 8. International justice offers judicial clarity and control. Traditional African practices provide a sense of cultural resonance and community responsibility. Setiloane speaks of the latter as "a certain kind of power."[59]

Power of a Different Kind

I spoke with Daphne Madiba, a Lutheran priest in the Limpopo Province in South Africa, about the meaning of culture and music in traditional ceremonies. She spoke of missionary influence and traditional religious practices:

> Both traditions teach us of the deep spiritual and conflict-resolving significance of music. The ancestors speak in a manner that calms our spirits. We raise our voices and speak fast. Then our voices grow quiet, our eyes are opened to the needs of others and we are less angry. We learn to understand the needs of those who have done violent things. The language of the spirit is not Venda, Shangaan, or English. It is different. It is an unspoken language buried in silence, in music, and in the time-honored customs of our mothers and fathers who have entered the spirit world. It is power of a different kind.[60]

The peace-building culture and practices of others need to be assessed in terms not of what makes sense within our own rational credibility structures but of the contribution it makes to peace. It is this that persuaded the Office of the United Nations High Commissioner for Refugees in Uganda in February 2007 that the traditional reconciliation practices of the Acholi people needed to be explored in pursuit of lasting peace. Wanting to explore indigenous healing and reconciliation approaches as a way "to give peace a chance," the Ugandan government, which had earlier referred the case of the LRA to the ICC for indictment in 2005, resolved in 2007 to "engage" the ICC on whether this was in fact the most viable way of bringing the Northern Ugandan conflict to an end.[61]

The ultimate goal of transitional justice and peace building is the realization of an enduring peace characterized by individual and communal rights. Dinis Salamao Sengulane suggests that

> maybe traditional African healing and reconciliation practices provide no more than a quiet and secure place for people to withdraw from the anger and violence of society so as to think quietly, to resolve differences, to break the link with past evil, and to receive the support of their communities as they reenter society with a commitment to put right past wrongs and to live in harmony with others. . . . Those who share in these ceremonies claim that more happens. They believe that they are inwardly changed and supported by the living and the living dead to live better lives."[62]

Within certain communities these practices can augment other peace-building processes. The failure to explore such practices in African societies, not least in rural and traditional areas, can undermine a holistic approach to peace building. For sustainable peace building in Africa to become the order of the day, the complexities of the conflicts that haunt the continent need to be acknowledged.

The burning challenge facing the African states is the need for balance between holistic justice and political stability. This requires both the discipline inherent to Western notions of the rule of law as well as the patience and restoration that characterizes traditional African reconciliation practices. The difficulty is to get the balance right. This will require adjustment and flexibility by both Western and traditional African notions of the rule of law.

Transitional Justice in Africa

The strength of African justice and reconciliation mechanisms is that they are grounded in the social fabric of the communities they represent. They seek to overcome social polarization, and where appropriate they explore ways of reintegrating perpetrators into society. They regard community reconciliation as an ultimate goal against which censure, retribution, and restoration need to be measured.

To the extent that the goals of transitional justice are overcoming political polarization, rebuilding society and promoting civic trust through perpetrator accountability, and restoring the human dignity of victims, the exploration of complementary partnerships between the ICC and traditional African mechanisms for justice and reconciliation is both desirable and realistically possible.

Few scholars and practitioners have a principled objection to promoting a viable relationship between the ICC and domestic governments and judiciaries or traditional courts and the broader African population to ensure that these objectives are met. Difficulties emerge when it is assumed that international justice is the measure of all justice. This is particularly problematic on a continent that is burdened with the memory of colonialism and internationally imposed "solutions" to domestic problems that have resulted in the endless suffering of the African people. The question is how to accomplish a realistic level of complementarity between international and domestic institutions. This concern is addressed in the final chapter.

WHY RECONCILIATION IS IMPORTANT

Speak to us about reconciliation
Only if you first experience
The anger of our dying.

Talk to us about reconciliation
Only if your living is not the cause
Of our dying.

Talk to us about reconciliation
Only if your words are not products of your devious scheme
To silence our struggle for freedom.

Talk to us about reconciliation
Only if your intention is not to entrench yourself
More on your throne.

Talk to us about reconciliation
Only if you can cease to appropriate all the symbols
And meanings of our struggle.

—J. Cabazares, quoted by Walter Wink,
Healing a Nation's Wounds

Why is political reconciliation important? It provides a context for authentic, free, and fearless speech as a basis for making tough decisions on how to deal with the past in order for a new kind of society to emerge. It makes conversation that reaches across political and other divisions possible. It provokes former enemies and adversaries to explore new options for living together. It is central to African options for a shared peace.

A distinction between individual reconciliation and political or national reconciliation has been maintained throughout this book. It has been argued that political reconciliation, not least in the wake of prolonged political violence and war, is about a willingness to explore ways of changing negative attitudes and destructive behavior. Improved relationships between enemies can provide a new basis for addressing the causes of conflict, implementing goals that are immediately attainable, and developing strategies aimed at realizing those objectives that can only be met over a longer period of time.

A distinction has also been maintained between reconciliation and forgiveness. I have done so while recognizing the importance of political forgiveness as defined in several recent publications. Donald Shriver's formative work *An Ethic for Enemies* is subtitled *Forgiveness in Politics*. His point of departure is the liberation of forgiveness from its religious captivity that prioritizes the individual to the neglect of the political sphere.[1] Stressing that enmity between enemies is inevitable in the wake of conflict, he identifies forgiveness as an incentive to draw society beyond "the left over debris of national pasts" to a future yet to be realized.[2] For him, "political forgiveness" is a process in much the same way that "political reconciliation" is defined in the pages of this book. He captures the reality of postconflict political relations by quoting Rodney King in the aftermath of the 1992 Los Angeles riots as saying: "People, I just want to say, you know, can we all get along? . . . I mean, we're all stuck here for a while. Let's try and work it out." For this to happen, Shriver argues that some level of forgiveness is required.

In his major contribution to political theology, Miroslav Volf, like Shriver, also uses "forgiveness" to describe a cautious relationship between adversaries. He defines this level of forgiveness as being located at the "boundary between exclusion and embrace."[3] His axiom is reminiscent of the title of Martha Minow's book, *Between Vengeance and Forgiveness*. While addressing some similar themes, Volf's approach is different from that of Minow. Above all Volf is driven by a theological imperative to reach toward a level of engagement with former enemies and "ultimate others" that gives expression to New Testament ideals. Asked at the height of the Serbian-Croat conflict whether he, as a Croat, could embrace a Serbian fighter, he responded: "No, I cannot—but as a follower of Christ I think I should be able to."[4] At the same time, he writes of the need to "embrace" one's enemies in a more cautious and modest way at the level of dialogue and political reciprocity.[5]

Linguistic differences aside, my concern is to promote the political possibilities of what Shriver and Volf describe at the lower level of encounter between enemies. In continuity with this level of reconciliation, Kjell-Åke Nordquist defines reconciliation as a relational concept, requiring individuals and groups in conflict to agree to find mutually acceptable ways of resolving a conflict.[6] At the level of politics, he stresses that this requires a structural dimension, within which relations can be developed and solutions to conflicts can be explored. Conversely, he suggests that forgiveness is, at least initially, a one-sided act. His concern is that any sense of obligation to forgive often places pressure on individuals to forgive when they are not ready or able to do so. Forgiveness can, however, result in the examples of grace and magnanimity displayed especially by leaders who are prepared to do more than their followers to heal a nation's wounds.[7] The apology of President Willie Brandt at the Warsaw Ghetto monument in December 1990 opened a new narrative on post-Nazi responsibilities in Europe. When Nelson Mandela walked out of prison in February 1990, he captured the attention of the entire world in calling on South Africans to forgive one another.

In brief, the politics of forgiveness affirms the discussion introduced in chapter 3, where the importance of what Max Horkheimer called a "theological moment" and Paul Ricoeur the "poetics of existence" was considered.[8] Both identify the need for a political ideal to lure nations toward achievements not yet realized. Inspirational leaders often provide this incentive.

At a conference of North American academics some years ago, it was suggested by several social scientists present that I drop the word "reconciliation" from my presentation and substitute an alternative such as "social cohesion" or "trust building."[9] "Reconciliation carries too much religious baggage, and it has been abused by so many oppressive regimes that it has lost its integrity," I was told. A Chilean participant insisted that "reconciliation is an oppressive word in the lexicon of Latin America survivors. It requires victims to make peace with the past and to accept their continued exclusion from the present dispensation. It implies that our oppressors had a right to do to us what they did." Later that day, an elderly man who had seen the inside of Monrovian prison cells under three successive Liberian heads of state (William Tolbert, Samuel Doe, and Charles Taylor) observed that "enemies need one another to be made whole." Picking up on the conversation later, he suggested, "Enemies and opponents need to see themselves through the eyes of the other in order to overcome their anger." "If they refuse to understand the fears and motivations of one another, their anger will linger, fueling the spiral of violence that has consumed places like Liberia." He acknowledged that human nature is such that not many who have suffered are instinctively inclined to be reconciled with those who have caused their suffering, but he insisted that reconciliation is the only way to break the spiral of victims becoming perpetrators only to generate new victims. "Reconciliation is the realpolitik of sustainable peace building," he said.[10] His words have remained with me.

Reconciliation is ultimately about more than coexistence, trust building, social cohesion, and participatory democracy, although it is intimately related to each of these constructs. "Coexistence is a good start, trust building is essential, social cohesion is important and the goal is democracy, but I would like to think that the price I paid during the struggle years was for more than what these categories offer," Peter John Pearson, a Roman Catholic priest and activist in the South African fight against apartheid, told a seminar in Cape Town: "My fear is that if we merely coexist with our enemies, they remain enemies and sooner or later the conflict is likely to reignite," he observed. Reconciliation involves broadening the lens of peace building to find a way to move beyond a preoccupation with "me and my future" to "us and our future." It involves a commitment to transcend the political exploitation of polarizing identity categories that in so many situations give rise to conflict. "Reconciliation is the first step toward forgiveness, which remains an ideal that is rarely attained in a society that is still seeking to extract itself from conflict and war."[11]

Reconciliation is not about forgetting. It is about remembering—at least trying to remember in a constructive kind of way. Speaking on the occasion of the Deutscher Bundestag in 1996, President Roman Herzog observed: "The pictures of the piles of corpses, of murdered children, women and children, women and men, of starved bodies are so penetrating that they remain distinctly engraved, not just in the minds of survivors and liberators, but in those who read and view accounts of [the Holocaust] today. . . . Why, then, do we have to will to keep this memory alive? Would it not be an evident desire to let the wounds heal into scars and to lay the dead to rest? . . . History fades quickly if it is not part of one's own experience. [But] memory is living future. We do not want to conserve the horror. We want to draw lessons that future generations can use as guidance. . . . In the light of sober description, the worst barbarous act shrinks into an anonymous event. If we wish for the erasure of this memory, we ourselves will be the first victims of self-deception."[12]

For Herzog, remembrance was a deliberate exercise in the creation of something new. His counsel was that we need to remember in order not to repeat past atrocities. Terrence McCaughey, president of the former Irish anti-apartheid movement before 1994, tells of his time as a student at Tübingen University in Germany in the late 1950s. There had been a week of films on German politics from the Weimer Republic through to the rise and fall of Adolf Hitler, the first such series since the end of the war. Academic life almost came to a standstill. He tells of his Old Testament professor, Karl Elliger, addressing his class on the morning after the final presentation. "You young people no doubt think we were all stupid not to have seen what was happening," he said. "We have no excuses. But learn this: Evil never comes from the same direction, wearing the same face. I hope you will be wiser and more discerning than our generation when the threat of evil next comes around. You need to be vigilant." Turning to his notes, the professor quietly continued to lecture his students on the Book of Joshua.[13]

Reconciliation as *goal* is about recognizing our own susceptibility to evil, without excusing or condoning evil either in ourselves or in others. It involves exploring the possibility of a change in attitude and behavior in a quest for a sense of togetherness that transcends the binary political distinctions between black and white, Hutu and Tutsi, Serb and Croat, Palestinian and Israeli, victim and perpetrator—as well as dogmatic notions of good and evil. However, there is no postconflict situation in the world today where this goal has been realized. That is why this book focuses on the *process* of political encounter as a means of achieving this elusive goal. Underlying this focus is the realization that if the *goal* of a new paradigm does not motivate and sustain a people in their struggle, they are in danger of being trapped in the binary categories that gave rise to the conflict. Unless an emerging nation is prepared to strive with all its human and creative resources at every opportunity to make what is new, it is unlikely to extricate itself from the heritage of a past from which it needs to escape. In the words of Elliger, the conflict is likely to reemerge, albeit with a different face. Mandela expressed a similar sentiment when he stressed the importance of understanding the "causes, motives, and perspectives" of those responsible for past evil. He warned that unless the essential concerns of perpetrators and victims are addressed, they are likely, in one form or another, to give rise to future conflict.[14]

Alex Boraine insists that "reconciliation is not something that is achieved and can hang on the wall like some picture representing the past and even the future. It is a process—a process which began before the life of the [Truth and Reconciliation Commission]. The process of reconciliation began at the negotiation table with the basic acceptance by all parties that we have to share territory called South Africa with our former enemies."[15] It indeed began in a cautious and tentative way long before negotiations began. Reconciliation is the beginning and the end of a process within which the enemies of yesterday need to explore what it means to cooperate in resolving the issues that initiated and sustained the conflict. Never easy, reconciliation does not presuppose agreement on all solutions to all such issues. It does presuppose a willingness to address these concerns politically rather than in blood. This requires a willingness to think new thoughts and imagine new solutions.

Imagining the New

Among the first casualties of protracted conflict is the loss of political imagination and the inability to see beyond entrenched violence. At best it is hoped that a way can be found to stop the fighting, to create a buffer zone between enemies, and to impose a cease-fire. This is often a crucial step in pursuit of higher, self-sustaining notions of peace. But for sustainable peace to emerge, more than an agreement to stop the killing is required. Antagonists need to see one another differently and find ways of creating a different kind of future.

Reminiscent of John Paul Lederach's discussion on moral imagination (discussed in chapter 3), John Sampson, a Namibian artist whom I first met years earlier when he was a student in Cape Town, walked me through his studio in Windhoek. We spoke of the political change in postindependence Namibia and about future political options facing that country. The conversation shifted to his work as an artist. "A new way of seeing things is a bit like a work of art or a poem," he said. "It needs to be pondered, sometimes fought with, perhaps admired—even when it is not fully understood. Politicians, battle-hardened generals, former SWAPO [South West Africa People's Organization] guerrillas, and skeptical academics sometimes dismiss my work as fantasy and romantic nonsense. But that is where creativity begins. That is perhaps the humble contribution that the poet and artist can make to the tough world of politics."[16]

Identity is an important political category in African politics. It is an entrenched reality that needs to be creatively and realistically accommodated in any sustainable reconciliation process. However, the adverse politicization of race, ethnicity, and identity is a different matter. Used as a mobilizing factor often by both those in power and those seeking to claim power, it heightens conflict, although some would argue that this level of intensification is necessary, not least in asymmetrical conflicts, to bring matters to a point where issues can be dealt with openly. Frank Chikane, the former director-general in the South African presidency, spoke of the problem inherent to moving from a "mobilizing strategy" to a "nation-building strategy" at the time of the South African transition.[17] He referred to young black activists and students in the days of the struggle who in an endeavor to make the country ungovernable demonstrated their refusal to support the apartheid infrastructure by not paying train fares out of Soweto. Acknowledging the importance of this strategy, he pondered what needed to be done to persuade activists to support the emerging new political infrastructure and pay their train fares once the struggle was over. Of course the politicization of difference and identity in political struggle runs deeper than paying train fares and utility accounts, and yet Chikane's analogy holds. Identity and strategy negatively employed have the capacity to undermine a postconflict peace-building process. In a period of unresolved conflict, resistance is often enough. In reconstruction, more is required. This often involves the need for a change of political strategy, a change in relations among antagonistic groups, and an openness to the possibility that one's own identity and that of one's opponents can change. It involves exploring the possibility of changing an identity of resistance and confrontation into an identity of democratic participation in a nation-building exercise that recognizes the need for critical participation in state structures.

Mahmood Mamdani reminds us that Vladimir Lenin chided Rosa Luxemborg for being so preoccupied with combating Polish nationalism that she could not see beyond it.[18] In so doing, he argued, she risked being locked in the world of the rat and the cat. The rat sees no more malicious enemy than the cat, and the cat knows of nothing more delicious than the rat. The outcome is that even if the rats manage to defeat the cats, the impulse of their victim mentality is to seek revenge. They simply exchange places with the cat. Mamdani suggests: "You can turn the world upside down, but still fail to change it. To change the world, you need to break out of the world view of not just the cat, but also the rat, not just the settler but also the native."[19]

The distinction that Mamdani makes between ethnicity as cultural identity, which he sees as "consensual and multiple," and political identity, which is "imposed and enforced," has pertinence beyond Rwanda and other parts of the world where identity politics has the capacity to undermine peace. Briefly, and at the risk of simplifying his analysis, he argues that it is the political identity imposed in the colonial era that hardened the boundaries between "Hutu" and "Tutsi."[20] These identities were perpetuated in the 1959 social revolution when the Hutu, trapped in a colonial victim mentality, traded places with their colonial masters and gave expression to their hegemonic aspirations by dominating the Tutsi. When the Rwandan Patriotic Front/Army (RPF/RPA) defeated the Juvénal Habyarimana regime in 1994 they, too, he argues, perpetuated the binary distinctions that underlie generations of conflict in Rwanda. Building on an ideology of "never again" excluding or committing genocide, they failed to seize the opportunity to create a new sense of Rwandan identity. The outcome is that "the jailer comes to be tied to the jail as much as is the prisoner."[21] The result is that no one is free. The cycle of civil war and genocide continues to dominate the thinking of both the victims and victors.

The problem inherent in identity politics, which is invariably driven by political interests, is that when a potential turning point emerges that offers an opportunity to create a new kind of national identity, entrenched forms of politicized difference militate against this happening. The unifying national identity so desperately needed in many postconflict countries is undermined. The result is that resentments and unresolved memories wait to be avenged when the occasion is seen to be opportune. In brief, the use of identity construction, although useful as a mobilizing agent in one situation, can be a severe liability in another.

Identity politics is particularly pertinent in a world where the vast majority of conflicts, many of which result in mass atrocities, are intrastate rather than between countries. This is a situation that persuades a number of scholars to argue that issues of ethnic diversity and power sharing in intrastate situations require a new set of incentives and rewards that allow adversarial groups to reduce their demands for cultural and social autonomy as the only basis for the shared recognition of all identities. Andreas Wimmer and his colleagues suggest that ethnic conflicts have become "a testing ground for a new morality of promoting peace, stability and human rights across the globe."[22]

As suggested in an earlier chapter, this may well be the major challenge facing the twenty-first century. Certainly on the African continent—where the

Berlin Conference at the close of the nineteenth century imposed national boundaries that paid no heed to ethnic, monarchical, or any other borders or spheres of influence—increased attention needs to be given to the ethnographic dimensions of both intrastate and interstate conflicts. Means and ways need to be developed to enable individuals and groups with different identities to find ways of engaging one another in mutually beneficial ways. At the same time, it must be recognized that what sometimes are portrayed and masquerade as ethnic conflicts are essentially conflicts related to material resources, regional influence, or political opportunism. The nature and complexity of such disputes aside, there is little doubt that ethnic and related differences, both perceived and real, are matters that cannot be ignored in the pursuit of sustainable peace on the African continent.

Diane Enns develops identity politics in relation to broader identity concerns within the context of peace building.[23] In so doing she alerts us to the feminist, multiculturalist, and antiracism discourses, not least in North America, that stress the need to recognize and challenge the exploitative differences that exist among groups before it is possible to agree on a basis for transcending such differences. Quoting Patricia Williams, Enns argues that in North America colorblind sameness fails to challenge the racist, cultural, and economic disparities that separate racial and ethnic groups.[24] Similar forms of reconciliation are rejected by Latin American and other critics of reconciliation. It is this that makes the identity debate, both before and after a conflict, contested and in need of careful steering in nation-building exercises. An identity-based conflict, like any other, is about power and privilege, with issues of culture, ethnicity, and religion being used to incite potential followers to action. Given its visceral and emotional power, identity issues can scarcely be ignored in a situation where they have been used to fuel conflict.

It is neither feasible nor expedient to ask individuals or communities to surrender the multiple identities they choose. This is what gives people a sense of worth, without which they are in danger of losing their humanity.[25] The question is how to create a society within which different *consensual identities* are respected and given equal status, as opposed to *politicized identities* that are imposed and enforced by a dominant state. For this to happen, Mamdani argues that the stranglehold on history *writing* and *making* needs to be broken. This requires political conflicts, killings, and genocides to be understood and interpreted in historical context. To fail to address the causes, motives, and perspectives of conflict is to fail to break the recurring cycle of conflict. This is not easy at a political level. Hegemonic states are invariably able to count on the support of journalists, academics, priests, and others who influence and shape the attitudes of the broader population. It is this support, Mamdani suggests, that led to the Rwandan genocide being carried out by spouses, family, workmates, neighbors, friends, nurses, doctors, judges, and human rights activists. The killers were believers, suitably conditioned to carry out their civic duty.

It is the perpetuation and internalization of a colonially imposed ideology of "indigenous Hutus" and "alien Tutsis" that persuades Mamdani to make the claim that the crime of colonialism involved more than the "expropriation of the native." "The greater crime," he writes, "was to politicize indigeneity."[26] This resulted in the Hutu majority, acting in accordance with colonially imposed categories, coming to regard themselves as having the right as an "indigenous" population to drive out the "alien" Tutsi. Nuances aside, the Tutsi in turn imposed victor's justice in their overthrow of Hutu domination in 1994.

The new government stressed its commitment to "Rwandicity" and Rwandan unity, outlawing monoethnic political parties and other forms of ethnic separation. Faced at the same time with the influx of returning Tutsi exiles, RPF leaders allowed them to claim the property of Hutu landowners who had fled their homes as the RPF army advanced. The complexities of post-1994 land policy notwithstanding, it is economic benefit and land preference, linked as they are to ethnic identity, that persuades analysts that the identity politics of colonial rule and Hutu power are being perpetuated in post-1994 Rwanda. It is this that persuades Zinaida Miller to emphasize—without making any dire predictions about future genocides or civil war—that careful attention must be given to conflict prevention by addressing issues of access to land and related forms of economic exclusion in post-conflict situations.[27] Above all, in a situation where politicized identity is historically entrenched, the temptation to use issues of ethnicity to mobilize the poor against the privileged classes is always there. Miller quotes a worker for a nongovernmental organization in Rwanda:

> We have to be able to teach the history in a way that doesn't make each event equivalent to the last one, so that we can understand the complexities. The former government twisted history and abused it; unfortunately, instead of adding complexity and nuance, the current government seems to think the answer is just to twist it back the other way. But that isn't the answer. We need to be able to look at Tutsi monarchies and Hutu power and genocide and colonialism and understand each one and how they've influenced the others without saying monarchy was the same as genocide. But unless we understand all of it as continuing events in a history, we can't understand at all.[28]

The important question is how to replace those categories that have the capacity to generate and perpetuate conflict with those that enable sustainable forms of peace to emerge. In Mamdani's words, how can the "victor's justice" be replaced with the "survivor's justice"? This, he argues, involves the difficult task of those "blessed with life" after a civil war being required to create a new way in which former enemies and adversaries are able to live together in harmony by drawing all those willing to explore the possibility of creating something new into a new democratic process.[29] The complexity and difficulty of such a process is reflected in the failure of so many postconflict states to realize this objective, with the inclusivity of states promised at the time of liberation giving way to factionalism, exclusion, and conflict.[30]

This is what legitimate political reconciliation is all about. The survivor's justice raises its own set of questions. Important among these is that of impunity, which needs to be considered in relation to the Rome Statute that gave rise to the International Criminal Court. A concept of evenhanded survivor's justice does, conversely, provide the rudiments of the "more" that is required after at least some perpetrators have been prosecuted or given amnesty.

A further concern arises from the implication that genocidaires and perpetrators, including victims turned perpetrators, are themselves often victims of a state-driven sense of duty so powerful that few are able to escape its impact. This is seen in the impact of Hutu power on grassroots people who participated in the genocide. Yet, as discussed in chapter 4, some brave individuals do act against dominant ideologies. The fact that they are few in number means, however, that postconflict nation building needs to concern itself not only with the empowerment and reparation of victims but also with the rehabilitation of perpetrators who continue to be part of postconflict societies. In many situations perpetrators are powerful members of the new society, carrying with them the privileges accumulated in the earlier dispensation. The question is how to enable such offenders to contribute to the desired new order.

Nation building in a postconflict situation requires both an incentive and the momentum that enables the perpetrators, victims, and bystanders alike to contribute to the creation of a dispensation that is able to break away from the politically imposed categories of the former state. For this to happen, the perpetrators need to acknowledge the injustices and inequalities that victimize people. The emerging new state needs to empower the victims and survivors to rebuild their lives. The victims need also to accept that in the new dispensation they cannot afford to view themselves as "impotent victims without responsibility," although they do deserve sympathy, maximum support, and appropriate reparations.[31] It also needs to be understood that the violence to which some victims may resort in postconflict situations is often a consequence of their victimization. This does not mean, however, that they can escape societal guilt or responsibility.

For Rwanda to transcend its heritage of conflict and genocide, it is often argued that the Tutsi government needs to surrender its monopoly of power, making itself vulnerable to a Hutu majority. The Tutsi leadership, however, fears a repeat of the Hutu driven genocide of 1994. The situation is well captured by International Alert: "On the majority side of the equation [Hutu] there is a profound sense of grievance at their long-standing exclusion and a determination that this must be corrected. On the minority side [Tutsi] there is a profound fear of exclusion/extermination and a determination to guard against it—all leading to a deadly competition for political power."[32] Rwanda is an example of the difficulty involved in breaking out of perceptions of the other that lock nations into latent if not overt forms of violence. It is a difficulty understood in other countries in the African Great Lakes region, the Horn of Africa, South Africa, the Israeli-Palestinian conflict, and in the situation that prevails in the former Yugoslavia and elsewhere. A first step toward overcoming a standoff of this nature involves the kind of engagement and trust building I discuss in chapter 3.

Frantz Fanon's *Black Skin White Masks* captures the need for this level of trust building and risk in a final passage that transcends the anger and the anxiety portrayed in many of the earlier pages of his book, in which he reflects on the history of the colonialism and racism he experienced in Martinique, in France, and in Algeria: "No attempt must be made to encase man, for it is his destiny to be set free. The body of history does not determine a single one of my actions. I am my own foundation. . . . The disaster and inhumanity of the white man lie in the fact that somewhere he has killed man. . . . I, the man of color, want only this: That the enslavement of man by man cease forever . . . Superiority? Inferiority? Why not quite simply attempt to touch the other, to feel the other, to explain the other to myself."[33]

In *The Wretched of the Earth*, published nine years later, Fanon will talk of "absolute violence" as a revolution that can only come from peasants or the *fellaheen*. This signals his disappointment with the postcolonial new bourgeois leaders.[34] Advocates of justice and reconciliation need to take heed.

Challenge and Invitation

As if responding to Fanon, Govan Mbeki placed "having and belonging" at the heart of political reconciliation.[35] He spoke of the need to ensure that those with least to lose are given reason to believe that their needs can be met from within the new order and that those who have most to lose are assured of a place within the new dispensation. It is a balance that requires a level of statecraft involving both *challenge* and *invitation*. The challenge, above all in countries emerging from periods of oppressive rule, involves dealing creatively and in a proactive manner with issues of political and economic exclusion where for historic and structural reasons particular groups did not share in the political decision making or reap the economic benefits of society. I told Oom Gov, as Mbeki was affectionately known, of a meeting in Belfast that I had attended as part of a South African delegation where a crusty and determined old Irish priest, steeped in the Irish troubles, insisted to a group of staunch young republicans that "when the fervor of the present settles down, you will discover you cannot eat a flag." Laughing heartily, Mbeki remarked: "I hope that priest understands that unless the Sinn Fein and the Unionists begin to talk to one another, the political and economic inclusion of which he talks will be no more than a pipe dream." (Sinn Fein and the Unionists have of course since then entered into a political agreement and initiated democratic rule in Northern Ireland.)

Mbeki spoke of a "renewed people" for whom the old divisions of race and class would give way to a "new sense of togetherness"—an ideal on which we should not compromise. He went on to say that "for political reconciliation to be sustainable beyond the excitement of the early phase of rapprochement and negotiations [that South Africa was experiencing at the time], the economy needs to be restructured in such a way that the poor and socially excluded begin to share in the material benefits of the nation's wealth." He also stressed that for economic growth and equitable distribution to happen, there needed to be political and social engagement and civic trust between the different sections of society:

> People, all people, both black and white, Hutu and Tutsi, Shona and Ndebele need to feel that they are part of the emerging new dispensa-tion. They need to feel free to participate in the decision-making pro-cess in a robust and spirited way. If people do not feel comfortably "at home" in their respective countries, they will not only be reluctant to work for the common good but will also cause considerable trouble. The tragedy is that this is often only realized after an extended period of conflict and violence is over, which leaves its imprint on the attempt to create an inclusive society.[36]

With the passion that came from his many years of struggle, Mbeki stressed that "South Africa must belong, economically, politically, and socially, to all who dwell within it. If we do not get this right, we will not realize the ideals to which we dedicated our lives."

Having

To "have" clearly involves having access to economic and material re-sources that are sufficient to meet one's basic needs. It involves being skilled to earn a living wage, having access to educational opportunities and to adequate health care, housing, transportation, and related infrastructural resources. It also involves having basic human rights, which include both individual and political rights as well as socioeconomic rights. However, for this to be available and implemented, good governance, human security, and service delivery need to be in place.

In transitional societies that endeavor to recover from conflict, war, and oppressive rule, it takes time for these things to be realized. Health care facilities need to be developed, roads need to be constructed or repaired, schools need to be established or reopened, a transport system needs to be set up, and clean water, electricity, and sanitation need to be provided. The list is endless. Add to these the need to train doctors, teachers, and engineers, plus the inevitable need to establish the rule of law, democratic elections, and a judiciary with adequately trained judges committed to upholding human rights.

The evidence in most transitional and developing countries is that people, not least the poor, are incredibly patient while waiting for these developments to take place. Their demands are largely modest. They want adequate housing, jobs, and schooling for their children. Sadly, few African countries, including South Africa, have been able to meet these demands. For this to happen, countries need to be governed by the rule of law, and they need to affirm such human rights as freedom from hunger, disease, and ignorance—in short, all people must have access to the basic necessities of life. Differently stated, economic development, social cohesion, and good governance are three sides of the same triangle.

The 1991 United Nations *New Agenda for the Development of Africa* acknowledged this reality: "Peace is an indispensable prerequisite for development. Peace initiatives by African countries should be encouraged and pursued in order to bring an end to war, destabilization and internal conflicts so as to facilitate the creation of optimal conditions for development. The international community as a whole should endeavor to cooperate with and support the efforts of African countries for a rapid restoration of peace, normalization of life for uprooted populations and national socio-economic reconstruction."[37]

Sue Brown and Funekile Magilindane develop the significance of this linkage by arguing that "a seldom-specified prerequisite for economic regeneration is the ability of ordinary citizens to look beyond immediate survival in order to plan future activities. Few are going to build, save or put extra work into anything but self-preservation or defense if they have no reason to expect that they can retain the benefits of their hard work. As farmers will not plant if they cannot anticipate harvest, citizens cannot be expected to help build a new social framework if they cannot imagine a future without poverty and an endless struggle for mere survival." They conclude: "The more predictable the social framework, the livelier the economy that is able to develop."[38]

The dominant model of transitional justice is clearly relevant to the creation of this kind of society. It affirms the importance of human rights, the rule of law, an equitable social order, and related human rights. The problem is that it does not always put the same level of energy or resources into these needs as it does into the need to apprehend, prosecute, and, where appropriate, ensure that the perpetrators of gross violations of human rights are punished.

The result is that other forms of impunity—including historical, political, moral, and economic impunities—are neglected. Each of these concerns must be given adequate attention. Unless economic impunity is addressed through economic transformation and growth, the possibility of sustaining the rule of law and redressing material forms of past suffering becomes increasingly remote. To the extent that the transitional justice debate neglects the economic side of this transition, it undermines its own principled commitment to sustainable peace. For such peace to prevail, the divisions that tear the social fabric of African societies apart need to be addressed specifically and actively. The sources of conflicts vary, but they almost always include economic inequality.

Speaking at a graduation ceremony at the University of Cape Town in 1995, shortly before the establishment of the Truth and Reconciliation Commission, Alex Boraine said:

> For the words of reconciliation to be heard, they must be accompanied by economic justice. . . . Every time the Land Claims Court meets, every time the Department of Agriculture releases land to people who have been deprived for so long, it speaks of new opportunity and reconciliation. Every time a simple home is erected so that people who were once squatting in bushes can have some shelter, it speaks not merely of goodwill, of possessions, but is a genuinely concrete action which helps to reconcile a deeply divided society. . . . Reconciliation without the anchor of restitution is not merely false reconciliation, not only a travesty of justice—that is, to victims of people who have suffered— but it is to confirm people in their suffering rather than to affirm them in their survival and create new opportunities for the future.[39]

South Africa has failed to meet these challenges with the sense of purpose once hoped for. The Truth and Reconciliation Commission, in turn, failed to address the issues of economic disparity with the same sense of urgency that it tackled the issues central to its mandate, namely "killing, torture, abduction or severe ill-treatment." It did, however, call on the government to take the necessary actions to "accelerate the closing of the intolerable gap between the advantaged and disadvantaged in society."[40] It further recommended that "a scheme be put in place to enable those who benefited from apartheid policies to contribute towards the alleviation of poverty." Without calling specifically for a wealth tax, it recommended that "urgent consideration be given by government to harnessing all available resources in the war against poverty."[41] The decisive question that fell outside of the commission's mandate was how to reshape economic relations to ensure that this happens. There can be no lasting peace without economic justice; but neither can there be economic justice without sustainable peace. This challenge needs to be as centrally located to the transitional justice debate as concerns about closing down on the legal impunity of perpetrators of what the commission defined as gross violations of human rights.

Belonging

If economic inclusivity is the material ingredient required to promote political reconciliation, the transcending of ethnic divisions is the social or subjective side of the process. The list of communities caught up in religious and ethnic identity concerns is a long one—the conflict in Northern Ireland; the Serbs, Muslims, and Croats in the Balkans; the Kurds in Iran and Iraq, the Sikhs in Northern India and Kashmir; the Tamils in Sri Lanka; the concerns of Tibetans; and the Basque communities in Spain and elsewhere. In African countries, states ranging from Rwanda, Burundi, and the Democratic Republic of the Congo in the African Great Lakes region to the Sudan and other countries of the Greater Horn, West Africa, and in the Southern African region face significant ethnic challenges. Add to these examples the sense of exclusion experienced by Pakistanis in Britain; Hispanics in the United States; aborigines in Australia; Maoris in New Zealand; the Inuit in Canada; the French speakers in Quebec; and the Khoi-San, Afrikaner, and other minority groups in South Africa and the extent of the identity issues in nation-building processes is obvious.

International instruments on group and minority rights, beginning with the recommendation of the UN Subcommittee on the Prevention of Discrimination and the Protection of Minority Rights as early as 1954, signal an increasing awareness by the international community that groups excluded from the dominant culture of their environment on the basis of ethnicity, religion, and language constitute a serious threat to national and regional stability. This underlines the need to include in the nation-building process all those who have the capacity to undermine peacemaking and democracy, without allowing them to jeopardize or delay the emergence of an equitable and just new order through the promotion of divisive ethnic politics.

In a culturally heterogeneous nation, which means most if not all modern nations, the challenge of political pluralism is at the forefront of nation building. A state that seeks to neutralize, exclude, absorb, or expel those whose national or tribal origins differ from that of the majority or ruling minority ultimately destroys its own vitality. Three options suggest a way beyond the monolith of statism, national chauvinism, and cultural domination: liberalism, multiculturalism, and cultural openness. Let us briefly consider each one.

Liberalism

The dominant model of nation building in the Western World continues to be a particular brand of individualistic liberalism, which suggests that there is room for all to participate in the body politic on the basis of the affirmation of individual human rights. In brief, liberals often play down the political importance of issues of language, religion, culture, and other "thick" sources of belonging such as memory, ethnicity, race, class, and gender, suggesting that where individual rights are in place contentious issues such as race, gender, and class—those very things that some would argue constitute the essential ingredients of what it means to be human—can be kept out of the political mix. The problem is that those who have a strong sense of culture, religion, identity, and race, sometimes in the absence of economic, intellectual, and language resources with which to compete with the liberal elite, are disempowered and excluded from what has aptly been called the "naked public square." It is this exclusion in the name of a liberal notion of there being "room for all" that often gives rise to ethnic, racial, cultural, or religious forms of chauvinism, by way of reaction.

Mark Amstutz helpfully argues that the focus of liberalism on individual rights and responsibilities fosters accountability and order in situations of relative political stability within which an overarching sense of inclusivity is claimed and recognized by all participating groups. In emerging democracies, conversely, where violence is entrenched through generations of intergroup conflict, it needs to be counterbalanced with communal bonds and responsibilities.[42] This more so in African societies, where traditionally the individual exists in and through his or her community. This requires both the community to take responsibility for individual wrongs and the individuals to be responsible to the community of which they are a part.

Differently stated, the opponents of liberalism argue that what is alleged to be a nonpartisan, culture-free liberal state is in reality thick with cultural and related overtones. It is marvelously easy to confuse *our* particular culture and tradition with what we see as universal human nature. We persuade ourselves that our culture is God's culture, universally given for the benefit of the entire human race, whereas it takes those who do not share our presuppositions to verify how inclusive our culture really is. This is why we need to listen most attentively to those who occupy the margins of the public square. They tend to see the fault lines of the public square more clearly than those who are most comfortably at home within it. It is this sense of exclusion in the name of liberalism that is seen by many as little more than surface-level transformation that results in multiculturalism being seen as a credible alternative to those forms of liberalism that play down cultural difference as a basis for coexistence.

The problem is that in societies built on this assumption, minority voices are all too often simply not heard. It is assumed that liberalism is the voice not only of reason but of all reasonable people, including those "reasonable people" who cling to the margins of society. The South African poet Antjie Krog, reflecting on the bitter struggle for inclusion by various groups in the long history of her native land, ponders the question: "How long does it take / for a voice / to reach another?"[43] How long, we may ask, does it take for the voices of the politically oppressed, culturally ignored, or economically excluded to be heard? While these voices are ignored, suggests the Ghanaian novelist Chinua Achebe, "in the distance the drums [of discontent] continue to beat."[44]

It takes those relegated to the margins of the public square to challenge the presuppositions of those who occupy the center. It takes dissident groups to see the fault lines in "color-blind" models of social existence that those at the center of power cannot see. For their voices and concerns to be heard, it is essential for them to have a social and political space from which to engage the dominant group. It is this that has persuaded some to see multiculturalism that seeks to give space to different cultures as a viable alterative to liberalism.

Multiculturalism

Apartheid was, of course, built on multiculturalism of a particular kind, a kind that entrenched group difference. Still today, Afrikaner *boerestaat* politics and other narrow expressions of nationalism continue to affirm the right to be different. "So let them be Zulus, Afrikaners, or Jews. That's okay by me, as long as I am given the same space to be," is a typical response. The problem is that the attempt to build a society in which different cultures and ethnic groups live in parallel rather than explore the possibilities of engaging one another has its own set of problems. Human nature and politics being what they are, the affirmation of exclusive identities lends itself to ethnic or group narcissism. Reconciliation demands more than parallel coexistence.

Multiculturalism further fails to address the ambiguities of identity. Not everyone in any particular ethnic group shares the same monolithic identity. Few ethnic groups, whether Xhosa, Hutu, or Neur, are homogeneous. They include the wealthy, the poor, intellectuals, men, women, workers, and owners of businesses, each of whom often have more in common across cultural and ethnic lines than they have with others in their own particular group.

Cultures also evolve. They are dynamic realities, not least in the border zones where cultures engage one another at both a voluntary and an involuntary level. The stories of South African townships such as Soweto, Mamelodi, Gugulethu, and Kwa-Mashu illustrate the point. These urban centers receive workers from the Eastern Cape, Venda, Qwa Qwa, and rural KwaZulu-Natal who encounter urbanized neighbors and people from other ethnic groups, including legal and illegal immigrants from the Congo, Zimbabwe, Nigeria, Malawi, and elsewhere. There are established and emerging entrepreneurs, gangsters, thieves, frightened people, and aspirant middle-class new arrivals in the city. These township dwellers often need to speak Afrikaans to clinch a job, English to get their kids into school, *tsotsi-taal* in the shebeens, and Xhosa, Venda, or Zulu to mama back home. These are cultures in the making that transcend and belie the rigidities of the cultural purists, who like to place traditional cultures side by side on a neat multicultural continuum. This suggests that multicultural engagement soon gives way to cultural evolution. Individuals and cultures are formed through interaction with other individuals and cultures. These are complex processes that create a space where social change is possible and new identities begin to emerge without force or imposition.

Different situations demand different solutions. Sudan is not South Africa, any more than Rwanda is Spain. It is clear, however, that a multiculturalism that fails to address the integration and evolution of identities, above all in postconflict societies, is ultimately little more than a veneer over the struggle of one culture to dominate another. Multiculturalism seeks to counter liberalism's unity *over* diversity with a sense of unity *in* or *through* diversity—but it fails to explore trajectories beyond separate identities. At worst, it can be little more than a ruse for living with subtle but entrenched separation, what South Africa once defined as "separate but equal" identities. The challenge is how to engage difference while allowing cultural change and integration. At best, multiculturalism allows for a coexistence of a kind. However, it is not reconciliation in the sense of engaging one another, influencing one another, and keeping open the possibility of finding a level of trust and mutually beneficial integration of cultures in the future.

Cultural Openness

Max Weber reminds us that culture is more than a light coat that rests on our shoulders to be discarded at will.[45] It is story, memory, symbol, language, and a place within which we live, move, and have our being. In this sense, culture is the ordinary. It is inherited, and it is taught. It evolves through encounters and dialogue. It is imposed and it is free choice.

Ironically, it is when we try to protect and defend our culture that it is most vulnerable. When we allow it to be, finding itself in relation to other cultures, it comes into its own. In South Africa, Afrikaans is stronger today than it ever was under the chauvinistic days of language protection and imposition. And yet it is different, as all languages are different.

The importance of difference is to create a space where those rooted in different languages and cultures can participate in the public square. It is at the same time important to ensure that no one group, either by default or by design, dominates another or undermines the inclusivity of the public square. This requires a realization by all participants that culture has the capacity to awaken a people. In Fanon's words, culture is "the sentence which expresses the heart of the people, . . . [becoming] the mouthpiece of a new reality in action."[46] For there to be sustainable peace, everyone needs the freedom to compose that sentence. Cultural openness is about social engagement through the sharing of stories, with no specific intent other than to share ourselves. The outcome may be no more than gaining an appreciation of the other. It may also be a conscious or unconscious exploration of pondering tomorrow's identity.

South Africans have made a somewhat laissez-faire start to reaching toward a new identity rather than a principled and directed one. This is most clear in relation to national symbols, names of cities and towns, landmarks, and statues—although this is beginning to be addressed. Some who visit South Africa, not least from other African countries, are intrigued to find that a statue of the Boer leader General Louis Botha on his horse still presides over the entrance to the presidential offices in Cape Town, that streets are still named after Hendrik Verwoerd and other icons of apartheid, and that there is still a city called Pretoria that struggles to rename itself Tswane. Monuments have not been torn down, and few statues honoring past leaders have been put into discrete places of storage. The question is, Where to go from here? How does one include, complement, and capture a new vision that reaches beyond the past to an inclusive future? John Ruskin once said, "Great nations write their autobiographies in three manuscripts, the book of deeds, the book of words, and the book of art. Not one of these books can be understood unless we read the two others, but of the three the only trustworthy one is the last."[47] He goes on to suggest that it is primarily the actual buildings, monuments, and memorials built within a particular nation at a particular time that capture the true ethos of that time and place. If this be so, who or what is a nation in transition? At best, it is a nation in becoming.

Culture and identity in Africa and elsewhere are complex things. Wars have been fought in the name of such. To suppress an identity eventually leads to revolt in the deep Camusian sense that compels the victim after the two hundred and seventieth stroke of the whip to shout "enough" and to fight back.[48]

But what is this thing called culture that provides what Weber says is more than a "light coat" that is integral to who we are? I offer six brief observations: (1) Culture comes from the Latin word *cultura*, meaning farming or agriculture that involves the complex process whereby nature is intentionally interfered with in an attempt to create a better product. (2) We are all born into our culture, it is there waiting for us; we drink it in like we drink our mother's milk. (3) Cultures are living things, always in flux. (4) Cultural groups are never homogeneous; we all differ from our closest kinfolk. (5) No one finds it particularly easy to change culture; most of us are culturally a bit reactionary. (6) A dynamic culture that includes people through dialogue and encounter can be a liberating but fearful adventure.[49]

Perhaps no nation in the world has found the answer to the quest for inclusive nation building, although some have learned better than others to cope with difference. Nations that are in transition from deep if not deadly conflict driven in one way or another by the issue of ethnicity and identity need to be particularly sensitive to the possibility of lapsing back into ethnic and identity issues. This makes reconciliation an important category in the transitional justice debate. To coexist is better than to kill, but the danger of coexistence is that it does not ultimately get beyond the "them and us." Herein lies a danger that can reignite past animosity and violence in postconflict situations.

More important than determining what level of engagement and exchange is required to transcend the binary categories within which the past conflict is vested is the commitment to a process that looks beyond the will to merely coexist, passing one another by on the other side of the street. It is this vision— one that entertains the possibility of learning to live together in a more integrated and open-ended manner—that lies at the heart of political reconciliation. It is something that no country in transition from a violent past can afford to ignore. Erik Doxtader suggests that "reconciliation promises a beginning, the creation of that which we can neither hold nor control. It is something that goads our imagination and extends our knowledge. We quantify reconciliation at the risk of rendering it banal."[50] This involves a process of engagement, conversation, imagination, and the taking of successive steps. J. H. Oldham and John Bennett referred to these steps as "middle axioms" that anticipate "the next step" that can reasonably be taken at a given time in creation of a society that opens new opportunities for sustainable peace.[51] Their work anticipates the importance of the dialect between political reconciliation and forgiveness that is affirmed in this book.

What, Then, Is Reconciliation?

Reconciliation is both *process* and *goal*. As *process* it is inevitably uneven, lapsing into counterproductive and even violent ways of redressing a conflict. It requires restraint, generosity of spirit, empathy, and perseverance. It is about exploring ways of gaining a deeper and more inclusive understanding of the problems that are the root cause of a conflict. It is about opening the way to better understanding, respect, and trust building. Above all, it is about finding ways to connect people across what are often historic and entrenched barriers of suspicion, prejudice, and inequality. This could lead to an adaptation or change of values and a new or less rigid sense of identity and outlook on life.

The *goal* of reconciliation at the level of *having* is the creation of a socioeconomic situation in which people have equal access to essential social services and basic material necessities. At the level of *belonging*, it involves the transcending of identity barriers where entrenched privilege subordinates or excludes others. Put differently, reconciliation is about sharing the resources of life that are available in a given place at a given time. John Paul Lederach captures this in his suggestion that reconciliation is constituted by both "a focus and locus."[52] Reconciliation has a narrow focus, which concerns relationship building as a context within which former enemies and adversaries can begin to address the problems that have driven them into violent conflict in pursuit of something new. At the same time, reconciliation is context specific, responding to core or particular problems in pursuit of a solution that is locally owned. The reconciliatory practice needs also to be shaped and attuned to local customs, which may include the kinds of rituals and customs outlined in the previous chapter.

Shortly after the report on the South African Truth and Reconciliation Commission was handed to President Nelson Mandela in October 1998, an editorial in the *New York Times* captured this reality: "Controversy has added to widespread complaints that the Commission has not helped the process of reconciliation. This is wrong. True reconciliation, which occurs when a society is no longer paralyzed by the past and people can work and live together, cannot be based on silence. No society can be restored to health by papering over as much pain as South Africans have suffered. A noisy and informed debate about the complicity and crimes of the apartheid era is necessary, even if uncomfortable."[53] Reconciliation often begins with noisy talk. It is a process that reaches toward a goal that is often beyond the comprehension of those who initiate it.

Reconciliation is an art rather than a science. Sometimes it happens. When it does happen, it is usually in the wake of hard work that begins with cautious first contacts between enemies via intermediaries, personal encounters, rapprochement, talks about possible talks, talks, negotiations, and trust building.

The focus of this book has been on process rather than goal. Similarly, the benchmarks of reconciliation modestly suggested here focus on how to get antagonists to agree on a path that suggests the possibility of sustainable peace. As approximations, the benchmarks may well occur in different sequences in varying contexts. All that is suggested here is that collectively they constitute the kind of commitment needed by former enemies and adversaries who seek to learn to live together in peace. Thus:

- Reconciliation does not necessarily involve forgiveness. Antagonists need not forgive one another or love one another in order to explore the beginning of new relationships.
- Reconciliation interrupts an established pattern of events. At the lowest level, political reconciliation may simply involve an agreement to stop killing one another. At a more advanced level, it explores ways to prevent the killing from reoccurring. Beyond that, it seeks to put a structure in place for sustainable peace building.

- Reconciliation is about timing. It often requires time for mourning and a release of anger. A nation also needs time to recognize and redress the wounds of the past. It is equally important to seize the moment for healing when it comes.
- Reconciliation is about breaking the silence on the past. It is not easy to speak when those around you are holding their silence or when there is a price to be paid for speaking. Sometimes language cannot capture the suffering and the unspoken cries that need to be heard. Yet words, or an acknowledged silence, can be the beginning of a process of moving on.
- Reconciliation is about the future. Breaking the silence of the past—sometimes requiring that one breaks ranks with one's allies—can open a space within which to talk about the future.
- Reconciliation entails understanding. Understanding does not necessarily lead to reconciliation—and yet when the story of a perpetrator is thoughtfully and truthfully told, empathetically heard, and deeply understood, it can open the way to explore a different way for perpetrators and victims to engage one another.
- Reconciliation involves acknowledging the truth. Acknowledgment is sometimes more important than knowledge of the facts. It sometimes becomes the basis for an apology.
- Reconciliation is about memory. The past lives on, shaping the present and threatening the future. It needs to be confronted for its control to be challenged.
- Reconciliation is about justice. There is perhaps no such thing as pure justice in an imperfect world. Justice, at the most practical level, is about fair play, which needs to be implemented in as courageous and evenhanded a way as possible.

In terms of conflict-resolving mechanisms, reconciliation begins where force, adjudication, and arbitration begin to give way to negotiation, mediation, and social interaction. Ultimately reconciliation is about sustainable peace. It is about the internalization of peace-building attitudes at the national, communal, and individual levels. Reconciliation in this sense is often the only realistic alternative to the escalation of violence in countries seeking to extricate themselves from situations of violence and civil war.

There is no blueprint for initiating or jump-starting the reconciliation process—from reaching beyond the confines of entrenched cultural, economic, and political enclaves in which former enemies, or those who live as strangers in a hostile and divided land, seclude themselves. Sometimes the alienation between opposing groups is so deep that it requires adversaries to stare into the looming abyss of destruction to discover that they need one another to survive. In other situations, there emerges a moment of sanity that interrupts what seems like a relentless journey into the darkest night. Both situations require the acknowledgment of the humanity of the other that can only emerge as enemies sit under the same tree and talk—with authenticity, courage, imagination, and hope—(re)discovering the bond of a common humanity.

This discernment of a human bond even when first glimpsed at a distance has the potential to open a space where adversaries can begin to revisit the social constructs of identity, dominance, or victimhood that separates them from one another. It is a bond that rarely emerges from within the ghettoes of isolation. It is activated, nurtured, and brought to fruition only as adversaries venture beyond their zones of comfort though encounters, trust building, and courageous dialogue.

SEEKING CONSENSUS

A duty to prosecute all human rights violations committed under a
previous regime is too blunt an instrument to help successor governments which must struggle with the subtle complexities of re-establish-
ing democracy. . . . Rather than a duty to prosecute, we should think of
the duty to safe-guard human rights and prevent future violations by
state officers or other parties."

—Carlos Santiago Nino, *Radical Evil on Trial*

All but the most sinister members of society regard sustainable peace, involving a process of former enemies finding some form of accommodation or reconciliation, as a goal worth striving for. The most ardent advocates of prosecution
for genocide, crimes against humanity, and war crimes argue that retribution is
required to establish the rule of law as a basis for sustainable peace. Others argue
that the prosecution of perpetrators can in some situations jeopardize the possibility of sustainable peace.

The tension in this regard tends to be between lawyers who fear the implications of impunity and the advocates of peace building and reconciliation
who fear the collapse of political rapprochement and a resumption of violence.
The question is how to transcend both fears, ensuring accountability without
destabilizing countries torn apart by deep conflict. Neither the most principled
human rights lawyers nor the advocates of peace building and reconciliation
ultimately disagree that both justice *and* reconciliation are needed for peace to
be sustainable. The essential question is which comes first, and whether the
focus of transitional justice ought to be on punitive justice or on a more holistic
sense of inclusive or restorative justice.

Human rights actors focus on a principled outcome—a state in which
human rights standards, including the prosecution of perpetrators, are upheld.
Advocates of peace building and reconciliation, conversely, emphasize a process of dialogue aimed at promoting a culture of the rule of law and human
rights. Human rights actors tend to direct their strategies toward systems of

law (whether local, regional, or international), whereas reconciliation advocates tend to see the limitations of legal judgments, evaluating them as much by their political and socioeconomic impact on society as by the degree to which they satisfy strict legal standards of justice.

Human rights groups seek to be an objective, impartial voice calling to justice all those who commit human rights abuses. Reconciliation advocates place an emphasis upon relationship building and the need to hear all voices—even the voices of those who have committed human rights abuses—as a basis for the creation of political stability and institutional transformation, without which justice has little chance of being realized. Human rights actors tend to see the quest for justice and the rule of law as the critical foundation for peaceful coexistence, while reconciliation advocates tend to see mutual understanding and the capacity to live together as the critical foundation for forward-looking justice and establishing the rule of law.

In brief, human rights actors tend to define impunity narrowly in an attempt to close down on future gross violations of human rights. Reconciliation and peace-building actors, conversely, tend to view impunity and accountability more broadly, applying this to a range of postconflict priorities that need to be addressed in a political transition. Such priorities include developing the structures and institutions needed to implement the rule of law and protect human rights, establishing an economy capable of sustaining these institutions, and promoting democratic structures that will enable former enemies and adversaries to begin to build trust as a basis for realizing these objectives.

Despite recognizing the importance of prosecutions as a corrective to impunity, the ultimate goal of transitional justice is surely to balance political reconciliation with justice. Aryeh Neier, president of the Open Society in New York and an ardent supporter of the prosecution of those primarily responsible for gross violations of human rights, suggests that it is hard to quarrel with Desmond Tutu when he contends that the South African process of "providing amnesty in exchange for acknowledgement and full disclosure [of perpetrations], with prosecutions as an alternative for those who do not acknowledge and disclose, served the country better than a process that would have relied solely on prosecutions."[1]

Recognizing the UN position that amnesties cannot be granted with respect to international crimes, the transitional justice debate cannot afford to lose sight of the reality within which different conflicts are rooted.[2] It needs to accept that each particular historical context within which gross violations of human rights have been committed will inevitably shape the immediate demands of that society.

Local understanding, local ownership, and local commitment are the eye of the needle through which the norms of international law need to pass if peace is to prevail. The process of attaining balance between the universal and the particular is, of course, complex. It takes time. And it requires a serious encounter between those promoting international law and those favoring local initiatives for resolving conflict.

Unless carefully coordinated, the tensions between the advocates of prosecution and those prioritizing reconciliation can lead to an unnecessary confrontation between two equally important steps in the political transition. The different ingredients that make for sustainable peace includes accountability for past gross violations of human rights and the rule of law, as well as an inclusive sense of human rights that includes social, political, and economic rights. These rights have to be weighed one against the other—recognizing that trade-offs will inevitably be necessary. Those who support amnesty of one kind or another for past crimes need at the same time to ask whether past offenders are able and willing to make a positive contribution to the new order. This is not an assumption that can be taken for granted.

It is still too early to ascertain whether internationally imposed prosecutions have brought sustainable peace in Africa or elsewhere in the world. The jury is, in turn, still out on whether countries like South Africa that have settled their conflicts in a nonpunitive manner can sustain the momentum for peace that have earned them the admiration of the world. In the case of South Africa, the apartheid regime negotiated its demise and saw Nelson Mandela inaugurated as its first democratically elected president.

The question is whether and how a level of complimentarity can be realized between international law and nonprosecutorial mechanisms for justice and reconciliation. Specific to this particular book is the question of whether African countries such as the Democratic Republic of the Congo (DRC), Sudan, Uganda, and other nations at war with themselves can be enabled to move beyond their respective entrenched conflicts, which to date neither international nor local approaches alone have demonstrated an obvious ability to ameliorate. For this to happen, the proponents of both international and local forms of justice need to address a range of challenges, which include the following:

- The need for a higher level of transparency and debate concerning the priorities of the International Criminal Court (ICC). When the ICC opened investigations in Northern Uganda, the prosecutor indicated that the ICC's intervention would help end the war, stating that the ICC's role was to contribute directly to peace. When, however, the leader of the Lord's Resistance Army (LRA), Joseph Kony, indicated a willingness to enter into peace negotiations, provided charges against him were dropped, this provoked the prosecutor to say that it is his job to prosecute, not to make peace. What, then, is the role prosecutor, and how does it affect Article 16 and Article 53 of the Rome Statute?

The intervention of the ICC in Sudan, for example, is seen by many African leaders as intrusive interference in the affairs of a sovereign nation by Western powers with economic and related interests in the country and the region. Equally important, it is seen as undermining the mediation and peace initiatives undertaken by concerned African countries and the African Union, whose peacemaking initiatives are crucial in bringing stability to the continent.[3] This concern can only be addressed through more public awareness, greater international transparency, and clarity on the intents of the ICC. The debate on ways of resolving entrenched conflict in Africa and elsewhere is not over. As suggested in the prologue to the present volume, "options for peaceful transition can never be taken off the table." Without this level of debate, agreement on an inclusive sense of justice that meets the demands of both the international community and the people of the country concerned is unlikely to be achieved.

- An examination and analysis of the intervention of the international community in a particular situation in relation to conflicts in other situations. To what extent, for example, does the arrest of the former Liberian dictator Charles Taylor, through the agency of the Sierra Leonean Special Court, entrench other dictators in their positions in refusing to accept political asylum or amnesty as a "reward" for surrendering power—fearing that they may face the same fate as Taylor? To what extent ought local and regional leaders to be consulted in deciding whether justice or peace ought to be prioritized in situations of entrenched armed conflict and mass atrocities?

- The need for greater cooperation between the ICC and national courts. Without this, the legitimacy and efficacy of ICC indictments on the continent will continue to be questioned. Diane Orentlicher refers to the philosopher Bishop George Berkeley's question of "whether a tree really fell in the forest if no one heard it fall." She asks questions of whether prosecutions constituting a crucial pillar in a program of transitional justice can play their intended role if they operate at a remote distance from the public and speak only in the largely inaccessible language of legal judgment.[4] This suggests that the ICC needs to invest more energy into empowering, and where necessary sensitizing, local judicial mechanisms to the demands of international justice.

- The implications of the international community employing the ICC for purposes of political leverage. Steps taken by the ICC in the Central African Republic (CAR), the DRC, Sudan, and Uganda (countries where the ICC is operative) have clearly persuaded those who are either indicted or likely to be indicted to take the accusations against them seriously. Certainly Omar al-Bashir and Joseph Kony responded to international, regional, and national pressure in a manner not seen earlier. The expansion of the LRA's aggression into the DRC, South Sudan, and the CAR along with its continuing activity in Uganda, conversely, confirms the views of those who see Kony as seeking to exploit the Juba talks to his own benefit. It suggests that he has little real interest in seeking a just settlement to the conflict in Northern Uganda. The question is what kind of peace deal would be required for rebel leaders and other perpetrators, of which Kony and his cohorts are but a few, to make peace? If the demands are too severe, the incentive to negotiate is taken away. If left too flexible, they could exploit Article 16 to undermine the ICC's impact.

- The extent of the legitimacy of international law in local or domestic situations, especially in isolated communities that are struggling to bring an end to armed conflict, war, and mass atrocities. Jürgen Habermas argues that moral and legal values do not emerge from some normative metaphysical or universal source. Law, whether international or customary, is a social construction attainable through debate, persuasion, and inclusive legal discourse involving the participation of everyone concerned.[5] Lon Fuller, writing earlier (at the time of the first wave of African independence), argues that law at its best is based on societal consensus concerning the "best route to a better future," giving expression to "who we want to be" and the "kind of community we aim to have."[6] Though the moral legitimacy of international law is broadly accepted and established, the efficacy of international law needs to be assessed contextually, ensuring that where implemented it is to the benefit of the victims of past suffering. The South African negotiated settlement was reached because the leaders of the antiapartheid struggle prioritized "political justice over criminal justice."[7] If the Rome Statute that gave rise to the ICC had been ratified and imposed on South Africa at the time, this settlement would not have enjoyed the level of international support that enabled it to happen.

- The context within which international law is applied. My concern is not to explore the nature of the legitimacy of international law in relation to state sovereignty. Rather, it is first to raise questions concerning the contextual limitations of legal prosecution in the prevention of gross violations of human rights. Second, it is to explore realistic ways of redressing these limitations. Third, it is to support the need for the establishment of a modus operandi that allows for the complementary functioning of international and national prosecutions as well as alternative accountability structures. These may be traditional African mechanisms, hybrid structures such as the Rwandan *gacaca* courts, or truth commissions. In brief, broad-based, inclusive legal discourse needs to be intensified between those who promote the imposition of international law in Africa and intellectuals, leaders, and others who raise questions about the demands of the ICC, as a basis for reconsidering the dominant prosecutorial trend within the transitional justice debate.

- The fact that only Africans have been indicted by the ICC since its inception in 2002. This elicits sentiments within the transitional justice debate that often distracts from the thoughtfulness that is needed to promote justice and sustain peace. The abiding memory of colonialism has provoked many Africans and others to accuse the proponents of international law of new colonial designs. Questions are raised as to why certain African rebel leaders have been indicted to the exclusion of others, and why some heads of state are seen to be exempted from prosecutions while others are not. In this regard, the situations in the CAR, the DRC, Sudan, and Uganda clearly demand international attention. Greater candor and transparency by the ICC in this regard could contribute to resolving the resultant level of suspicion among many Africans.

  The fact that there is no evidence of the ICC investigating the involvement of global powers in the war crimes committed in these and other countries has resulted in accusations of political bias against the court. Evidence of apparent condoning of torture, indefinite detention without trial, the use of chemical weapons, and the killing of innocent people by major powers and their allies in Africa, Iraq, the Middle East, and elsewhere puts a lie to the suggestion that Western nations are willing to enforce human rights law in their own countries and elsewhere. Conversely, the question needs to be asked why leaders of some African countries that have signed the ICC Rome Treaty are not prepared to act more decisively against al Bashir, Kony, and others who show a flagrant disregard for the human rights of fellow Africans in Dafur, Uganda, the DRC, and elsewhere. Other African leaders, Robert Mugabe visibly among them, have in turn remained in power for as long as they have precisely because of the tolerance and support for their survival by other African leaders.[8]

- The continuing underlying dichotomy between African communitarianism and colonial forms of liberal individualism. Western notions of law and individual responsibility were an inherent part of colonialism. In the process, traditional legal mechanisms were suppressed. With few exceptions, resistant traditional leaders were replaced by hand-picked collaborators. Postcolonial leaders rarely saw the need to deviate from such practices.

- It is too late and would be quite wrong to attempt to undo centuries of history. Times and needs have changed. The challenge is to find ways to identify and introduce such communal values and practices into international law that can contribute to the creation of the kind of social cohesion and stability that so many African countries need. In most situations, this requires the use of what Bruce Ackerman describes as "political capital" to promote future needs, rather than spending the limited resources of emerging democracies on punitive justice. "Moral capital is better spent in educating the population in the limits of the law," he writes. "There can be no hope of comprehensively correcting the wrongs done over a generation or more. A few crude, bureaucratically feasible reforms will do more justice, and prove less divisive, than a quixotic quest after the mirage of corrective justice."[9]

Options for cooperation between the ICC and the traditional African mechanisms for justice and reconciliation require continuing engagement between the exponents of both. The observation of Kofi Annan, the former secretary-general of the United Nations, referred to in chapter 1, on the mandate of the ICC and the South African Truth and Reconciliation Commission (TRC) is pertinent in this regard. He suggests that it is "inconceivable . . . that the ICC [which had at the time of the TRC not yet been ratified by the required sixty countries] would seek to substitute its judgment for that of a whole nation that is seeking the best way to put a traumatic past behind it and build a better future."[10] Locating the South African TRC within the country's broader political transition, Boraine concludes: "If one compares South Africa before and after 1994, one has to concede that we are not the same country, that the major conflict, which hopelessly and devastatingly divided our society, has been resolved."[11] Despite the TRC's many limitations and a host of new challenges facing the nation, it is the 1994 level of political change promoted by the TRC process that continues to attract the attention of countries in conflict across the African continent and elsewhere in the world. The unanswered question is whether the establishment of the ICC has eliminated the possibility of a similar settlement from occurring in other situations of conflict.

Tim Allen points out that for traditional justice mechanisms to be included in an Ugandan settlement, for example, they need to become part of the formal Ugandan justice system, which would presumably subject them to certain judicial checks and balances.[12] The Agreement on Accountability and Reconciliation negotiated in Juba between the Government of Uganda and the LRA takes a first step in this direction by acknowledging the role of the Acholi people and other traditional mechanisms in the judicial settlement of the Northern Ugandan conflict. It does not show how or by what criteria this could happen. Careful legal, political, and moral work involving African and international players waits to be done in this regard. The fact that Kony has failed to negotiate in good faith and has ultimately refused to sign the agreement should not be allowed to prevent this work from continuing. Whatever happens to Kony and the other LRA leaders, there are community and national leaders in Uganda and neighboring countries who also need to be held accountable for their deeds and there are communities that need to be reconciled. Without this, major governance and economic concerns are unlikely to be resolved. It is argued by Ugandan authorities and their allies that only once the already deeply fractured LRA has been eliminated can peace be negotiated in the region. At the same time it is clear that the long-outstanding political, social, and economic demands of the Acholi will be need to be addressed by the government of Uganda to ensure sustainable peace in the region. A formal court would hardly be able to include the latter in its judgment, whereas traditional African courts lend themselves to making this level of reform part of a settlement.

A holistic understanding of transitional justice presupposes a complex, multifaceted process. It involves the accountability of perpetrators, truth recovery, institutional reform, reparations, civic trust, and reconciliation—recognizing that there is extensive debate regarding the specificities and context of each of these ingredients. The ultimate goal of any transitional justice exercise is sustainable peace and reconciliation, requiring a permanent end to past abuses and the realistic restoration of the lives of the victims of such abuses. This requires the emergence of a society that seeks to provide for the material well-being and human dignity of all its citizens.

As argued in the introduction to this volume, transitional justice is not simply about establishing an acceptable trade-off between justice and peace. It is primarily about different forms of justice within a specific context that is judged to be conducive to sustainable peace. Except in rare situations, this form of justice contains a mix of truth, accountability, and political reconciliation, in the sense of being prepared to work with one's opponents to enable a society to move from autocratic rule to the beginning of democracy.

Reconciliation is a tough, slow-moving process. It requires a decisive beginning, creative enough to bring former enemies to a point where they are willing to explore a shared solution to the conflict, which often has the capacity to consume a society in violence but not to bring peace. It requires a commitment to an inclusive regime of human rights, as an incentive to deepening peace. Its goal is a society within which enemies begin to engage one another as fellow citizens—and even friends.

Peace building invariably involves political concessions, deal making, and moral compromises. The African contribution to this process is to turn a necessity into a potential for virtue by favoring maximum inclusivity and the pursuit of reconciliation in dealing with issues of conflict and national security. It offers the opportunity to rise above violent conflict and abuse through the repairing of relationships and the rediscovery of the humanity of even those who seem to have sacrificed their right to be regarded as human. More specifically, *ubuntu* offers the world a set of values that deserve to be included in the mix that lies at the root of the transitional justice debate. It is decidedly not the Holy Grail solution to deep-seated conflict. To ignore what it offers is, however, to dismiss an option for peace in situations around the world that cry out for political transitions that involve more than prosecutions. Africa at the same time needs to face the reality that where perpetrators are not willing to make peace, they must face the strong arm of retribution and exclusion from society.

NOTES

Introduction

1. John Paul II, "Memory and Reconciliation: The Church and the Faults of the Past," quoted by Amstutz, *Healing of Nations*, ix.

2. Mamdani, "Human Rights Fundamentalism."

3. Mozambique and Namibia, conversely, offered blanket amnesty to perpetrators as a basis for ending their respective conflicts and are arguably no less "reconciled" than South Africa.

4. Galtung, "Twenty-Five Years of Peace Research," 145.

5. High Court of South Africa, North Gauteng High Court, Pretoria, Case 15320/ 9, April 28, 2009.

6. UN Economic and Social Council, Commission on Human Rights, 61st Session, *Promotion and Protection of Human Rights*, 5.

7. Bhargava, "Moral Justification of Truth Commissions," 60.

8. Irae Baptista Lundin, Madrid, October 2005.

9. Stafford, "For a Lost Child."

Prologue

1. Rome Statute of the International Criminal Court, available at www.un.org/ law/icc/statute/romefra.htm.

2. The arrest of Jean-Pierre Bemba is not for the activities of his militia in the DRC but for his support of rebel forces in an attempted coup in the Central African Republic.

3. Laurent Nkunda was arrested in Rwanda following a joint Rwandan-DRC military initiative, and the DRC has asked for his extradition. The question is whether Rwanda will comply; whether the DRC intends to prosecute him in Kinshasa as a renegade Congolese soldier, which would signal a growing domestic capacity not to rely on the ICC for prosecutions; or whether he will ultimately face trial in The Hague on charges of genocide, crimes against humanity, or war crimes.

4. The fact that Zimbabwe, like Sudan, has not signed the Rome Statute will involve the direct intervention of the UN Security Council.

5. McAdams, "Transitional Justice."

6. Williams, *Moral Luck.*

7. Orentlicher, "Settling Accounts."

8. Orentlicher, "Settling Accounts Revisited," 18–19.

9. Zalaquett, "Balancing Ethical Imperatives and Political Constraints," 1425.

10. Villa-Vicencio and Doxtader, *Pieces of the Puzzle*, 66–72.

11. Sooka, "Holding Peace and Justice in Tandem."

12. United Nations, *Agenda for Peace.*

13. UN Security Council, *Rule of Law and Transitional Justice*, 4. Also see United Nations, *Agenda for Peace.*

14. Office of the United Nations High Commissioner for Human Rights, *Rule of Law Tools for Post-Conflict States.*

15. Brounéus, *Reconciliation*, 54–55.

16. Wallensteen and Nordberg, *Report of the Dag Hammarskjöld Symposium*, 18.

17. Piet Meiring describes the different approaches to issues of justice and rec-onciliation by lawyers, the clergy, and others in the South African TRC. See Meiring, *Pastors or Lawyers?*

18. Wallensteen and Nordberg, *Report of the Dag Hammarskjöld Symposium*, 18.

19. Draft copy, "Decision on the Meeting of the African Parties to the Rome Stat-ute of the ICC," Libya, July 7–8, 2009. See also *African News* 486 (May 2009), 10–43.

Chapter 1

1. Agreement on Accountability and Reconciliation between the Government of the Republic of Uganda and the Lord's Resistance Army, Juba, Sudan, June 29, 2007. See also Baines, "Haunting of Alice."

2. Rome Statute of the International Criminal Court, www.un.org/law/icc/statute/romefra.htm.

3. Ibid. Also see Lovat, *Delineating the Interests of Justice.*

4. Huyse and Salter, *Traditional Justice and Reconciliation*, 192.

5. Dani Nabudere, at a seminar at the University of Cape Town, July 2003.

6. See Mamdani, "Lessons of Zimbabwe."

7. An important and accessible overview of African history is Meredith, *State of Africa.*

8. See www.oxfam.org.uk/resources/policy/conflict_disasters/bp107_africasmissing billions.html.

9. Breytenbach, "Imagine Africa."

10. Nkrumah, *Revolutionary Path*, 235. See also Agyeman, "African Publius."

11. Fanon, *Wretched of the Earth*, 183.

12. Tendai Biti, at a symposium, "Zimbabwe: What Now?" Institute for Justice and Reconciliation, Cape Town, May 2008.

13. Jinadu, *Explaining and Managing Ethnic Conflict*, 7.

14. Ibid., 23.

15. Chris Landsberg, "South Africa and the Making of the African Union," 200.

16. Ibid., 204.

17. Obi, *No Choice but Democracy*, 17.

18. Dani Nabudere, Cape Town, July 2003.

19. Ignatieff, *Human Rights as Politics*, 33.

20. Saki Macozoma, at an Institute for Justice and Reconciliation Symposium: Money and Morality, October 3, 2006.

21. Fired, *Beyond "Never Again,"* 119.

22. Luttwak, "Give War a Chance," 36.

23. Fantu Chenu, Nordic African Institute, Uppsala, October 25, 2007.

24. Ignatieff, *Warrior's Honor*, 87.

25. Baker, "Conflict Resolution versus Democratic Governance," 566.

26. Kofi Annan, speaking at the University of the Witwatersrand Graduation Ceremony, September 1, 1998.

27. A senior Rwandan justice official, Kigali, March 2006.

28. Quoted by Meredith, *State of Africa*, 154.

Chapter 2

1. Ramesh Thakur, "Politics vs. Justice at The Hague," *International Herald Tribune*, August 15, 2002.

2. Kissinger, *World Restored*, 138.

3. Dinka elder, Juba, August 1, 2007.

4. Ohlson, *Power Politics*; Ohlson, "Understanding Causes of War and Peace," 134.

5. Lederach, *Building Peace*, xv.

6. The Boipatong massacre carried out by mainly Zulu hostel dwellers in June 1992 and the Bisho massacre in the Ciskei "independent" homeland by the Ciskei defense force in September 1992 were seen by the ANC to be undertaken with the complicity of the South African police.

7. Quoted in a phone-in program on Cape Talk Radio, August, 2003.

8. Robert Mugabe, Zimbabwe Independence 1980, www.sokwanele.com/node/75.

9. Mongesi Guma,, Cape Town, July 2006.

10. Dani Nabudere, Cape Town, July 2003.

11. Rapoport, *Origins of Violence*.

12. Galtung, "Violence, Peace and Peace Research."

13. Burton, *Conflict: Resolution and Provention*, 3.

14. Lederach, *Preparing for Peace*, 17–19.

15. See Avruch, *Culture and Conflict Resolution*, 88–100.

16. Fisher, Ury, and Patton, *Getting to Yes*, 19.

17. Bailey, "Tertius Luctans," 82.

18. See Gharajedaghi, *Systems Thinking*. For an application of this to the 1994 South African political settlement in 1994, see Heald, "Learning from Enemies."

19. Lederach, *Little Book of Conflict Transformation*, 30.

20. Lederach, *Moral Imagination*.

21. Cyril Ramaphosa, Johannesburg, May 1994.

22. Theuns Eloff, symposium discussion, School of Business Administration, Witwatersrand University, July 2007.

23. Woman at a seminar, Kigali, November 2007.

24. Roelf Meyer, Pretoria, May 2007.

25. Saunders, *Politics Is about Relationship*, 7.

26. Havel, "Power of the Powerless."

27. A young woman at a seminar on the role civil society plays in peace building, Freetown, September 19–21, 2003.

28. Kalungu-Banda, *Leading Like Mandela*, 48.

29. Habib, "Economic Policy and Power Relations," 28.

30. Miller, *Constructing Sustainable Reconciliation*.

31. Seminar on political change at the Pontificia Universidade Catolica do Parana in Curitiba, Brazil, September 1994.

32. Reported by Johann Hari in the *Sunday Independent*, May 14, 2006.

33. Darby and MacGinty, *Contemporary Peace-Making*.

34. Tuchman, *March of Folly*.

35. Havel, "Power of the Powerless."

Chapter 3

1. Zartman, *Elusive Peace*, 338.

2. Wallensteen, *Understanding Conflict Resolution*, 133.

3. Lyons, *Demilitarising Politics*, 6.

4. The complexities involved in the transformation from armed struggle to political party in the case of the Farabundo Mart Liberation Front in El Salvador, Renamo in Mozambique, the Revolutionary National Front in Sierra Leone, and the Khmer Rouge in Cambodia is considered in an important PhD thesis by Mimmi Soderberg Kovacs; see Kovacs, "From Rebellion to Politics."

5. Ohlson, "Understanding Causes of War and Peace"; also see Ohlson, *Power Politics and Peace Policies*.

6. Foucault, *Fearless Speech*, 169.

7. Ibid., 83.

8. Mac Maharaj, Berlin, September 2006.

9. Lévinas, *Ethics and Infinity*, 89.

10. Lévinas, Fornet, and Gomez, "Philosophie, justice et amour," 8–9.

11. Sartre, *In Camera*.

12. Roelf Meyer, Pretoria, April 2007.

13. See Heald, "Learning from Enemies," 253–54.

14. Arendt, *Origins of Totalitarianism*, 300.

15. Lyotard, "Other's Rights," 136–38.

16. Aloisea Inyumba, Kigali, September 2006.

17. Quoted by Sparks, *Tomorrow Is Another Country*, 204.

18. Heald, "Learning from Enemies," 120.

19. *Cape Argus*, August 24, 1994.

20. Charland, "Constitutive Rhetoric."

21. Nelson Mandela in his closing address to the Thirteenth International AIDS Conference, Durban, 2000.

22. Deng, *Dinka Cosmology*, 165.

23. Deng, "Reaching Out," 192.

24. The *umushingantahe* is an institution made up of people who are respected in their community as people of wisdom and integrity; *umushingantahe* (singular), *abashingantahe* (plural).

25. Ntahombaye et al., *Bashingantahe Institution in Burundi*.

26. Roelf Meyer, Pretoria, April 2007.

27. Havel, "Word about Words," 4.

28. Lederach, *Moral Imagination*, 39.

29. "The TRC Ten Years On," conference organized by the Institute for Justice and Reconciliation, Cape Town, April 2006.

30. Krog, *Country of My Skull*, 42.

31. Itumeleng Mosala, at "TRC Ten Years On."

32. Le Guin, *Wave in the Mind*, 34.

33. Schank, *Tell Me a Story*, 17.

34. Havel, "Word about Words," 5.

35. Kahane, *Solving Tough Problems*, 129.

36. José Chipenda, at "Reflecting on African Peace Initiatives," a conference organized by the Institute for Justice and Reconciliation, Cape Town, September 2005.

37. See Kahane, *Solving Tough Problems*, 91–92, 122–23; and Senge et al., *Presence*.

38. Bennett, *Christian Ethics*, 76–77.

39. In 1997, a Mr. Soobramoney, an ailing, terminally ill patient, sought the Constitutional Court's backing, under Section 27 of the Constitution, for life-prolonging medical treatment when he was turned away by Addington Hospital in Durban because its available facilities were overextended and his terminal condition was judged by the health authorities to place him too low on the priority list to qualify for treatment. The Court refused to overrule the judgment of the hospital and that of the KwaZulu-Natal health authorities. The Cape High Court, conversely, subsequently gave some hope to those seeking relief against the socioeconomic rights entrenched in the Constitution. Irene Grootboom and 899 other applicants, of whom 510 were children, were evicted from an informal settlement known as New Rust in the Western Cape, where this private land had been earmarked for building low-cost housing. They applied to the Court

for an order requiring the government to provide them with adequate shelter or housing until they obtained permanent accommodation. The Cape High Court granted
the order under Section 28 of the Constitution, which guarantees the right of children to, among other things, shelter. Taken on appeal to the Constitutional Court,
there was found to be no violation of the rights of the child (Section 28) in this instance, with the state contending that this was the primary obligation of the parents
and families and, only failing such care, of the state. At the same time, it ruled that
the state had no core obligation to provide basic shelter that is enforceable immediately and on demand, although it is required progressively within its resources to do
so. It nevertheless found the eviction to be unreasonable to the extent that "no provision was made for relief to the categories of people in desperate need," and required
the government, under Section 26(2) of the Constitution, to provide temporary relief to the people concerned.

40. Berman, *Interaction of Law and Religion*, 24.

41. Horkheimer, *Die Sehnsucht nach dem ganz Andern*, 60.

42. Ricoeur, "Can Forgiveness Heal?" 35.

43. Saunders, *Politics Is about Relationship*, 65.

44. Desmond Tutu, at "TRC Ten Years On."

Chapter 4

1. Nelson Mandela, Pretoria, September 1998.

2. Collier et al., *Breaking the Conflict Trap*, 83. See also Miller, *Constructing Sustainable Reconciliation*.

3. Cited by Enver Surty, minister of justice and constitutional development, at
"The TRC Ten Years On," conference organized by the Institute for Justice and Reconciliation, Cape Town, April 2006.

4. Sooka, "Holding Peace and Justice in Tandem."

5. Krog, *Country of My Skull*, 42.

6. Danieli, *International Handbook of Multigenerational Legacies of Trauma*, 678.

7. Salazar, "How to Recognize Evil in Politics."

8. Ibid.

9. Interviews conducted by the Institute for Justice and Reconciliation between
2000 and 2003. These interviews culminated in the publication by Foster, Haupt, and
de Beer, *Theatre of Violence*.

10. Charland, "Reconciliation, Identity and Impiety."

11. Govan Mbeki, Cape Town, April 2000.

12. Soyinka, *Burden of Memory*.

13. Ibid., 81; italics added.

14. Mamdani, "Reconciliation without Justice." Also see Mamdani, "Truth according to the Truth and Reconciliation Commission."

15. Mamdani, "Reconciliation without Justice," 5.

16. French, "Unchosen Evil," 4–41. Also see Cooper, "Collective Responsibility, 210.

17. Goldhagen, *Hitler's Willing Executioners*, 34, 45–48.

18. The long debate that preceded the defining of "gross violations of human rights" that the TRC was required to investigate is outlined by the Truth and Reconciliation Commission, *Truth and Reconciliation Commission of South Africa Report*, vol. 1, 48–93. It narrowed the definition to "(a) the killing, abduction, torture or severe ill-treatment of any person; or (b) any attempt, incitement, instigation, command or procurement to commit an act referred to in paragraph (a), which emanated from conflicts of the past and which was committed during the period 1 March 1960 to 10 May 1994 within or outside the Republic, and the commission of which was advised, planned, directed, commanded or ordered, by any person acting with a political motive." The TRC interpreted the mandate in a narrow sense, deciding not to explicitly investigate racism, forced removals, job reservation, and related issues that gave rise to the gross violations of human rights are defined above—coming under criticism from critics. These included Soyinka and Mamdani, as referred to above.

19. Nelson Mandela, Joint Sitting of Both Houses of Parliament, May 24, 1994, cols. 1–15.

20. I am indebted to the careful documentation and analysis of this conversation by Doxtader, *With Faith in the Works of Words*.

21. Ibid., 271.

22. Ibid., 261.

23. Ibid., 249.

24. Asmal, Asmal, and Roberts, "Truth, Reconciliation and Justice."

25. For the former president's submission to the TRC, see Doxtader and Salazar, *Truth and Reconciliation in South Africa*, 301–19. Also see www.doj.gov.za/trc/trc_frameset .htm.

26. Leon Wessels, Cape Town, December 2007.

27. For the Democratic Party's submission to the TRC, see www.doj.gov.za/trc/ trc_frameset.htm.

28. This was in a memorandum submitted to the TRC at the Armed Forces hearing in Cape Town on October 9, 1997; see www.doj.gov.za/trc/index.html.

29. Sachs, "Fourth D. T. Lakdawala Memorial Lecture."

30. I. Mohammed, Judgment in Constitutional Court of South Africa, Case CCT 17/96, July 25, 1996.

31. Roberts, *Injustice and Rectification*.

32. Shriver, "Long Road to Reconciliation."

33. Nyameka Goniwe, Conference on Reparations and Memorialisation: The Unfinished Business of the TRC, Cape Town, October 2000.

34. Sipho Tshabalala, at "TRC Ten Years On."

35. Gibson, *Does Truth Lead to Reconciliation?*; Gibson and MacDonald, *Truth—Yes, Reconciliation—Maybe*.

36. Thembi Simelane-Nkadimeng, at "TRC Ten Years On."

37. See Office of the United Nations High Commissioner for Human Rights, *Options for Accountability*. Also see Agreement on Accountability and Reconciliation between the Government of the Republic of Uganda and the Lord's Resistance Army, Juba, Sudan, June 29, 2007.

38. Ash, "The Truth about Dictatorship," 40.

39. Marrus, "History and the Holocaust."

40. Ayindo, "Retribution or Restoration for Rwanda?"

41. Ignatieff, *Warrior's Honor*, 170.

42. Saunders, *Politics Is about Relationship*, 7.

43. Alexander, *Ordinary Country*, 171.

44. Achebe, *Morning Yet*.

Chapter 5

1. Magona, *Mother to Mother*, 77.

2. Sindiwe Magona, Cape Town, August 2008.

3. Quoted by Sparks, *Mind of South Africa*, 14.

4. Boon, *African Way*, 13.

5. Zakes Mda, at a symposium on identity organized by the Institute for Justice and Reconciliation, Cape Town, October 2003.

6. De Vere Allen, *Swahili Origins*.

7. van den Heuvel, Mangaliso, and van de Bunt, *Prophecies and Protests*.

8. J. Sachs, in *Port Elizabeth Municipality v. Various Occupiers*, 2004 (12) BCLR 1268 (CC), par. 37.

9. *State v. Makwanyane*, Constitutional Court of South Africa (CCT/3/94), June 1995.

10. Mokgoro, "Ubuntu and the Law."

11. Sono, *Dilemmas of African Intellectuals*, 7.

12. Fanon, *Wretched of the Earth*, 178.

13. Havel, "Power of the Powerless," 1.

14. Ibid., 4.

15. Louw, "African Concept of *Ubuntu*," 169.

16. Cavarero, *Relating Narratives*.

17. Posel, "TRC's Unfinished Business," 87.

18. Ibid., 86, quoting Foucault.

19. Ibid.

20. Bohler-Müller, "Beyond Legal Metanarratives."

21. Ibid.

22. Shaun Johnson, *Native Commissioner*, 77ff.

23. A military officer, September 2006.

24. Kearney, *On Stories*, 1.

25. Ash, *Truth about Dictatorship*, 40.

26. Minow, *Between Vengeance and Forgiveness*, 9.

27. Ibid., 87.

28. Heald, "Learning from Enemies," 214.

29. Ibid., 265, quoting de Bono, *Conflicts*, 19–20.

30. Roelf Meyer, Pretoria, April 2007.

31. Ruth Mompati, in an interview published by Villa-Vicencio, *Spirit of Freedom*. Mompati was again interviewed in July 1998.

32. Tutu, *No Future without Forgiveness*, 31.

33. Kennedy, *Dark Sides of Virtue*, 18.

Chapter 6

1. Saunders, *Politics Is about Relationship*, 7.

2. Some scholars find the term "traditional" problematic, suggesting it implies that the practices are static, whereas they adjust to the needs, challenges, and insights of the times; others affirm the notion of "traditional" as necessary within the context of Western-driven notions of change.

3. UN Economic and Social Council, Commission on Human Rights, 61st Session, *Promotion and Protection of Human Rights*, 5.

4. Murithi and Hudson, *United Nations Mediation Experience*, 23.

5. Kennedy, *Dark Sides of Virtue*, 20.

6. Zartman, *Traditional Cures for Modern Conflicts*, 3.

7. Life and Peace Institute and University of Burundi, *Traditional Institutions for Conflict Resolution*.

8. Tarekegn Adebo, Uppsala, October 2007.

9. People committing category one crimes include those who are alleged to be involved in planning, organizing, inciting, supervising, or instigating genocide and other crimes against humanity; these are referred to the national courts or the International Criminal Tribunal in Arusha. Since 2008, however, some category one cases have been dealt with by *gacaca* courts, where those accused of "lesser" crimes (which includes complicity in genocide) are tried in the *gacaca* courts. For a discussion on the *gacaca* courts see Clarke, "Hybridity, Holism and Traditional Justice."

10. Schirch, *Ritual and Symbol in Peacebuilding*, 109.

11. Tarekegn Adebo, Uppsala, October 2007.

12. Ntahombaye et al., *Bashingantahe Institution in Burundi*; Nindorera, "*Ubushingantahe* as a Base for Political Transformation."

13. Agreement on Accountability and Reconciliation between the Government of the Republic of Uganda and the Lord's Resistance Army, Juba, Sudan, June 29, 2007.

14. Irae Baptista Lundin, Maputo, May 2008.

15. Dinis Salamao Sengulane, speaking at the Institute for Justice and Reconciliation's Consultation on State-Led Transitional Justice Mechanisms, Johannesburg, June 2007.

16. Schirch, *Ritual and Symbol in Peacebuilding*, 105f; 165. Schirch draws, inter alia, on MacLean, *Triune Concept of the Brain*; and McLaughlin, McManus, and d'Aquili, *Brain, Symbol and Experience*. Also see Sacks, *Musicophilia*.

17. Crawford-Browne, "Trauma, Healing and Reparations."

18. Honwana, "Children of War," 139.

19. Schechner, *Future of Ritual*, 233.

20. Ibid.

21. Freda Haddad, Cape Town, July 1999.

22. Dinis Salamao Sengulane, Johannesburg, June 7–9, 2006.

23. Schirch, *Ritual and Symbol in Peacebuilding*, 107.

24. The work of the Institute for Justice and Reconciliation is acknowledged in what follows. See Batchelor, "African Traditional Peacebuilding Systems"; Batchelor, "Traditional Peacebuilding Systems in Transition."

25. Fanon, *Wretched of the Earth*, 188.

26. The Juba Agreement specifically identifies these rituals, practiced among the Acholi, the Iteso, Langi, and Madi, as options for inclusion in settling the conflict between the Ugandan government and the LRA.

27. International Center for Transitional Justice, *Conciliation Resources*; International Center for Transitional Justice, *Forgotten Voices*.

28. Ogulu Odama, at a conference on religion in African conflicts and peace-building initiatives: problems and prospects for a globalizing Africa, sponsored by the Joan B. Kroc Institute for International Peace Studies, Notre Dame University, Jinja, March 31–April 3, 2004.

29. *The Economist*, October 21, 2006, 56–57.

30. International Center for Transitional Justice, *Forgotten Voices*.

31. Press release, August 16, 2007, based on a survey conducted by the Berkeley-Tulane Initiative on Vulnerable Populations, a joint project of the Human Rights Center, University of California, Berkeley, and the Tulane Payson Center for International Development and the International Center for Transitional Justice, www.ictj.org/images/content/7/3/738.pdf.

32. Ibid. Also see Justice and Reconciliation Project, *Cooling of Hearts*.

33. Odama, at a conference on religion in African conflicts and peace-building initiatives.

34. I rely on the insights and nomenclature of the Life and Peace Institute in Uppsala and on Badal, *Local Traditional Structures*.

35. Quoted by Francis Deng, Cape Town, December 2004.

36. Southern Sudan Peace Commission Strategic Plan, September 2007.

37. Clement Janda, at a conference organized by the New Sudan Council of Churches, Juba, December 2006.

38. Deng, "Reaching Out," 121.

39. Deng, Cape Town, December 2004.

40. William Tolbert III, Monrovia, 2004.

41. Clarke, "Ethnicity, Leadership and Conflict Mediation."

42. Muchukiwa, "Pacification Institutions," 14–17.

43. Arsano, "Traditional Capacity for Conflict Management," 18–30. The Borana are part of the larger Oromo ethnic group that extends beyond Ethiopia into neighboring countries.

44. Yacob Arsano, Uppsala, October 2007.

45. Nürnberger, *Living Dead and the Living God*. James Kombo writes of a similar perspective among the Luo ethnic group in Southern Sudan. See Kombo, "Peace in the Traditional Luo Society," 31–39.

46. Gabriel Setiloane, Maokeng in the Free State Province, January 2004.

47. Eppel, "Healing the Dead," 267.

48. Igreja, "Peace, Justice and Healing in Post-War Mozambique."

49. Nokuzola Mdende, Cape Town, July 2008.

50. James Kok Ruea, concluding address at a strategic planning meeting for the Southern Sudan Peace Commission, Juba, July 13, 2007.

51. This person spoke with me in Kinshasa, December 2007.

52. Bohler-Müller, "Beyond Legal Metanarratives."

53. Lederach, *Building Peace*, xv.

54. Community worker, Juba, July 2007.

55. This resulted in cases of sexual violence being excluded from *gacaca* jurisdiction in 2004, although reinstated to *gacaca* in 2008. It is not clear what changes have been introduced to address the earlier problems. For a discussion of the *gacaca* courts, see Clarke, "Hybridity, Holism and Traditional Justice."

56. Beatrice Aber, Juba, July 2007.

57. Traditional leader in Bor in South Sudan, Juba, July 2007.

58. James Kok Ruea, Juba, 13 July 2007.

59. Gabriel Setiloane, Maokeng, January 2004.

60. Daphne Madiba, Hammanskraal near Pretoria, June 2004.

61. "Uganda: Government to Seek Review of ICC Indictments against LRA Leaders," June 21, 2007, www.irinnews.org/Report.aspx?ReportId=72861.

62. Dinis Salamao Sengulane, Johannesburg, June 7–9, 2007.

Chapter 7

1. Shriver, *Ethic for Enemies*. Also see Shriver, *Honest Patriots*.

2. Shriver, *Ethic for Enemies*, 3–9. See also Villa-Vicencio, *Theology of Reconstruction*, 32–48.

3. Volf, *Exclusion and Embrace*.

4. Ibid., 9.

5. Ibid., 215.

6. Nordquist, "Reconciliation as a Political Concept."

7. See Tavuchis, *Mea Culpa*; and Barkan and Kam, *Taking Wrongs Seriously*.

8. Horkheimer, *Die Sehnsucht nach dem ganz Andern*, 60; Ricoeur, "Can Forgiveness Heal?" 31–35.

9. These suggestions were made at a conference at the Joan B. Kroc Institute for International Peace Studies, University of Notre Dame, South Bend, IN, September 2003.

10. Ibid.

11. Peter John Pearson, Cape Town, September 2006.

12. Presse und Infromationsdienst der Bundesregierung, January 23, 1996, translated and quoted by Kayser, "Improvising the Present."

13. Karl Elliger, Dublin, March 10, 1999.

14. Nelson Mandela, Pretoria, September 1998.

15. Boraine, *Country Unmasked*, 376.

16. John Sampson, Windhoek, June 2007.

17. Frank Chikane, Cape Town, 1992.

18. Mamdani, *When Victims Become Killers*, 132.

19. Mamdani, "Making Sense of Political Violence." 16.

20. Mamdani argues that although Tutsi privilege existed before the colonial period, the entrenchment and politicization of ethnic divisions was intensified during the colonial period. The Kayibanda regime entrenched the colonial ideology, making a distinction between "indigenous" Hutus and "alien" Tutsis. Habyarimana, who came to power in the 1973 coup, took the process a step further in denationalizing those Tutsis who went into exile. When the Rwanda Patriotic Army invaded Rwanda from Uganda, he justified his actions as a defender of the nation against the exiles who, he argued, wanted to restore the monarchy and impose Tutsi domination. However, with the collapse of the Rwandan economy and political destabilization in the country, he came under increasing pressure to liberalize his policy toward the Tutsi. This allowed radical Hutus who had been sidelined by Habyarimana to regain influence, resulting in the formal establishment of Hutu power. Tensions between the two Hutu groups increased, while exiled Tutsis, facing increasing opposition to their presence in Uganda, moved further into Rwandan territory. With Habyarimana's death in a plane crash over Kigali while returning from peace talks in Arusha, Hutu power triumphed and the genocide was unleashed.

21. Mamdani, *When Victims Become Killers*, 272.

22. Wimmer et al., *Facing Ethnic Conflict*, 1. Also see Enns, *Identity and Victimhood*.

23. Enns, *Identity and Victimhood*.

24. See Williams, *Seeing a Color-Blind Future*; and Enns, *Identity and Victimhood*, 5.

25. Fanon, *Wretched of the Earth*, 188.

26. Mamdani, *When Victims Become Killers*, 14.

27. Miller, *Constructing Sustainable Reconciliation*.

28. Ibid., 2.

29. Mamdani, *When Victims Become Killers*, 273.

30. Melber, *Limits to Liberation*.

31. Enns, *Identity and Victimhood*, 17.

32. International Alert, quoted by Wohlgemuth, "Conflict Prevention in Burundi," 88.

33. Fanon, *Black Skin White Masks*, 230–31.

34. Fanon, *Wretched of the Earth*.

35. Govan Mbeki, Cape Town, April 2000.

36. Ibid.

37. UN General Assembly, *New Agenda*.

38. Quoted by Villa-Vicencio and Doxtader, *Pieces of the Puzzle*, 115.

39. Boraine, *Country Unmasked*, 351.

40. Truth and Reconciliation Commission, *Truth and Reconciliation Commission of South Africa Report*, vol. 5, 308.

41. Ibid.

42. Amstutz, *Healing of Nations*, 212.

43. Krog, "Country of Grief and Grace," 95.

44. Achebe, *Things Fall Apart*, 32.

45. Weber, *Protestant Ethic*.

46. Fanon, *Wretched of the Earth*, 178.

47. Quoted by Clark, *Civilisation*, 1.

48. Camus, *Rebel*.

49. I am indebted to a former colleague, James Moulder, for the parameters of this definition.

50. Doxtader, "It Is 'Reconciliation' If We Say It Is," 1. The idea is developed further by Doxtader, "Reconciliation: A Rhetorical Conception."

51. See Forrester, *Beliefs, Values and Policies*, 22.

52. Lederach, *Building Peace*, 30.

53. *New York Times*, October 31, 1998; quoted by Boraine, *Country Unmasked*, 342.

Chapter 8

1. Aryeh Neier, "A Review of the Truth Commission of South Africa Report," quoted by Boraine, *Country Unmasked*, 296.

2. UN Security Council, *Rule of Law and Transitional Justice*.

3. Draft copy, "Decision on the Meeting of the African Parties to the Rome Statute of the ICC," Libya, July 7–11, 2009.

4. Orentlicher, "'Settling Accounts' Revisited."

5. Habermas, *Between Facts and Norms*, 222.

6. Fuller, "Positivism and Fidelity to Law," 630.

7. Mamdani, "Human Rights Fundamentalism," 18.

8. See also Adams, *Hushed Voices*.

9. Ackerman, *Future of Liberal Revolution*, 73.

10. Kofi Annan, speech at the Witwatersrand University Graduation Ceremony, September, 1, 1998.

11. Boraine, *Country Unmasked*, 345.

12. Allen, "Ritual (Ab)use?" 51.

BIBLIOGRAPHY

Achebe, Chinua. *Morning Yet on the First Day of Creation*. New York: Anchor Press, 1975.
———. *Things Fall Apart*. New York: Anchor Books, 1986.
Ackerman, Bruce. *The Future of Liberal Revolution*. New Haven, CT: Yale University Press, 1992.
Adams, Heribert. *Hushed Voices: Unacknowledged Atrocities*. Unpublished manuscript.
Adebajo, A., A. Adedeji, and C. Landsberg, eds. *South Africa in Africa: The Post-Apartheid Era*. Durban: University of KwaZulu-Natal, 2007.
Agyeman, Opoku "The African Publius." *Journal of Modern African Studies* 23, no. 3 (September 1985): 371–88.
Alexander, Neville. *An Ordinary Country: Issues in the Transition from Apartheid to Democracy in South Africa*. Pietermaritzburg: University of Natal Press, 2002.
Allen, Tim. "The International Criminal Court and the Invention of Traditional Justice in Northern Uganda." *Politique Africaine*, no. 107 (2007): 147–66.
———. "Ritual (Ab)use? Problems with Traditional Justice in Uganda." In *Courting Conflict? Justice, Peace and the ICC in Africa*, edited by Nicholas Waddell and Phil Clark. London: Royal African Society, 2008.
———. *Trial Justice: The International Criminal Court and the Lord's Resistance Arm*. London: Zed Books, 2006.
Amstutz, Mark R. *The Healing of Nations: The Promise and Limits of Political Forgiveness*. Lanham, MD: Rowman & Littlefield, 2005.
Arendt, Hannah. *The Origins of Totalitarianism*. New York: Harcourt Brace, 1951.
Arsano, Yacob. "Traditional Capacity for Conflict Management: The Case of the Boran of Southern Ethiopia." In *Traditional Institutions for Conflict Resolution and Promotion*, edited by University of Burundi and Life and Peace Institute. Bujumbura: University of Burundi and Life and Peace Institute. 2001.
Ash, Timothy Garton. "The Truth about Dictatorship." *New York Review of Books*, February 19, 1998, 35–40.
Asmal, Kader, Louise Asmal, and Ronald Roberts. *Reconciliation through Truth. A Reckoning of Apartheid's Criminal Governance*. Cape Town: David Philip, 1996.
———. "Truth, Reconciliation and Justice: The South African TRC in Retrospective." *Modern Law Review* 63, no. 1 (2000): 1–24.

Avruch, Kevin. *Culture and Conflict Resolution.* Washington, DC: United States of Peace Press, 2006.

Ayindo, Babu. "Retribution or Restoration for Rwanda?" *Africa News,* January 1998, http://web.peacelink.it/afrinews/22issue/p4.html.

Badal, Ralph K. *Local Traditional Structures in Sudan.* Nairobi: Life and Peace Institute, 2006.

Bailey, G. F. "Tertius Luctans: Idiocosm, Caricature and Mask." In *Conflict Resolution: Cross-Cultural Perspectives,* edited by Kevin Avruch, P. W. Black, and J. Scimecca. New York: Greenwood Press, 1991.

Baines, Erin. "The Haunting of Alice: Local Approaches to Justice and Reconciliation in Northern Uganda." *International Journal of Transitional Justice* 1 (2007): 91–114.

Baker, Pauline. "Conflict Resolution versus Democratic Governance." In *Managing Global Chaos,* edited by Chester Crocker, Fen Osler Hampson, and Pamela Aall. Washington, DC: United States Institute of Peace Press, 1996.

Barkan, Elazer, and Alexander Kam, eds. *Taking Wrongs Seriously.* Stanford, CA: Stanford University Press, 2006.

Bassiouni, M. C., ed. *Post-Conflict Justice.* Ardsley, NY: Transnational Publishers, 2002.

Batchelor, Diana. "African Traditional Peacebuilding Systems: Recurring Themes." Occasional Paper. Cape Town: Institute for Justice and Reconciliation, 2005.

———. "Traditional Peacebuilding Systems in Transition: Roots and Restoration in African Soil." Occasional Paper. Cape Town: Institute for Justice and Reconciliation, 2005.

Bennett, John. *Christian Ethics and Social Policy.* New York: Charles Scribner's Sons, 1946.

Berman, Harold. *The Interaction of Law and Religion.* Nashville: Abingdon Press, 1974.

Betts, R. "The Delusion of Impartial Intervention." *Foreign Affairs* 73, no. 6 (1994): 20–33.

Bhargava, Rajeev. "The Moral Justification of Truth Commissions." In *Looking Back, Reaching Forward: Reflections on the Truth and Reconciliation Commission in South Africa,* edited by Charles Villa-Vicencio and W. Verwoerd. Cape Town: University of Cape Town Press, 2000.

Biggar, N., ed. *Burying the Past: Making Peace and Doing Justice after Civil Conflict.* Washington, DC: Georgetown University Press, 2001.

Bizos, George. *No One to Blame? In Pursuit of Justice in South Africa.* Cape Town: David Philip, 1998.

Bohler-Müller, Narnia. "Beyond Legal Metanarratives: The Relationship between Storytelling, *Ubuntu* and Care." *Stellenbosch Law Review* 18, no. 1 (2007): 133–60.

Boon, Mike. *The African Way: The Power of Interactive Leadership.* Johannesburg: Zebra Press, 1996.

Boraine, Alex. *A Country Unmasked: Inside South Africa's Truth and Reconciliation Commission.* Cape Town: Oxford University Press, 2000.

Boraine, A., and J. Levy, eds. *The Healing of a Nation?* Cape Town: Justice in Transitions, 1995.

Borer, T. A., ed. *Telling the Truths,* Notre Dame, IN: University of Notre Dame Press, 2006.

Braithwaite, J. *Restorative Justice and Responsive Regulation.* Oxford: Oxford University Press, 2002.

Breytenbach, Breyten. "Imagine Africa." Opening remarks at Conference on Vitalizing African Cultural Assets, Gorée Island, March 5–7, 2007.

Brounéus, Karen. *Reconciliation: Theory and Practice for Development Co-operation.* Stockholm: Swedish International Development Cooperation Agency, 2003.

Burton, John, ed. *Conflict: Resolution and Provention,* vol. 1 of Conflict Series. London: Macmillan, 1990.

———. *Conflict: Human Needs Theory,* vol. 2 of Conflict Series. London: Macmillan, 1990.

———. *Conflict: Basic Human Needs,* vol. 3 of Conflict Series. New York: St. Martin's Press, 1990.

Camus, Albert. *The Rebel: An Essay on Man and Revolt.* New York: Vintage International, 1991.

Cavarero, Adriana. *Relating Narratives, Storytelling and Selfhood.* New York: Routledge, 2000.

Charland, Maurice. "Constitutive Rhetoric: The Case of the Peuple Québécois." *Quarterly Journal of Speech* 73, no. 2 (1987): 133–50.

———. "Reconciliation, Identity and Impiety." Paper presented at symposium on "Coming to Terms with Reconciliation," University of Wisconsin–Madison, November 10–11, 2006.

Chazan, N., P. Lewis, R. Mortimer, D. Rothchild, and J. Stedman. *The Rise of a Party-State in Kenya: From "Harambee!" to "Nyyayo."* Berkeley: University of California Press, 1992.

Clark, Kenneth. *Civilisation.* New York: Harper & Row, 1969.

Clarke, Phil. "Ethnicity, Leadership and Conflict Mediation in Eastern Democratic Republic of the Congo: The Case of the Barza Inter-Communautaire." *Journal for Eastern African Studies* 2, no. 1 (2008): 1–17. http://dx.doi.org/10.1080/17531050701846682.

———. "Hybridity, Holism and Traditional Justice: The Case of the Gacaca Courts in Post-Genocide Rwanda." *George Washington International Law Review* 39 (2005): 765–837.

Collier, Paul, V. L. Elliot, Havard Hegre, Anke Hoeffler, Marta Reynal-Querol, and Nicholas Sambanis. *Breaking the Conflict Trap: Civil War and Development Policy.* New York: Oxford University Press for World Bank, 2003.

Comaroff, J., and S. Roberts. *Rules and Processes: The Cultural Context of Dispute in an African Context.* Chicago: University of Chicago Press, 1981.

Cooper, David. "Collective Responsibility, Moral Luck and Reconciliation." In *War Crimes and Collective Wrongdoing: A Reader,* edited by Aleksander Jovic. Malden, MA: Blackwell, 2001.

Crawford-Browne, Sarah. "Trauma, Healing and Reparations." Paper delivered at Institute for Justice and Reconciliation's Consultation on State-Led Transitional Justice Mechanisms, Johannesburg, June 7–9, 2007.

Crocker, C., and F. Hampson, eds. *Managing Global Chaos: Sources of and Responses to International Conflict.* Washington, DC: United States Institute of Peace Press, 1996.

Danieli, Yael. *International Handbook of Multigenerational Legacies of Trauma.* New York: Plenum Press, 1998.

Darby, John, and Roger MacGinty, eds. *Contemporary Peace-Making.* London: Palgrave Macmillan, 2003.

Davies, J. G. *When Men Rebel and Why.* New York: Free Press, 1971.

De Bono, Edward. *Conflicts: A Better Way to Resolve Them.* Harmondsworth, U.K.: Penguin Books, 1986.

De Brito, A. B., C. Gonzales-Enriques, and P. Aguilar, eds. *The Politics of Memory: Transitional Justice in Democratizing Societies.* Oxford: Oxford University Press, 2001.

Deng, Francis M. *Dinka Cosmology.* London: Ithaca Press, 1980.

———. "Reaching Out: The Dinka Principle of Conflict Management." In *Traditional Cures,* edited by I. William Zartman. New York: Brookings Institution Press, 1997.

Deng, Francis M, and I. William Zartman. *Conflict Resolution in Africa.* Washington, DC: Brookings Institution Press, 1991.

Des Forges, A. "Making Noise Effectively: Lessons from the Rwandan Catastrophe." In *Vigilance and Vengeance,* edited by Robert Rotberg. Washington, DC: Brookings Institution Press, 1996.

De Vere Allen, James. *Swahili Origins.* Athens: Ohio University Press, 1993. Available at www.swahilionline.com/culture/culture.htm.

Doxtader, Erik. "It Is 'Reconciliation' If We Say It Is: Discerning the Rhetorical Problem in the South African Transition." Paper presented at 2000 Meeting of Association for Rhetoric and Communication in Southern Africa, Lusaka.

———. "Reconciliation: A Rhetorical Conception." *Quarterly Journal of Speech* 89, no.4 (2003): 267–92.

———. *With Faith in the Works of Words: The Beginnings of Reconciliation in South Africa, 1985–1995.* Cape Town: David Philip, 2008.

Doxtader, Erik, and Phillipe-Joseph Salazar. *Truth and Reconciliation in South Africa: The Fundamental Documents.* Cape Town: David Philip, 2007.

Doxtader, Erik, and Charles Villa-Vicencio, eds. *Through Fire with Water: The Roots of Division and the Potential for Reconciliation in Africa.* Cape Town: David Philip, 2003.

———. *To Repair the Irreparable: Reparation and Reconstruction in South Africa.* Cape Town: David Philip, 2004.

Drumbl, M. A. *Atrocity, Punishment, and International Law.* Cambridge: Cambridge University Press, 2007.

Dyzenhaus, D. *Judging the Judges, Judging Ourselves: Truth, Reconciliation and the Apartheid Legal Order.* Oxford: Hart, 1998.

Enns, Diane. *Identity and Victimhood: Questions for Conflict Management Practice.* Berkhof Occasional Paper 28. Berlin: Berkhof Research Center for Constructive Conflict Management, 2007.

Eppel, Shari. "Healing the Dead: Exhumation and Reburial as Truth-Telling and Peace-

Building Activities in Rural Zimbabwe." In *Truth Telling and Peace-building in Post-Conflict Societies*, edited by T. Anne Borer. Notre Dame, IN: University of Notre Dame Press, 2006.

Fanon, Frantz. *Black Skin White Masks: The Experiences of a Black Man in a White World*. New York: Grove Press, 1967.

———. *The Wretched of the Earth*. New York: Grove Press, 1963.

Fired, Eva, ed. *Beyond "Never Again."* Stockholm: Swedish Government, 2005.

Fisher, R. *Interactive Conflict Resolution*. Syracuse, NY: Syracuse University Press, 1997.

Fisher, Roger, William Ury, and Bruce Patton. *Getting to Yes: Negotiating an Agreement without Giving In*. Boston: Houghton Mifflin, 1991.

Fletcher, L. E., and H. M. Weinstein. "Violence and Social Repair: Rethinking the Contribution of Justice to Reconciliation." *Human Rights Quarterly* 24 (2002).

Forrester, Duncan B. *Beliefs, Values and Policies: Conviction Politics in a Secular Age*. Oxford: Clarendon Press, 1989.

Foster, Don, Paul Haupt, and Maresa de Beer. *The Theatre of Violence: Narratives of Protagonists in the South African Conflict*. Cape Town: HSRC Press, 2005.

Foucault, Michel. *Fearless Speech*, edited by David Pearson. Los Angeles: Semiotext(e)/MIT, 2001.

French, Peter. "Unchosen Evil and Moral Responsibility." In *War Crimes and Collective Wrongdoing: A Reader*, edited by Aleksander Jovic. Malden, MA: Blackwell, 2001.

Fuller, Lon. "Positivism and Fidelity to Law." *Harvard Law Review* 71, no. 4 (1958): 630–72.

Galtung, Johan. *Peace by Peaceful Means: Peace and Conflict, Development and Civilization*. London: Sage, 1996.

———. "Twenty-Five Years of Peace Research: Ten Challenges and Some Responses." *Journal of Peace Research* 22, no. 2 (1985): 141–58.

———. "Violence, Peace and Peace Research." *Journal of Peace Research* 6, no. 3 (1969): 167–91.

Gastrow, P. *Bargaining for Peace: South Africa and the National Peace Accord*. Washington, DC: United States Institute of Peace Press, 1995.

Gharajedaghi, J. *Systems Thinking: Managing Chaos and Complexity*. Boston: Butterworth Heinemann, 1999.

Gibson, James L. *Does Truth Lead to Reconciliation? Testing the Considered Assumptions of the TRC Process*. Bloomington, IN: Midwest Political Science Association, 2004.

———. "Truth, Justice, and Reconciliation: Judging the Fairness of Amnesty in South Africa." *American Journal of Political Science* 46, no. 3 (2002): 540–56.

———. "Truth, Reconciliation, and the Creation of a Human Rights Culture in South Africa." *Law and Society Review* 38 (2004): 5–40.

Gibson, James L., and Helen MacDonald, eds. *Truth—Yes, Reconciliation—Maybe: South Africans Judge the Truth and Reconciliation Process*. Cape Town: Institute for Justice and Reconciliation, 2001.

Gobodo-Madikizela, P., A. Collins, and G. Eagle, eds. *Critical Psychology in Africa. The International Journal of Critical Psychology*. London: Lawrence & Wishart, 2006.

Goldhagen, Daniel. *Hitler's Willing Executioners.* London: Little, Brown, 1996.

Goldstone, Richard. *For Humanity: Reflections of a War Crimes Investigator.* New Haven, CT: Yale University Press, 2000.

Goleman, D. *Emotional Intelligence: Why It Can Matter More Than IQ.* New York: Bantam, 2006.

Graybill, L. *Truth and Reconciliation in South Africa: Miracle or Model?* Boulder, CO: Lynne Rienner, 2002.

Gurr, T. R. *Minorities at Risk: A Global View of Ethnopolitical Conflicts.* Washington, DC: United States Institute of Peace Press, 1993.

Habermas, Jürgen. *Between Facts and Norms: Contributions to a Discourse Theory on Law and Democracy.* Cambridge, MA: MIT Press, 1998.

Habib, Adam. "Economic Policy and Power Relations in South Africa's Transition to Democracy." *World Development* 28, no. 2 (2000): 245–63.

Havel, Václav. "The Power of the Powerless: In Memory of Jan Patocka." In *The Power of the Powerless,* edited by John Keane. Armonk, NY: M. E. Sharpe, 1985. Available at www.vaclavhavel.cz/index.php?sec=2&id=.

———. "A Word about Words." Address given in 1989. Reprinted in *New York Review of Books,* January18, 1990. Available at www.vaclavhavel.cz/index.php?sec=2&id=1.

Hayner, P. *Unspeakable Truths: Confronting State Terror and Atrocity.* New York: Routledge, 2001.

Heald, Geoffrey. "Learning from Enemies: A Phenomenological Study of the South African Constitutional Negotiations from 1985 to 1998." PhD thesis, University of the Witwatersrand, 2006.

Honwana, Alcinda. "Children of War: Understanding War and War Cleansing in Mozambique and Angola." In *Civilians in War,* edited by Simon Chesterman. Boulder, CO: Lynn Rienner, 2001.

———. "Negotiating Post-War Identities: Child Soldiers in Mozambique and Angola." In *Contested Terrains and Constructed Categories,* edited by G. Bond and N. Gibson. Boulder, CO: Westview Press, 2002.

Horkheimer, Max. *Die Sehnsucht nach dem ganz Andern: Ein interview mit Kommentaar van Helmut Gumnoir.* Hamburg: Furche, 1975.

Hume, C. *Ending Mozambique's War: The Role of Mediation and Good Offices.* Washington, DC: United States Institute of Peace Press, 1994.

Humphrey, M. *The Politics of Atrocity and Reconciliation.* London: Routledge, 2002.

Huntington, S. *The Clash of Civilizations and the Remaking of World Order.* New York: Simon & Schuster, 1996.

Hutchins, Edwin. *Culture and Inference: A Trobriand Case Study.* Cambridge, MA: Harvard University Press, 1980.

Huyse, Luc, and Mark Salter, eds. *Traditional Justice and Reconciliation after Violent Conflict: Learning from African Experiences.* Stockholm: International Institute for Democracy and Electoral Assistance, 2008.

Ignatieff, Michael. *Blood and Belonging: Journeys into New Nationalism.* London: Vintage Books, 1994.

———. *Human Rights as Politics and Ideology.* Princeton, NJ: Princeton University Press, 2001.

———. *The Warrior's Honor.* New York: Henry Holt, 1997.

Igreja, Victor. "Peace, Justice and Healing in Post-War Mozambique: Magamba Spirits in Gorongosa." Paper delivered at Centre for Conflicts Resolution Conference, Peace versus Justice? Truth and Reconciliation Commissions and War Crimes Tribunals in Africa, Cape Town, May 17–18, 2007.

International Center for Transitional Justice. *Conciliation Resources, Coming Home: Understanding Why Commanders of the Lord's Resistance Army Choose to Return to a Civilian Life.* New York: International Center for Transitional Justice, 2006.

———. *Forgotten Voices: A Population-Based Survey on Attitudes about Peace and Justice in Northern Uganda.* New York: International Center for Transitional Justice, 2005.

Jinadu, A. Adele. *Explaining and Managing Ethnic Conflict in Africa: Towards a Cultural Theory of Democracy.* Claude Ake Memorial Paper Series 1. Uppsala: Uppsala University and Nordic Africa Institute, 2008.

Johnson, Shaun. *The Native Commissioner.* Johannesburg: Penguin Books South Africa, 2006.

Jones, B. D. *Peacemaking in Rwanda: The Dynamics of Failure.* London: Lynne Reinner, 2001.

Justice and Reconciliation Project. *The Cooling of Hearts: Community Truth-Telling in Acholiland.* Special Report. Gulu: Justice and Reconciliation Project, 2007.

Kahane, Adam. *Solving Tough Problems: An Open Way of Talking, Listening and Creating New Realities.* New York: Berrett and Koehler, 2004.

Kalungu-Banda, Martin. *Leading Like Mandela: Leadership Lessons from Nelson Mandela.* Cape Town: Double Storey Books, 2006.

Kayser, Undine. "Improvising the Present: Narrative Construction and Re-construction of the Past in South Africa and Germany." Honors thesis, Centre for African Studies, University of Cape Town, 1997–98.

Kearney, Richard. *On Stories.* New York: Routledge, 2002.

Kennedy, David. *The Dark Sides of Virtue: Reassessing International Humanitarianism.* Princeton, NJ: Princeton University Press, 2004.

Kennedy, P. *Preparing for the Twenty-First Century.* London: Harper Collins, 1993.

Kissinger, Henry A. *A World Restored: Metternich, Castlereagh and the Problems of Peace, 1812–1822.* Boston: Houghton Mifflin, 1973.

Kombo, James. "Peace in the Traditional Luo Society." In *Traditional Institutions for Conflict Resolution and Promotion*, edited by University of Burundi and Life and Peace Institute. Bujumbura: University of Burundi and Life and Peace Institute, 2001.

Kovacs, Mimmi Soderberg. "From Rebellion to Politics: The Transformation of Rebel Groups to Political Parties in Civil War Peace Processes." PhD thesis, Uppsala University, 2007.

Kritz, N. *Transitional Justice: How Emerging Democracies Reckon with Former Regimes.* Washington, DC: United States Institute of Peace Press, 1995.

Krog, Antjie. "Country of Grief and Grace." In *Down to My Last Skin*. Johannesburg: Random House, 2000.

———. *Country of My Skull*. Johannesburg: Random House, 1998.

Kumar, K., ed. *Rebuilding Societies after Civil War: Critical Roles for International Assistance*. Boulder, CO: Lynne Rienner, 1997.

Landsberg, Chris. "South Africa and the Making of the African Union and NEPAD: Mbeki's 'Progressive African Agenda.'" In *South Africa in Africa: The Post-Apartheid Era*, edited by Adekeye Adebajo, Adebayo Adedeji, and Chris Landsberg. Durban: University of KwaZulu-Natal Press, 2007.

Lederach, John Paul. *Building Peace: Sustainable Reconciliation in Divided Societies*. Washington, DC: United States Institute of Peace Press, 1997.

———. *The Little Book of Conflict Transformation*. Intercourse, PA: Good Books, 2003.

———. *The Moral Imagination: The Art and Soul of Building Peace*. Oxford: Oxford University Press, 2005.

———. *Preparing for Peace: Conflict Transformation across Cultures*. Syracuse, NY: Syracuse University Press, 1995.

Le Guin, Ursula. *The Wave in the Mind: Talks and Essays on the Writer, the Reader and the Imagination*. London: Random House, 2004.

Lévinas, Emmanuel. *Ethics and Infinity*. Pittsburgh: Duquesne University Press, 1985.

Lévinas, Emmanuel, R. Fornet, and A. Gomez. "Philosophie, justice et amour: Entretien avec Emmanuel Lévinas." *Esprit* 8/9 (1983): 8–17. In English: "Philosophy, Justice, and Love," in *Is It Righteous to Be? Interviews with Emmanuel Lévinas*, edited by Jill Robins. Stanford, CA: Stanford University Press, 1983.

Life and Peace Institute and University of Burundi, eds. *Traditional Institutions for Conflict Resolution and Promotion of Peace in the Great Lakes and Horn of Africa Regions*. Bujumbura: Life and Peace Institute and University of Burundi.

Louw, Dirk. "The African Concept of *Ubuntu* and Restorative Justice." In *Handbook of Restorative Justice*, edited by D. Sullivan and L. Tifft. New York: Routledge, 2006.

Lovat, Henry M. *Delineating the Interests of Justice: Prosecutorial Discretion and the Rome Statute of the International Criminal Court*. Bepress Legal Series Working Paper 1435. Berkeley, CA: Berkeley Electronic Press, 2006. http://law.bepress.com/expresso/eps/1435.

Luttwak, Edward N. "Give War a Chance." *Foreign Affairs* 78, no. 4 (July–August 1999): 36–44.

Lyons, Terrence. *Demilitarising Politics: Elections on the Uncertain Road to Peace*. Boulder, CO: Lynne Rienner, 2005.

Lyotard, Jean-François. "The Other's Rights." In *On Human Rights: The Oxford Amnesty Lectures*, edited by Stephen Shute and Susan Hurley. New York: Basic Books, 1993.

MacLean, Paul D. *A Triune Concept of the Brain and Behaviour*. Toronto: University of Toronto, 1972.

Magona, Sindiwe. *Mother to Mother*. Cape Town: David Philip, 1998.

Mamdani, Mahmood. "Human Rights Fundamentalism." *Mail and Guardian*, March 20–26, 2009, 18–19.

———. "Lessons of Zimbabwe." *London Review of Books*, December 4, 2008. www.lrb.co
.uk/v30/n23/mamd01.html.

———. "Making Sense of Political Violence in Postcolonial Africa." *Identity, Culture and Politics* 3, no. 2 (2002): 2–24.

———. "Reconciliation without Justice." *Southern Africa Review of Books*, November–December 1996, 3–5.

———. "The Truth according to the Truth and Reconciliation Commission." In *The Politics of Memory: Truth, Healing and Social Justice*, edited by I. Amadiume and A. An-Naim. London: Zed Books, 2000.

———. *When Victims Become Killers: Colonialism, Nativism, and the Genocide in Rwanda*. Cape Town: David Philip, 2001.

Mandela, Nelson. *Long Walk to Freedom*. London: Little, Brown, 1994.

Marrus, Michael. "History and the Holocaust in the Courtroom." Paper delivered at conference, "Searching for Memory and Justice: The Holocaust and Apartheid," Yale University, February 8–10, 1998.

McAdams, A. James. "Transitional Justice: The Issue That Won't Go Away." Paper delivered at an international conference at the Munk Centre for International Studies at the University of Toronto, Toronto, March 19–20, 2009.

McLaughlin, Charles D., John McManus, and Eugene G. d'Aquili. *Brain, Symbol and Experience: Towards a Neurophenomenology of Human Consciousness*. Boston: Shambhala, 1990.

Meiring, P. G. J. *Pastors or Lawyers? The Role of Religion in the South African Truth and Reconciliation Process*. Centurion, South Africa: Sabinet, 2002.

Melber, Henning, ed. *Limits to Liberation in Southern Africa: The Unfinished Business of Democratic Consolidation*. Cape Town: HSRC Press, 2003.

Mendez, J. E. "Accountability for Past Abuses." *Human Rights Quarterly* 19 (1997): 255–82.

Meredith, Martin. *The State of Africa: A History of Fifty Years of Independence*. London: Jonathan Ball, 2005.

Miller, Zinaida. *Constructing Sustainable Reconciliation: Land, Power and Transitional Justice*. Occasional Paper. Cape Town: Institute for Justice and Reconciliation, 2007. www.ijr.org.za/publications/publications-v2-1.

Minow, Martha. *Between Vengeance and Forgiveness*. Boston: Beacon Press, 1998.

Mitchell, C., and M. Banks. *Handbook of Conflict Resolution: The Analytical Problem Solving Approach*. London: Pinter, 1996.

Mokgoro, Yvonne. "Ubuntu and the Law in South Africa." *Potchefstroom Electronic Law Journal* 1 (1998): 1–11.

Muchukiwa, Bosco. "Pacification Institutions and Their Legitimacy: The Case of Southern Kivu Communities in the Democratic Republic of the Congo." In *Traditional Institutions for Conflict Resolution and Promotion*, edited by University of Burundi and Life and Peace Institute. Bujumbura: Life and Peace Institute and University of Burundi, 2001.

Murithi, Tim, and Judi Hudson, eds. *The United Nations Mediation Experience in Africa*,

Centre for Conflict Resolution and the United Nations Department for Political Affairs. Policy Advisory Group Seminar Report. Cape Town: Centre for Conflict Resolution, 2006. http://ccrweb.ccr.uct.ac.za/fileadmin/template/ccr/pdf/Vol_16-UNMEA _Report_Final.pdf.

Murphy, J. G., and J. Hampton. *Forgiveness and Mercy.* Cambridge: Cambridge University Press, 1994.

Nabudere, D. *Restorative System of Justice and International Humanitarian Law.* Mbale: Marcus-Garvey Pan Afrikan Institute, 2008.

Nadler, A.. T. Malloy, and J. D. Fisher, eds. *The Social Psychology of Intergroup Reconciliation.* New York: Oxford University Press, 2008.

Neier, Aryeh. *War Crimes: Brutality, Genocide, Terror, and the Struggle for Justice.* New York: Random House, 1998.

Nindorera, Agnes. "*Ubushingantahe* as a Base for Political Transformation in Burundi." Boston Consortium on Gender, Security, and Human Rights Working Paper 2, Boston, 2003.

Nino, Carlos Santiago. *Radical Evil on Trial.* New Haven, CT: Yale University Press, 1996.

Nkrumah, Kwame. *Revolutionary Path.* New York: International Publishers, 1973.

Nordquist, Kjell-Åke. "Reconciliation as a Political Concept: Some Observations and Remarks." In Multidisciplinary Perspectives on Peace and Conflict Research, edited by Francisco Ferrandiz and Antonius Robben. Bilbao: University of Deusto Press, 2005.

Nordstrom, C., and J. Martin, eds. *The Paths to Domination, Resistance and Terror.* Berkeley: University of California Press, 1992.

Ntahombaye, Phillipe, Adrien Ntabona, Joseph Gahama, and Liboire Kagabo. *The Bashingantahe Institution in Burundi: A Pluridisciplinary Study.* Bujumbura: Life and Peace Institute, 1999.

Nürnberger, Klaus. *The Living Dead and the Living God.* Pretoria: CB Powell Bible Centre, 2007.

Obi, Cyril I. *No Choice but Democracy: Prising the People out of Politics in Africa?* Claude Ake Memorial Paper Series 2. Uppsala: Uppsala University and Nordic Africa Institute, 2008.

Office of the United Nations High Commissioner for Human Rights. *Options for Accountability for Reconciliation in Uganda.* Geneva: United Nations, 2007. Available at www.northernuganda.usvpp.gov/peacerec2.html.

———. *The Rule of Law Tools for Post-Conflict States: Truth Commissions.* Geneva: United Nations, 2006.

Ohlson, Thomas. *Power Politics and Peace Policies: Inter-State Conflict Resolution in Southern Africa.* Department of Peace and Conflict Research Report 50. Uppsala: University of Uppsala, 1998.

———. "Understanding Causes of War and Peace." *Journal for International Relations* 14, no. 1 (2008): 133–60. http://ejt.sagepub.com/cgi/content/abstract/14/1/133.

Orentlicher, Diane. "Independent Study on Best Practices, Including Recommendations, to Assist States in Strengthening Their Domestic Capacity to Combat All Aspects of Impunity." UN Document E/CN.4/2004/88, 19(f), February 27, 2004.

———. "Settling Accounts: The Duty to Prosecute Human Rights Violations of a Prior Regime." *Yale Law Journal* 100 (1991): 2537–2616.

———. "Settling Accounts Revisited: Reconciling Global Norms with Local Agency." *International Journal for Transitional Justice* 1, no. 1 (2007): 10–22. http://ijtj .oxfordjournals.org/cgi/content/full/1/1/10.

Phat, Rachana. *The Khmer Rouge Rice Fields: The Story of Rape Survivor Tang Kim.* DVD. Phnom Penh: Documentation Center of Cambodia, 2004.

Posel, Deborah. "The TRC's Unfinished Business." In *Truth and Reconciliation in South Africa: 10 Years On*, edited by Charles Villa-Vicencio and Fanie du Toit. Cape Town: David Philip, 2006.

Prunier, G. *The Rwanda Crisis: History of a Genocide 1959–1994.* New York: Columbia University Press, 1995.

Quinn, Joanna. "Social Reconstruction in Uganda: The Role of Customary Mechanisms in Transitional Justice." *Human Rights Review* 8, no.4 (2007): 389–407.

Rapoport, Anatol. *The Origins of Violence.* New York: Paragon House, 1989.

Ricoeur, Paul. "Can Forgiveness Heal?" In *The Foundation and Application of Moral Philosophy*, edited by Hendrik J. Opdebeeck. Leuven: Peeters, 2000.

Roberts, Rodney C. *Injustice and Rectification.* New York: Peter Lang, 2002.

Robertson, G. *Crimes against Humanity: The Struggle for Global Justice.* London: Penguin Books, 1999.

Roht-Arriaza, N., ed. *Impunity and Human Rights in International Law and Practice.* New York: Oxford University Press, 1995.

Ross, M. *The Culture of Conflict.* New Haven, CT: Yale University Press, 1993.

Rothman, J. *From Confrontation to Cooperation: Resolving Ethnic and Regional Conflict.* Newbury Park, CA: Sage, 1992.

———. *Resolving Identity Conflicts in Nations, Organizations, and Communities.* San Francisco: Jossey-Bass, 1997.

Rupesinghe, K., ed. *Conflict Transformation.* London: Macmillan, 1995.

Sachs, Albie. "Fourth D. T. Lakdawala Memorial Lecture." New Delhi, December 18, 1998.

Sacks, Oliver. *Musicophilia: Tales of Music and the Brain.* New York: Vintage Books, 2008.

Salazar, Philippe-Joseph. "How to Recognize Evil in Politics." Paper presented at symposium on "Coming to Terms with Reconciliation," University of Wisconsin–Madison, November 10–11, 2006.

Sartre, Jean-Paul. *In Camera.* London: Vintage Books, 1961.

Saunders, Harold H. *Politics Is about Relationship: A Blueprint for the Citizens' Century.* New York: Palgrave Macmillan, 2005.

Schabas, W. A. "Amnesty, the Sierra Leone Truth and Reconciliation Commission and the Special Court for Sierra Leone." *University of California, Davis, Journal of International Law and Policy*, Fall 2004, 145–69.

Schank, R. *Tell Me a Story: A New Look at Real and Artificial Memory.* New York: Scribner's, 1990.

Schechner, Richard. *The Future of Ritual: Writings on Culture and Performance.* New York: Routledge, 1993.

Schirch, Lisa. *Ritual and Symbol in Peacebuilding.* Bloomfield, CT: Kumarian Press, 2005.

Senge, Peter, Otto Scharmer, Joseph Jaworski, and Betty Sue Flowers. *Presence: An Exploration of Profound Change in People, Organizations, and Society.* New York: Doubleday, 2004.

Shriver, Donald W., Jr. *An Ethic for Enemies: Forgiveness in Politics.* New York: Oxford University Press, 1995.

———. *Honest Patriots: Loving a Country Enough to Remember Its Misdeeds.* New York: Oxford University Press, 2008.

———. "Long Road to Reconciliation: Some Moral Steppingstones." Paper delivered at Oxford University, September 14–16, 1998.

Shutte, A. *Philosophy for Africa.* Cape Town: UCT Press, 1993.

———. *Ubuntu: An Ethic for a New South Africa.* Pietermaritzburg: Cluster Publications, 2001.

Slye, Ronald. "The Legitimacy of Amnesties under International Law and General Principles of Anglo-American Law: Is a Legitimate Amnesty Possible?" *Virginia Journal of International Law* 175 (2003): 173–247.

Smock, D., and C. Crocker. *African Conflict Resolution: The U.S. Role in Peacekeeping.* Washington, DC: United States Institute for Peace Press, 1995.

Sono, Themba. *Dilemmas of African Intellectuals in South Africa.* Pretoria: Unisa Press, 1994.

Sooka, Yasmin. "Holding Peace and Justice in Tandem." Paper presented at Centre for Conflict Resolution Conference: Peace versus Justice? Truth and Reconciliation Commissions and War Crimes Tribunals in Africa, Cape Town, May 17–18, 2007.

Soyinka, Wole. *The Burden of Memory, the Muse of Forgiveness.* Oxford: Oxford University Press, 2000.

Sparks, Allister. *The Mind of South Africa: The Story of the Rise and Fall of Apartheid.* London: Mandarin, 1990.

———. *Tomorrow Is Another Country.* Johannesburg: Struik Book Distributors, 1994.

Stafford, William. "For a Lost Child." In *Learning to Live in the World: Earth Poems.* New York: Harcourt, Brace, 1994.

Tavuchis, Nicholas. *Mea Culpa: A Sociology of Apology and Reconciliation.* Stanford, CA: Stanford University Press, 1991.

Tishkov, Valery. *Chechnya: Life in War-Torn Society.* Berkeley: University of California Press, 2004.

Torpey, J. *Politics and the Past: On Repairing Historical Injustices.* Lanham, MD: Rowman & Littlefield, 2002.

Truth and Reconciliation Commission. *Truth and Reconciliation Commission of South Africa Report.* Cape Town: Truth and Reconciliation Commission, 1998.

Tuchman, Barbara. *The March of Folly: From Troy to Vietnam.* London: Abacus, 1984.

Tutu, Desmond. *No Future without Forgiveness.* New York: Doubleday, 1999.

Umbreit, M.S. *What Is Restorative Justice?* Minneapolis: Center for Justice and Peacemaking. University of Minnesota, 1999.

UN Economic and Social Council, Commission on Human Rights, 61st Session. *The Promotion and Protection of Human Rights, Impunity: Report of the Independent Expert to Update the Set of Principles to Combat Impunity.* Report E/CN.4/2005/102. New York: United Nations, 2005. http://daccessdds.un.org/doc/UNDOC/GEN/G05/109/00/PDF/G0510900.pdf?OpenElement.

UN General Assembly, 46th Session. *New Agenda for the Development of Africa.* New York: United Nations, 1991. http://daccessdds.un.org/doc/RESOLUTION/GEN/NR0/582/39/IMG/NR058239.pdf?OpenElement.

UN General Assembly, 59th Session. *In Larger Freedom: Towards Development, Security and Human Rights for All—Report of the Secretary-General.* UN Document A/59/2005. New York: United Nations, 2005. http://daccessdds.un.org/doc/UNDOC/GEN/N05/270/78/PDF/N0527078.pdf?OpenElement.

United Nations. *An Agenda for Peace: Preventive Diplomacy, Peacemaking and Peacekeeping: A Report of the Secretary-General Pursuant to the Statement Adopted by the Summit Meeting of the Security Council.* UN Document A/47/277–S/24111. New York: United Nations, 1992. www.un.org/docs/SG/agpeace.html.

———. *The Causes of Conflict and Promotion of Durable Peace and Sustainable Development in Africa: Report of UN the Secretary-General to the United Nations Security Council.* New York: United Nations, 1998. www.un.org/ecosocdev/geninfo/afrec/sgreport/index.html.

UN Security Council. *The Rule of Law and Transitional Justice in Conflict and Post-Conflict Societies: Report of the Secretary-General.* UN Document S/2004/616. New York: United Nations, 2004. http://daccessdds.un.org/doc/UNDOC/GEN/N04/395/29/PDF/N0439529.pdf?OpenElement.

Ury, W. *The Third Side: Why We Fight and How We Can Stop.* New York: Penguin Books, 2000.

Van den Heuvel, Henk, Mzamo Mangaliso, and Lisa van de Bunt, eds. *Prophecies and Protests: Ubuntu in Global Management.* Amsterdam and Pretoria: Rozenberg Publishers and Unisa Press, 2006.

Van Zyl, Paul. "Dilemmas of Transitional Justice: The Case of South Africa's Truth and Reconciliation Commission." *Journal of International Affairs* 52, no. 2 (1999): 647–64.

Villa-Vicencio, Charles. *The Spirit of Freedom: South African Leaders on Religion and Politics.* Berkeley: University of California Press, 1996.

———. *A Theology of Reconstruction: Nation-Building and Human Rights.* Cambridge: Cambridge University Press, 1992.

Villa-Vicencio, Charles, and E. Doxtader, eds. *Pieces of the Puzzle.* Cape Town: Institute for Justice and Reconciliation, 2004.

———. *The Provocations of Amnesty: Memory, Justice and Impunity.* Cape Town: David Philip, 2003.

Villa-Vicencio, Charles, and Fanie du Toit, eds. *Truth and Reconciliation in South Africa: Ten Years On.* Cape Town: David Philip, 2006.

Villa-Vicencio, Charles, and W. Verwoerd, eds. *Looking Back, Reaching Forward: Reflections on the Truth and Reconciliation Commission in South Africa.* Cape Town: University of Cape Town Press, 2000.

Volf, Miroslav. *Exclusion and Embrace: A Theological Exploration of Identity, Otherness, and Reconciliation.* Nashville: Abingdon Press, 1996.

Waddell, N., and P. Clark, eds. *Courting Conflict? Justice, Peace and the ICC in Africa.* London: Royal African Society, 2008.

Wallensteen, Peter, ed. *Preventing Violent Conflict: Past Records and Future Challenges.* Uppsala: Department of Peace and Conflict Research, Uppsala University, 1998.

Wallensteen, Peter. *Understanding Conflict Resolution: War, Peace and the Global System.* London: Sage, 2002.

Wallensteen, Peter, and Olle Nordberg, eds. *Report of the Dag Hammarskjöld Symposium on Respecting International Law and International Institutions.* Uppsala: Dag Hammarskjöld Foundation, 2005.

Weber, Max. *The Protestant Ethic and the Spirit of Capitalism.* New York: Scribner's, 1976.

Williams, Bernard. *Moral Luck: Philosophical Papers, 1973–1980.* Cambridge: Cambridge University Press, 1981.

Williams, Patricia. *Seeing a Color-Blind Future: The Paradox of Race.* New York: Noonday Press, 1977.

Wilson, John P., and Thomas Rhiannon Brwynn. *Empathy in the Treatment of Trauma and PTSD.* New York: Brunner-Routledge, 2006.

Wilson, Richard. *The Politics of Truth and Reconciliation in South Africa: Legitimatizing the Post-Apartheid State.* Cambridge: Cambridge University Press, 2001.

Wimmer, Andreas, Richard Goldstone, Donald L. Horowitz, Ulrike Joras, and Conrad Schetter. *Facing Ethnic Conflict: Toward a New Realism.* Toronto: Rowman & Littlefield, 2004.

Wink, Walter. *Healing a Nation's Wounds.* Uppsala: Life and Peace Institute, 1966.

Wohlgemuth, Lennart. "Conflict Prevention in Burundi." In *Preventing Violent Conflict: Past Records and Future Challenges*, edited by Peter Wallensteen. Uppsala: Department of Peace and Conflict Research, Uppsala University, 1998.

Zalaquett, José. "Balancing Ethical Imperatives and Political Constraints: The Dilemma of New Democracies Confronting Past Human Rights Violations." *Hastings Law Journal* 43 (1992).

Zartman, I. William. *Ripe for Resolution: Conflict and Intervention in Africa.* New York: Oxford University Press, 1985.

———. *Traditional Cures for Modern Conflicts: African Conflict Medicine.* Boulder, CO: Lynne Rienner, 2000.

Zartman, I. William, ed. *Elusive Peace: Negotiating an End to Civil War.* Washington, DC: Brookings Institution Press, 1995.

Zartman, I. W., and J. Rasmussen, eds. *Peacemaking in International Conflict: Methods and Techniques.* Washington, DC: United States Institute of Peace Press, 1997.

Zehr, H. "Fundamental Concepts of Restorative Justice." In *Restorative Justice*, edited by Declan Roche. International Library of Essays in Law & Legal Theory, Second Series. Aldershot, U.K.: Dartmouth/Ashgate, 2003.

INDEX